Teaching
WEB
Search
Skills

Techniques and Strategies
of Top Trainers

Greg R. Notess

 Information Today, Inc.

Medford, New Jersey

Second printing, January 2007

Teaching Web Search Skills: Techniques and Strategies of Top Trainers

Library of Congress Cataloging-in-Publication Data

Notess, Greg R.
  Teaching Web search skills : techniques and strategies of top trainers /
by Greg R. Notess
        p. cm.
  Includes bibliographical references and index.
  ISBN 1-57387-267-9
  1. Internet searching--Study and teaching. I. Title.
  ZA4230.N68 2006
  025.04071--dc22

                                                                    2006019130

Printed and bound in the United States of America.

President and CEO: Thomas H. Hogan, Sr.
Editor-in-Chief and Publisher: John B. Bryans
Managing Editor: Amy M. Reeve
VP Graphics and Production: M. Heide Dengler
Book Designer: Kara Mia Jalkowski
Cover Designer: Michele Quinn
Copyeditor: Bonnie Freeman
Proofreader: Dorothy Pike
Indexer: Sharon Hughes

Dedication

To all Web searching teachers, trainers, instructors, and work-shop leaders, especially those who have talked with me about search engines, taken my classes, provided feedback on my Web site, and contributed ideas to this work. May you all have continued success in your training sessions!

And, as always, to Cecelia, Laura, and Mary.

Contents

Figures and Tables

About the Web Page
www.notess.com/teaching

Although many of the concepts, strategies, and teaching approaches discussed in this book will not change greatly over time, Web resources and their respective URLs will. To supplement and update the content presented here, the author maintains a companion Web site at www.notess.com/teaching. At the site, URLs mentioned in the book are listed by chapter and are periodically checked and updated.

If you are aware of any additional sites that would be helpful for teaching Web searching or if you encounter a dead or moved link, please contact the author at teaching@notess.com.

Preface

Teaching Web search engines is complex: The details constantly change, and there are many ways to teach the same point. In speaking with and observing other librarians who teach the subject, I have come to recognize a surprising diversity of approaches; sometimes we even offer conflicting advice! I have been teaching Web searching and conducting Internet training sessions since 1991, focusing on various Internet search engines. I have taught a variety of individuals and groups, including librarians, college students, market researchers, and scientists. Yet including only my own experiences and examples in this book would emphasize my personal teaching style, which may not be compatible with your own. I assert that good teaching is more an art than a science and that in the art of teaching, we can learn best by exploring the approaches of a variety of effective teachers and trainers.

Thus, in writing this book, I have drawn heavily on the experiences of a small but prominent group of expert Web search engine trainers. I have talked extensively with these individuals and surveyed their approaches to teaching Web searching. And I have had conversations with many others who teach Web search courses in a wide variety of settings. My intent is that rather than focusing on one pedagogical approach or instructional style, this book will offer a variety of styles, techniques, and examples. Just as we hope to make our students more information literate, my goal is to help you expand your Web searching literacy and Web search training vocabulary.

Many examples, anecdotes, and stories from the trenches are interspersed throughout (with a special collection in Chapter 13). Some are my own and many come from the trainers who contributed. The wide-ranging tales from the group reflect various teaching styles and personalities (and some conflicting ideas).

I will be citing the following individuals, each of whom I interviewed in depth, throughout the text (additional biographical information can be found in Appendix A):

- Joe Barker of the Teaching Library at the University of California, Berkeley; trainer for Infopeople

- Paul Barron, librarian and former technology director for Rockbridge (Virginia) County Schools

- Phil Bradley, an Internet consultant, trainer, Web designer, and author based in the U.K.

- John Ferguson and Alice Fulbright, reference librarians at Richland College Library, Dallas, Texas

- Ran Hock, a consultant, trainer, and author; principal of Online Strategies

- Jeff Humphrey, former Internet training specialist for INCOLSA, Indiana's statewide library network

- Diane Kovacs, an independent consultant and trainer; principal of Kovacs Consulting

- Gary Price, Director of Online Information Resources at Ask.com, former reference librarian at George Washington University, an independent consultant, and trainer, writer, and Webmaster and co-author of *The Invisible Web*

- Danny Sullivan, principal of Calafia Consulting and creator of Search Engine Watch

- Rita Vine, librarian and founder of Workingfaster.com, which provides custom training solutions and research portals

- Sheila Webber, lecturer in the Department of Information Studies, University of Sheffield, Western Bank, U.K.

These teachers, trainers, and instructors helped form many of the ideas presented in the book. To all of them and to others whose examples and experiences are included here, whether directly attributed or not, my great thanks.

Chapter 1

Web Searching and the Teaching Paradox

Web searching has brought together the general public, librarians, computer scientists, and pedagogues in the pursuit of information. The new Internet audience searches frequently and has little or no formal instruction in Web searching. The role of teaching efficient and effective Web searching has fallen largely to librarians and information professionals.

In many ways, training others to search the Web is simply an extension of the bibliographic instruction sessions librarians have taught for decades. Teaching how to search for information—whether in a printed index, a library card catalog, a commercial online search service, a bibliographic database on CD-ROM, a collection of electronic periodicals, a Web-based full-text aggregator, or a Web search engine—involves a number of basic principles.

Those of us in the information industry, whether we work in libraries or information centers or as independent researchers, have seen a rise in the demand for Web search training over the past several years. In the early days of the public Internet, many library users could and did safely ignore the Web as an information resource. But as the Web has come to predominate in information-seeking efforts of all types, the desire for training has risen apace.

Today, it is common for information professionals to provide Web searching workshops, courses, and lessons and to include Web search training in other types of instructional sessions. We teach Web searching in many different ways, and we have learned that while it applies the basic principles of all information research, it also poses some unique challenges and opportunities.

Web search engines change frequently. Individual search features come and go, and entire databases change periodically. Results differ from one moment to the next, even when they come from the same engine. It isn't unusual, in a hands-on class, for two students performing the same search on the same search engine at the same moment to get different results. Carefully crafted examples, designed to make an important instructional point, will work five minutes before the start of a session but fail to work when the instruction is underway.

This book is designed to provide an overview of key issues for those who teach Web searching, whether one-on-one or in group training sessions or through the use of online tutorials. Yet although the focus is on information for teachers and trainers, readers interested in improving their own search skills will find much useful information here, particularly in Chapters 7, 8, and 9, which cover search features and content issues, and in Chapter 10, which covers individual search engines.

Online Searching Background

Web searching has become a staple of information retrieval activity. Search engines rose to prominence along with the explosive growth of the World Wide Web in the mid-1990s. Search engines are the primary means by which millions of Web users seek information every day.

In spite of their close association today, online searching actually predates the world of the Web. As long ago as the 1970s, information professionals were using arcane command languages to search through large collections of online databases, both full text and bibliographic. DIALOG, LexisNexis, WESTLAW, MEDLARS, STN, ORBIT, and others were expensive systems. Using them effectively required intensive training on search syntax and an understanding of the scope and variety of available databases.

By the 1980s, information professionals had many products with sophisticated search interfaces. Also during the 1980s, CD-ROMs were commonly loaded on stand-alone computers for information searching, and eventually CD-ROMs were networked to provide broader access to the information content. Dial-up bulletin board systems, both commercial and free, were used to disseminate other information resources. Most of these systems had widely divergent search systems. Training sessions on these products were an essential beginning point for new users.

In those days, the buyers of these diverse information products wanted advanced search capabilities and a variety of output options. Products were typically designed for the advanced user and efforts to standardize search syntax were never fully successful.

Librarians were the initial audience for most of these systems, and soon they sought easier access and more user-friendly interfaces to provide direct database access for their communities. Throughout the 1980s and into the early 1990s, CD-ROMs and commercial search services became more available to segments of the public. As some of these products and services became easier to use, more users were able to perform searches without the benefit of a training session; still, one could not hope to become an advanced user without considerable instruction.

Also in the 1980s, consumer-oriented online services began offering information resources of their own with much simpler interfaces. Early versions of America Online (AOL), CompuServe, and similar systems included a variety of information offerings. They were subscription services and some information resources incurred additional costs. These early consumer information services were designed to be used with little or no training.

It was when the Internet began to have an impact on the information landscape that a tidal wave of changes began. As the 1990s progressed and more and more people found ways to get access to the Internet, the number of information resources grew exponentially. With huge numbers of people gaining access to the Net, many training classes focused on Internet basics such as e-mail, understanding addresses, Netiquette, and explanations of tools.

With the predominance of the Web, basic instruction on how to use the browser and how to navigate the Web became important. Users were taught how to install browser software, how links worked, and how to use bookmarks. Only after such basics had been covered did it make sense to talk about the process of searching for information online.

Internet Information Growth

While interest in online searching was growing, the Internet was developing and changing. The Internet actually dates back to 1969 and the beginning of the ARPANET, but it did not emerge as a significant information resource until the late 1980s. E-mail and Internet-based communication in general were certainly important aspects of the Internet, but few general-information sources were available. A sufficient body of information had to accumulate before the need for search engines became apparent.

As the Internet began to expand, librarians were among the first to see its potential for sharing information and providing access to information resources. One of the earliest efforts in this direction was telnet access to public library catalogs from the California and Colorado academic library systems. These catalogs came online in 1989, before Tim Berners-Lee had even released his World Wide Web to the growing Internet audience.

Other information resources were added as well, especially by the academic community, where researchers were seeking the advancement of their disciplines by sharing and collaboratively building databases that could be available to any online user.

As college campuses sought ways of providing information to students and the rest of the campus community, much attention in the early 1990s was focused on building campus-wide information systems Although several commercial options were also developed, the most successful system was a free protocol called gopher, from the University of Minnesota. Using a hierarchical, ASCII-based menu system, gopher was one of the first Internet tools for effectively sharing information within and among campuses and government agencies.

Gopher, telnet, ftp, and other complex Internet tools were the focus of Internet classes in the early 1990s. Early finding tools (not yet referred to as search engines) taught then included Archie, which searched ftp archives, and Veronica, which searched through gopher menu choices.

Origins of the Web

Meanwhile, Tim Berners-Lee, at the European Organization for Nuclear Research, had been working on another approach involving hypertext connections capable of supporting images that the physics community might need to share. When the World Wide Web and its associated hypertext transport protocol (http) and HyperText Markup Language (HTML) were introduced to the Internet community in late 1991, these protocols and languages didn't receive much attention. Most efforts seemed to focus on building content for gopher servers.

It was not until the development of Mosaic, a graphical Web browser, and subsequent versions that could be run on Windows and Macintosh operating systems that the Web quickly became the Internet publishing medium of choice. Suddenly all kinds of information appeared, from personal travel stories to computer product information to full-text government reports. As the Web came to dominate the Internet and as information multiplied, new tools for searching it were developed.

One of the problems with the first generation of finding tools was that they did not search the full text of files. Instead, these tools searched only the menus or titles. With the development of Web search engines like WebCrawler and AltaVista, however, users could search the full text of Web pages. This approach, combined with the automated crawling of Web pages, following one link after another, made for an easily built, very large searchable database of Web pages. And thus the search engines came to prominence.

Instructional Background

Librarians enjoy a wealth of literature on bibliographic instruction. This is not the place for a comprehensive survey of that trove. Instead, this book will focus on practical pedagogy related to teaching search techniques for the Web and the peculiarities of search engines. We will explore what works right now for those teaching Web searching and what techniques and strategies help when the subject matter of the instructional effort changes as fast as lightning.

The Teaching Connection

Some ask, why bother teaching search engines when they are designed to be extremely easy to use? The developers of search engines like Google expect a majority of users to use only one- or two-word queries, and they continually tweak the search engine ranking algorithms to provide useful results to such queries. Many Web searchers think they already know all the secrets of the search engines or feel that they can always find what they seek.

But a substantial number of people are more humble in evaluating their own skills. These people have questions and want training.

They ask for help at a reference desk, sign up for Web searching classes, and want to find out why their attempts at searching have not produced the results they need. The issues that face this group, including experience (or inexperience), personality type, divergent hardware and software usage, and many kinds of confusion, are outlined in Chapter 2.

When we try to help this group, we can profit from the advice of Phil Bradley, who notes that teaching Web searching is "an ongoing process—you can't teach Web searching. You can teach the concepts behind it and the strategies to employ, but ultimately it depends on the willingness of the students to put the concepts into practice in the longer term."

Teaching Simplicity

The box-and-button approach, seen on so many search engine sites, creates an instructional environment that is completely different from the one many librarians are familiar with. The commercial systems of the past were expensive and difficult for the uninitiated to use. The amount of training needed was daunting: Boolean searching, field explanations, set combinations, limiting, display options, and other capabilities could mean that for a single search system, hundreds of commands might be possible. Few were intuitive, and none offered the aura of simplicity we see from Web search engines.

Before the age of personal computing, print indexes and abstracting services were quite powerful tools for finding information. But again, use of such tools was far from intuitive. Different indexes used different sorting schemes and vocabularies and specialized indexes.

Today, search engine users click a single button to submit a search, and surveys show that people are often quite satisfied with the results. Indeed, most search engine industry watchers note that since the late 1990s, the relevance algorithms that search engines use to rank results pages have improved greatly.

Joe Barker remembers his early days teaching Web searching and maintaining his site at the University of California, Berkeley, when the new and growing information space on the Internet was a mystery to many people. There was a need then for training in basic Internet navigation. Few people knew about the information-finding tools that were available.

And even today, Joe gets about three requests per week from teachers of Web searching or Web site evaluation who want to use the materials on his Web site. It seems that in some ways the audience for search instruction has broadened and now includes many people who were not on the Web just a few years ago.

The State of Web Searching Today

We have recently entered the Google age, when one search engine tends to dominate the mindset of vast numbers of Internet searchers. The box-and-button approach has become so widespread that many of the older, expensive, commercial search systems have developed single box-and-button search screens themselves. All these systems have become much easier to use.

So why teach Web searching? If, as some would have us believe, people can just go to Google, enter a couple of words, click the search button, and magically get all the information they could possibly want, what remains to be taught?

The answer lies behind the seeming ease and speed of today's search engines. The colossal amount of information freely available on the Web is sometimes easy to find and at other times manages to hide from all but the most skilled searchers. But the truth is, the success of your quest depends completely on the kind of information you need and how important the right answer is.

In fact, Web search engines, even Google, are still a long way from providing access to all information. They do not even begin to search all the information available on the Internet. Although Google, Yahoo!, and MSN Search already index billions of Web pages, none of them provides accurate, authoritative answers to many questions. One indication of this dilemma is the press coverage of Web searching in recent years. While one article gushes over how easy it is to find information online, the next bemoans how incredibly difficult it is to find good data on the Web.

I have been teaching workshops on search engines and the Internet for more than a decade, and in the past few years, the demand for these workshops has increased and broadened. In the past we used to teach select groups of users—people with frequent searching needs who were willing to make an effort to learn the systems. Today, everyone with access to the Web seems to want to learn at least a little more about searching it.

Many Web surfers still use the first search engine they learned or, alternatively, the default engine provided by their browser or Internet access provider. Thus, many AOL users use AOL Search without ever knowing that they are searching a portion of the Google database. Internet Explorer users may just click the Search button and accept the default MSN Search option. Small Internet access providers may simply put a Yahoo! Search Marketing link on their home page, making it the default for their users. Although these companies increase their economic viability, their users may be unaware of the alternatives available.

Google users, confident they use the "best" search engine and can find all answers, eventually come across a difficult question—a school assignment to find information not available on the Web or a research problem at work requiring more details than the open Web offers—and suddenly the wonder tool fails.

I have talked with users who, after a few failures with a particular tool, give up on it and assume it will not work for other searches either. New employees often come to the job with experience in searching only for popular topics and they assume that the success they saw with those searches will be repeated when they try searching for work-related topics. Unfortunately, they are often disappointed.

Changing Patterns

Those of us who have been teaching Internet searching for a number of years have seen the content and approach of our sessions change greatly. We taught search tools like Veronica, Archie, and Jughead in the days when gopher and ftp dominated the Internet's information landscape. In the earliest days of the Web, search tools like the World Wide Web Worm and the Configurable Unified Search Engine (CUSI) were available but not widely known or used (Notess 1995). More recently, we taught AltaVista, Northern Light, Excite, and Infoseek.

Now many of these tools are gone. How long will it be before the latest tools are eclipsed by something new? Teaching Web searching is not easy, and curricula, lesson plans, outlines, and handouts have to be updated constantly. As Danny Sullivan of Search Engine Watch notes, one major problem with teaching Web searching is the time constraint. "There's simply so much to cover, and generally so little time to do it." Read on to explore the issues, find new concepts, experiment with different approaches, and wonder at the complexity of teaching Web search skills.

Chapter 2

Understanding Our Audience

The potential audience for Web search instruction is quite broad. Traditional bibliographic instruction has been aimed primarily at specific user groups doing bibliographic research in a defined subject area. Web searching, on the other hand, arouses interest from all kinds of users. Almost any Web user can benefit from some basic training in Web searching.

Those who typically teach only traditional library researchers need to give some thought to this broader audience. What kinds of people search the Web in addition to those doing traditional research? Here is a partial list:

- Online shoppers searching for specific products

- News hounds hunting for breaking headline news and older background

- Researchers looking for research progress reports before a study is finished

- Teens searching for popular information such as celebrity gossip, the latest releases of their favorite music groups, and reviews and summaries of new movies

- Travelers checking hotel prices and seeking sites that offer information about destination attractions

- Hobbyists looking for discussion groups and online communities of like-minded individuals

It is important to realize that these groups are not necessarily separate and distinct audiences. The corporate marketing manager who is looking for detailed market research on competitors in the morning could be searching for local political news, trying to buy an unusual collectible, checking the weekend's symphony schedule, and searching for a summer vacation destination in the evening.

Many of us do a wide variety of searching on the Web, but our Web searching is very different from searching traditional subject-focused databases. If someone is going to search a medical research database like MEDLINE, we can make some basic assumptions, such as the desire for medical information from journal articles. For general Web searching, we cannot assume a common need. All we can assume is that a person is searching for *something*—a bit vague as a starting point.

On the other hand, this variety of interests can be a benefit for teachers because they can draw examples from topics intriguing to a broad cross section of the audience. The search techniques are pretty much the same whether someone is searching for information about a new neighbor or trying to track down safety information about a hazardous substance. If you use an example from popular culture, students may remember it when they have an important work-related search, even if the latter topic holds less interest for them personally.

Not all audiences will appreciate examples drawn from popular culture, but if you can get some sense of your audience ahead of time, you can usually find one or more topics that will interest most of the group. Understanding an audience and recognizing the makeup of a group is an important component in reaching them and holding their interest. Try to characterize some individuals and plan for their reactions.

General Audience Characteristics

In talking with many other Web searching trainers, I have been astounded by the diversity of our audiences. They range from school children to company CEOs, market researchers to college students, engineers to plumbers, and many, many others. Sometimes we encounter this diverse range in a single group.

Yet, perhaps surprisingly, the members of this wide diversity of audiences often fall into three general groups: the novice, the know-it-all, and the experienced user. As with most generalizations, these groupings neither capture everyone nor completely describe many of those who come close to one of the stereotypes. Still, it is useful for an instructor to consider these three groups and plan strategies to keep the attention of each while still accomplishing instructional objectives. I have often found that even in a session consisting of only three students, one will fall into each of these categories.

Novices

The beginning Web searcher, the computer shunner, the new researcher—all of these are included in the novice category. The novice is the student for whom some basic aspect of Web searching is new. Perhaps it is someone who does not yet know how to use a mouse or someone who has been a frequent user of instant messaging and e-mail but who has spent little time doing research on the Web. Some in the group may have used the Web for years but never used the browser address box to enter a universal resource locator (URL).

Despite the prevailing assumption that all members of the younger generation know how to do everything involving computers, plenty of younger students fall into the novice category. These young people may be extremely adept at finding MP3 files for their iPod or searching a peer-to-peer network such as BitTorrent, yet they may never have searched for textual information. And most young students do not yet have the life experience to understand the context of many questions.

Older students, especially those who have not used computers or the Web very much, will often present themselves as novices. But not all of them are, and once they learn certain basics, some move along at a rapid rate. Age itself is not a predictor of novice status.

Novices need special handling in an instructional setting because they may lack background or experience in simple computer navigation functions. Novices may need to learn some of the basics of computer use, Web navigation, and the different kinds of boxes and buttons. Movement of the mouse may be difficult, and the concept of clicking on certain words rather than others may be brand new to them.

Know-It-Alls

For lack of a better term, I use "know-it-all" to describe people who come into a training session with a bit of a chip on their shoulder. The know-it-alls think they know how search engines work and how best to use them. They may feel as if there is nothing very complicated about Web searching and that they have heard it all before.

Perhaps they do not really want to be at the session but were told to attend by their supervisor. Sometimes they sit in the back of the room and play on the Web at their own pace rather than follow the instructor-led examples. Or they may sit in the front and wait for a chance to contradict the instructor.

In academia, the know-it-all is rarely in the majority, but one or more seem to crop up in almost every class. Trainers encounter know-it-alls in a variety of settings, from the law firm to the public library. A librarian at an engineering firm told me that all the engineers in her firm match the know-it-all profile and make for an especially challenging instructional session.

The problems with this group are obvious. One helpful solution is to quickly demonstrate that you have some knowledge and understanding of search engines that they do not. If you know ahead of time that you may have a few (or more) know-it-all attendees, plan ahead. Check the latest search engine news for a very recent development to mention; either they will not have heard about it and will be impressed with your knowledge, or they will know about it and will realize your knowledge is up-to-date. Following the latest news will also help when unexpected results come up in the class. You may be able to explain such results by tying them to recent changes.

Another approach is to have a couple of advanced and rarely used search commands at hand to use in an example early on in the presentation. Show a few simple searches, and then try an example that uses a couple of the advanced techniques to find a page that would not otherwise be found. Or talk about something like Google Suggest and then ask how many have used it before. If the know-it-alls haven't used it before, you'll have a much better idea of their actual experience and knowledge.

In her full-day sessions, Rita Vine takes a similar approach. For many groups she teaches, Rita will find the top five or six subject-oriented Web sites, or "subject starters" as she calls them, in the subject area of the audience. Then she prepares exercises to help the audience discover the strengths and weaknesses of each of those sites. Rita says, "We generally incorporate that piece of the training session at or near the beginning because the information is so valuable to learners. I try to give them something very valuable within the first 15 minutes. This brings a renewed commitment to a session that they may otherwise have been hesitant or resistant to be part of."

The challenge is to find a way to convince the know-it-alls that they do not know it all and that you have at least a few tricks to teach them. Find a way to catch them at the beginning of the session, tempt them with a few tidbits that they do not know, and then reward them verbally when they share accurate information. If you can accomplish all of this, which is not always easy, you may leave the session with some new fans.

Experienced Users

The most enjoyable students to teach and, for some fortunate instructors, the bulk of the attendees in a search class are those I refer to as experienced users. These are the individuals who really want to learn about Web searching but who already have some basic experience with computers and the Web. They know how to use a mouse, navigate on the screen, and use the standard functions in a Web browser, and they even know the name of the Web browser and the operating system that they use.

The experienced users are already online searchers who have used one or more search engines. But they are also humble enough to admit that they don't know everything, and they want to learn more about Web searching. They may even be successful with searches for popular topics. But they may have had less success with other kinds of searching in which the results are more important to them, personally or professionally.

These are the people who ask intelligent questions. They take notes and want to try hands-on exercises. And they are the easiest to teach because they want to learn and already understand the basics.

Pairing Strategies for Hands-On Workshops

In Chapter 3 we will look at various types of instructional sessions and their strengths and weaknesses. In a hands-on instructional setting, having a mixture of novices, know-it-alls, and experienced users in the same class presents some pedagogical problems. How can you teach the novices the basics they need while keeping the know-it-alls in check?

A strategy I tried once (and quickly dropped) was to pair a novice with a know-it-all. I thought the challenge of helping the novice would keep the know-it-all on track and at the right pace to get through the exercises. The know-it-all could certainly teach the novice the basics of using a mouse, starting up a Web browser, clicking on links, and using the back buttons, right? Wrong. Unfortunately, the know-it-all simply took control of the keyboard and mouse. Then instead of following along with the examples, the know-it-all just pulled up a few favorite sites, saying to the novice, "Just start here." So the novice, still wondering how to use a mouse, was not paying attention to me and was impressed with how well the know-it-all could use the computer. The know-it-all was ignoring me, showing off to the novice, and even contradicting (inaccurately, of course) some of the points I was teaching. I ended up having to work individually with each of these students to get them back on track with the rest of the class.

Separate those two groups! The pairing strategy can work, but pair a novice with an experienced user. Give clear directions to the experienced user to demonstrate whatever basics the novice may need, and check in with them frequently. What do you do with the know-it-alls? Pair them up together on one computer and let them argue about the best search strategy or the disadvantages of a particular search engine. After giving them a little time to butt heads, check in with them; you can be the arbiter, and you may be able to gain their respect by giving them sufficient information to settle their dispute.

Audience Assessment

In addition to categorizing your audience members, it is wise to discover at least a bit about their experience and background ahead of time or as early in the session as possible. For some groups, you may be able to get an accurate assessment from the session organizer. For others, you may not know anything until the session starts. How have the audience members been searching, using search engines, or browsing on the Web? Knowing the search tools they have been using before the session starts can help avoid complications later.

Certainly, the way students describe themselves or are described by others will not always be accurate. As consultant Gary Price says, "Many people say they are advanced, yet they don't know ... what the Google cache is ... or how to limit a search to a specific domain." Gary continues, "Many times you don't know what the real experience level is until the presentation gets started and you get the 'feel' of the room. ... Bottom line: Don't assume. Everyone wants to be advanced. A good trainer can quickly adapt to the audience."

Jeff Humphrey starts his classes by teaching Yahoo!. He does this to help assess the audience and adapt to it. "My sessions include everyone from circulation clerks who have barely used a mouse to librarians at major corporations who have been searching online for 20-plus years. Starting with Yahoo! allows me to better determine everyone's level of expertise."

Rita Vine explains that at the outset of a contract, trainers at her company, Workingfaster.com, "conduct some sort of needs assessment to be sure that we're addressing learner needs and, as appropriate, management needs." Since Rita usually conducts day-long contracted training sessions, this approach makes perfect sense. "We don't do anything fancy. Typically there are three phone discussions: one with someone identified as a low-skill learner, one with someone identified as a high-skill learner, and one with a manager. It works really well and takes little time."

If there is no opportunity for such an assessment before a session starts, the instructor can just ask a few questions at the beginning. In hands-on workshops with a limited number of attendees, I will typically ask the students to introduce themselves and answer a few questions, such as "What is your current favorite search engine?" To get a sense of the students' usual computing environment, I ask for a show of hands for Windows users, then Mac users, and finally UNIX or Linux users. If I have a Mac user in the audience, I'll need to address different mouse and keyboard issues (discussed later in this chapter).

Navigation Versus Search Confusion

With members of all three groups, as well as any who may fall somewhere in between or outside my classification, a number of issues can cause confusion because of the way the Web itself and Web browsers in particular have developed.

For some portion of our audience, the difference between searching and basic Web browser navigation is not always clear. Users often suffer from button confusion, box confusion, or address confusion.

Some Internet users do not frequent the Web. For the most part, they use only e-mail or instant messaging, or they browse the Web by clicking only on items on the default home page. Such users may not know the difference between the many buttons labeled Search and the various data entry boxes, or the difference between a URL and a search term.

One example that demonstrates the confusion between navigation and search occurred several years ago while I was working at the library reference desk. A patron wanted to know how to use the computers and, in particular, how to use them to get to a particular URL. (Actually, she did not even know she had a URL or any idea what the acronym stood for.)

After I showed her how to enter the URL in the browser's address box and then brought up the specific Web pages successfully at the

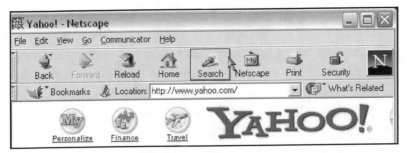

Figure 2.1   Netscape search button

reference desk, she went to try it for herself. Since she went to a public computer near the desk, I was able to check on her progress. Unfortunately, she was not successful in replicating what I had just shown her and grew frustrated by her failure.

I went over to her computer to see what the problem was. At that time, we had a version of Netscape on the public computers, just as at the reference desk. It turned out she was entering the URL into the correct box. However, since the Web was new to her, she then looked for somewhere to click on the screen rather than just pressing the Enter key as I had done (something I hadn't thought to emphasize). Seeing the Search button above the address box in the top tool bar (Figure 2.1), she clicked on it.

The Search button did bring up a new Web page—not for the URL she had painstakingly entered into the address box, however, but for the Netscape Search page. The Netscape Search page contained another box. Seeing the new box, she entered the URL there and clicked on the Search button above it. The Netscape Search page reloaded once more, with the unfortunate consequence of erasing the URL she had just entered for a second time.

Once I had observed this behavior, it was easy to correct. I had her enter the URL and press the Enter key, which successfully retrieved the page. Through her trial and error, I believe she learned this particular lesson well. There was a lesson in it for me, also.

Remembering What We Did Not Know

The previous story illustrates several aspects of user behavior that can be difficult to keep in mind. Most of us have used the Web for years. Most of us have used several versions of a given Web browser if not several different browsers over that time. We have used numerous other computer programs as well. Some of our behaviors have become automatic, and it is easy to forget that what is now second nature to us will not come instinctively to newer users.

This can be true even for experienced users, many of whom may use the same version of a Web browser in very different ways from the instructor. Each of the various browsers is designed to be easy to use. Together they offer several ways to achieve the same action. Developers of these browsers have tried to anticipate user mistakes and redirect users to useful places.

Most librarians tell me they never use their browser's search button. Most do not use the Go button that is sometimes available to the right of the address box. Most do not input search terms directly into the address box. Instead, they might install a specialized service like the Google Toolbar (available at toolbar. google.com) and use it to initiate all their searches. Because they do information-intensive work, they look for specialized search tools to expedite searching.

Yet as instructors, we need to remember that our own search and navigation behavior may be quite different from that of our students. Plenty of other people use the browser search button or whatever default their Internet access provider (such as AOL or MSN) might choose for them.

While the example given involved the use of Netscape, confusion can just as easily occur with Internet Explorer (IE). Click the search button on IE and a separate search pane opens up on the left-hand side of the screen (Figure 2.2). If the default has not been changed, it will go to an MSN Search box. Entering a URL into that box and clicking the search button in the tool bar will result in the disappearance of the search pane.

The browser companies eventually recognized this problem and recent versions of IE, Firefox, and Netscape feature a Go button to the right of the address box (see Figure 2.2 for the IE example).

To help yourself understand the challenge for new users, try this exercise: Plan a Web search for a piece of information you think will be easy to find. Write down each and every step you go through to find the information, beginning with turning on the computer. Then consider how difficult it would be to accomplish any or all of those steps if they were new to you. This should give you a good sense of the challenge facing some new users.

Figure 2.2 Internet Explorer search button and side panel

Box Confusion

Although it is second nature to many of us, the differences between the various boxes for data entry and the various buttons to click that help us search or navigate continue to be a significant source of confusion for many users. Consider, for instance, the old AOL home page (Figure 2.3). Four boxes were visible, highlighted in the figure for illustration purposes: the browser's address box, two boxes for signing into AOL, and a box for AOL Search.

The browser builders have long known about this potential for confusion. For just that reason, the address box can also function as a search box, depending on which version of a browser is being used and how it has been configured. If you type "green mints" into the address bar of IE, the default settings will automatically send the search to MSN Search.

For those new to the Web, it can take a while to understand the difference between browser boxes (the top highlighted box in Figure 2.3) and the various boxes on Web pages (the other three boxes in Figure 2.3). The bottom line in the minds of browser and search engine designers is that no matter what a user types into a given box, the results should be useful. While their approach is well intentioned, it can encourage incorrect behavior because it contributes to users confusing Web navigation with Web searching.

Address Confusion

URLs are the lifeblood of the Web. URLs are addresses for specific Web pages and can be entered directly into the browser's address box to go to a specific page. But users can also navigate to a Web site by simply typing the name of an organization (instead of the URL) into the browser's address box, getting search results, and then clicking on an appropriate results link.

Address confusion is similar to box confusion. The search engine companies are quite aware of the problem; a surprising number of search terms entered each day at the likes of Google,

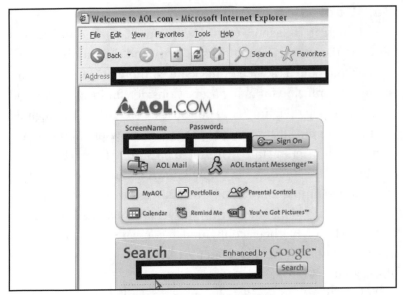

Figure 2.3   Old AOL home page with boxes highlighted

Yahoo!, and MSN consist of nothing more than a URL. People even enter http://www.google.com at Google! These novice users need to learn how to navigate to a site using a URL, how and when to use a search engine, and what the distinction is between these activities.

Button Confusion

While generally not as problematic as box confusion, button confusion can and does occur. If you refer once again to Figure 2.3, you will see seven buttons on the browser toolbar. In addition, the old AOL home page included several more buttons, such as Sign On, AOL Mail, AOL Instant Messenger, and Search. In fact, the AOL home page placed two buttons labeled Search in close proximity; one in the browser bar and the other on the Web page itself. Each Search button responds differently.

Google presents another case of button confusion. It takes the typical search engine approach of offering a single search box on its page but provides buttons labeled Google Search and I'm Feeling Lucky. Many people don't know that I'm Feeling Lucky takes them directly to the first page returned by a Google search; surprisingly, most Google users have never tried this button.

Part of the confusion with buttons can be that we just don't use them: With search engines, it is more convenient to press the Enter key after typing a query than to grab the mouse and click a button. (In the case of Google, simply hitting Enter defaults to the regular Google search.) The challenge to an instructor is to be aware of the different ways in which students may interact with a multibutton user interface.

Browser Differences and Problems

The majority of the Internet public now uses Internet Explorer (IE), but many people are using Web browsers such as Firefox, Mozilla, Opera, Netscape, and AOL. Even among the users of IE, there are differences: There are both PC and Mac users, and a fair portion of IE users at any given time will not have upgraded to the latest version of the browser.

It is important to note that various versions of a browser have different defaults and work differently. Even users of identical IE versions may experience differences due to settings and installation choices. In particular, users may experience different results in regard to the default search engine used, the way the search button behaves, the way the browser handles words entered into the address bar, and the availability of search engine toolbars.

Some software that may have been installed inadvertently can even hijack search engine results: When users enter the URL for Google or Yahoo!, they may get nothing or be sent to some other site. Programs like SpyBot (www.safer-networking.org) may be able to fix the problem in some cases but not always. For example, the QHOSTS trojan virus hijacks many popular search engine addresses. Fortunately, fixes are available at sites like software. brown.edu/dist/w-cleanqhosts.html.

Be aware of these types of problems and the differences students may experience outside the class so that you will know how to answer when they ask you why things work differently from one computer to the next.

Operating System and Hardware Issues

Like browsers, operating systems vary in terms of their default search functionality and capabilities. Although an operating system may have less direct effect on Web searching than a browser does, small details such as mouse functions and keystroke combinations can have an impact. Mac users may have questions about Sherlock, a Mac-specific search tool. As well, when talking about using the Windows Control key, you may need to mention that the Command or Apple key should be used on the Mac keyboard.

Most Mac users have a mouse with a single button. When these users are in a Windows lab, I often find them clicking the middle or right mouse button. Even Windows users have many mouse choices these days. If they are used to a simple, two-button mouse, and the lab computers provide a three-button mouse or one with a scroll wheel, some explanation may be in order. If the lab is using laptops or unusual pointing devices, expect to spend some time teaching the class how to use the trackball, touchpad, or finger mouse. Some of these devices are difficult for users to master quickly.

Adaptability and Change

Given all the issues I've already mentioned and the many different kinds of audiences we may teach, it should be clear that adaptability is a key component in successful Web search training. Not only do the search engines constantly change, but our audience changes as well. This is exemplified by Joe Barker's experience both at the University of California, Berkeley (UC Berkeley), where he teaches Web searching and maintains a Web site, and through the Infopeople project, for which he has classroom sessions and also online sessions via Blackboard. "The impact of my teaching in each venue is totally different—one [is] local and international [UC Berkeley], the other California librarians exclusively. I live two lives around teaching Web searching. Over the years, the UC Berkeley part has changed enormously. ... The whole Web site I developed grew out of the massive need for these classes back in 1996, and many who came to these classes used them like a manual or guide to learning the Web. I printed various pages from the site to make a kind of textbook for these courses. Now it is used more heavily by teachers and students around the world than at Berkeley." (Interested readers may want to visit "Finding Information on the Internet: A Tutorial" at www.lib.berkeley. edu/TeachingLib/Guides/Internet/FindInfo.html.)

For Joe, audience needs have changed considerably since 1996. Instead of focusing only on Web searching, he is "teaching the catalogs, journal index(es), maybe news, and *then* ... Web searching."

The expanding audience for Web search training mirrors the growing public interest in all aspects of the Internet. The audience and activity in its early years were heavily academic, but as the Web has become mainstream, the potential audience for search training has significantly broadened. In the years ahead, we can expect continuing and perhaps dramatic changes in our student demographics and in the search engines themselves. While this is a challenge for educators, it is also an exciting future that offers the opportunity to constantly update our teaching style, approach, and course content. As we enter this next phase, we should keep in mind that the better we understand our users, the more we can empower them.

Chapter 3

Choosing an Instructional Session Type

Teaching happens in all kinds of settings and situations. Choosing the most appropriate session type for a particular group is an important part of teaching. Several permutations are possible. The class can be a standard lecture with no Internet connection or even computers. The instructor may have a computer with Internet access and projection capabilities while the attendees do not. Or the class can be hands-on in which everyone has an Internet-connected computer.

Then there are online variants, including online interactive instruction and more static forms of training. Although distance education might seem to be a natural environment for teaching Web searching, each type of instructional setting has its unique problems, advantages, and special considerations.

In an ideal world, the type of instructional session would be based on the goals for the session and audience characteristics. A session would be designed to match the learning style of the audience as well as the instructor's purpose and intent. Yet in the real world of teaching and training, the type of session offered is typically decided by many factors—the facilities available, the number of attendees, the time and capabilities of the instructor, the amount of preparation time available to the instructor, the amount of time available for the session, and the functionality of the equipment. Even more important, sometimes the trainer's contract specifies a certain type of session without considering all the implications of the choice.

Hands-On Sessions

For many situations, a hands-on session is the ideal learning environment. In one such format, attendees each have an Internet-connected computer, and the instructor has one with projection capabilities. This format usually involves a lecture component followed by hands-on time, in which students practice elements explained in the lecture.

Advantages

The principal advantage of a hands-on session is that the students actually try out what is being taught to them. Most people learn better through practice, and the hands-on setting allows the students to experiment. If the exercise fails to work quite as neatly as the instructor's example, then the students can ask for clarification and try again. Hands-on practice provides many opportunities for student–teacher interaction.

For students with a tactile/kinesthetic learning style, the hands-on setting provides an opportunity to get physically involved with the material. Students type in the queries, use the mouse to move around the pages, try to go forward and backward on the Web as appropriate, and see the results of their tactile experience.

The great strength of the hands-on session is that it typically incorporates a lecture for the auditory learners, and for the visual learners, it uses examples displayed for all to see. All three groups have the opportunity to put concepts into practice, make mistakes, learn what went wrong, and try again.

If the classroom computer system is configured to send the instructor's screen to student computers, students can see examples up close. This capability is a significant advantage over classes with projection capabilities that are of low resolution or otherwise difficult to see.

In summary, hands-on sessions provide the following benefits:

- Students are able to try exercises.

- Tactile/kinesthetic learners benefit.

- Both auditory and visual learners benefit.

- Students are able to see examples up close.

Disadvantages

The hands-on approach to training does not work in every situation. First and foremost, the necessary facilities may not be available. Although a hands-on session can be reproduced to some extent through detailed pencil-and-paper exercises, the kinesthetic experience is quite different and may not translate well.

In addition to these limitations, hands-on training sessions are slow. If the instructor uses the typical approach of teaching a point and then having the class practice, each item takes longer to cover than it would in a lecture setting. Spending more time on a particular instructional topic limits the amount of material the instructor is able to cover in the class.

Hands-on sessions work very well with a dozen or fewer attendees, but as the class size grows, the instructor needs more time to monitor individual progress, deal with computer problems, and keep attendees on task and on the same page. Veteran instructor Paul Barron says, "More than 20 attendees in a hands-on training session is too many to monitor and help without slowing the class down too much." Personally I prefer fewer than 20 students.

A good hands-on session also requires careful planning on the part of the instructor because the exercises used should elaborate the instructional points and work smoothly. Finding the best exercises often takes considerable time. At the simplest level, the hands-on component can consist simply of having the students mimic whatever the instructor is doing. However, this technique can handicap the instructor, and students do not learn as well as they would if they were applying a demonstrated principle in a specific context.

Hands-on sessions are also vulnerable to malfunctioning computers, interrupted Internet connections, and search engine failures. Although search engine reliability has improved in recent years, hardware, software, and connectivity problems continue to plague instructional sessions. Sometimes every computer in the class goes down, though it is more common in my experience for one or two workstations to exhibit some kind of strange glitch. If extra computers are available, students can be moved, but such reassignments burn up precious class time.

In summary, plan hands-on sessions with the following disadvantages in mind:

- Adequate facilities are needed.

- Fewer subjects may be covered.

- More teaching time is required as class size grows.

- Careful planning by the teacher is required.

- Necessary equipment (computers, peripheral devices, and InternFet connectivity) is not always reliable.

Facilities

For the visual learners, proper setup of the learning environment is essential. Most hands-on environments have some type of projection capability. The projection's success depends greatly on the size and resolution of the image, the lighting in the room, and the visual ability of the attendees.

Depending on the audience group, the ability to control the student computers can be extremely helpful to the instructor. Classroom control software or even a software and hardware combination can let the instructor instantly lock all the student computers, send the screen from the instructor's station to the students' computers, display a specific student's station, and control other instructional aspects of the session.

The functionality of the classroom control system can have a strong impact on instruction. Those looking into a classroom control system should see the very useful "Classroom Control Systems" page at www.ala.org/ala/acrlbucket/is/iscommittees/ webpages/teachingmethods/classroomcontrol.htm (or snipurl. com/6ktr) from the Association of College and Research Libraries (Olson et al. 2005).

Planning

Good planning is a must for any successful hands-on session. Since typically less overall material will be covered, planning the outline of the material may take less time. But planning the exercises and other hands-on aspects of the class requires careful thought as well as testing ahead of time.

The first step in planning is to assess the hardware and software available for both the instructor and the students. What operating system and browsers are available and how will that affect any points in the outline? For example, the MSN Search toolbar requires Windows and Microsoft Internet Explorer (IE) Version 5 or later for installation, so you can't teach how to install it in a classroom of either Macs or Windows computers running only the Firefox browser. Even when the requisite operating system and browser are installed, you should check security settings ahead of time. Some labs are locked down so tightly that users cannot install anything.

If you are using a particular Web page for a hands-on class, you will need to get all the students to start there. Some trainers set their class home page as the default home page in the browser so that any time attendees get off track, they can click the Home button and get back to the starting point. Some instructors have all the attendees enter the URL, but if it is a long one, I recommend using a URL-shortening service like SnipURL.com or TinyURL. com to avoid the typing errors that can occur with long URLs.

Also consider your time constraints. Ran Hock, principal of Online Strategies, points out the difficulty of balancing hands-on lab time with lecture and demonstration. "In most of my courses that are hands-on (the majority of courses I teach), I encourage students to be hands-on throughout the session, and then I also devote portions to just hands-on teaching. How much time to give them in the latter is often problematic, especially when there is a lot of material to cover. A minimum amount of time is necessary for the hands-on experience to be effective. Give them too much time and some get bored, and then you can't cover the material necessary to accomplish the course goals."

One approach I have used for keeping a class together in the hands-on environment is to create a course page using frames. The intent is that there will always be a course navigational menu (on the left side or the top of the screen) so that wherever an exercise may lead them, the students can get to the next section when it is time to move on. For an example and the technical basics of this approach, see Chapter 11.

Exercises

When using exercises to reinforce points, plan an appropriate amount of time. Gary Price gives lecture and demonstration sessions more often than hands-on training, but in a training course in California for Infopeople, he conducted a hands-on session. Some of his exercises for that session could be accomplished relatively quickly—such as when he asked students to "take 10 seconds to find the definition of 'librarian' in Google" (an example that can show the dictionary connection capability of the search engine)—but for most examples he allowed about 10 minutes for every three questions, allocating another 7 minutes or so to go over the answers. I have often found that I spend more time going over the examples, answering questions about them, and explaining the points I was trying to make than the students take to actually do the exercises. So be sure to have enough time for the number of exercises being planned.

What kinds of exercises work well? That often depends on the style of the instructor. For phrase searching, I have often used a very basic exercise of searching a multiple word query, first without quotation marks, then with quotation marks, and having the group note the difference in the number and the relevance of results. For example, a search on the name of my town's founder, john bozeman, without quotation marks, yields about 100 times as many results as the phrase search "john bozeman". (Even though I know the numbers given by most search engines are quite inaccurate, the sheer difference in magnitude makes the example effective.)

For longer sessions, plan thoughtfully when to incorporate hands-on time. Jeff Humphrey, veteran trainer in Indiana's library network, recalls "doing a full-day session about Indiana-specific resources, covering about 75 to 80 resources, and leaving all the practice exercises for the end of the workshop. Not a good idea at 3:45 P.M. to ask people to recollect things covered at 10:00 A.M. without giving some reinforcement in between. I now give practice time about every 40 minutes during most of my workshops."

Lecture and Demonstration Sessions

When no computer lab or set of networked laptops is available, the lecture and demonstration session tends to be the fallback approach. Although a lecture may be considered low tech, it can be held virtually anywhere. Facility needs are basic—a room where people can sit (preferably) and hear the speaker.

Some aspects of Web searching can be taught in a straight lecture environment, but most trainers and students prefer having a lecture that is interspersed with integrated demonstrations. This method allows for question-and-answer periods in which the instructor can go online in response to a student's question and demonstrate the techniques along with providing a verbal answer.

Advantages

Certainly one major advantage of the lecture-demonstration approach is that an instructor can cover much more material than in a hands-on session. For an audience that wants to learn many new things about search engines, the lecture format is ideal. The instructor can make a point and move right along to the next topic, the perfect arrangement when time is limited or when the presentation is only a small part of a larger instructional session. The lecture format provides an opportunity to cover at least a few main points.

As with hands-on sessions, knowing audience needs and desires is crucial. For an audience that learns quickly, there is no need for repetitive exercises or demonstrations of every single small point. The lecture format allows you to breeze by the topics that everyone seems to know already and to slow down and focus on those topics that need more explanation, whereas in a hands-on session, it is easy to let the carefully planned exercises control the session's pace.

Lectures offer an additional advantage to searchers with intermediate skills as the instructor is likely to cover something of interest or something new. In a slower-paced, hands-on session, an instructor may choose to cover only about five or six features and examples. If an intermediate attendee already knows all those features, the whole session may seem unnecessary. But in a lecture, especially a fast-paced one that covers a large amount of material, the intermediate users can try out later those items that are new or of special interest.

Yet even if the audience includes students who would benefit from exercises and repetition, the lecture-demonstration format can be effective. As long as the students have sufficient motivation, the instructor can create exercises for them to do later, at their own computers, in order to reinforce what was said in the lecture.

A lecture can be prepared more quickly than a hands-on session. If your opportunities to teach Web searching come with little or no advance notice, this style works well. Those of us who teach frequently about search engines can often just "wing it" when given no forewarning that we will be teaching Web searching. If an academic librarian were planning a traditional bibliographic instruction session focusing on subject-specific sources and suddenly the professor announced the session should focus on Web resources exclusively, the librarian could pull out the Web searching lecture, along with a significant section on evaluation.

In summary, lecture-demonstration sessions offer the following advantages:

- Many topics can be covered and in a quick manner.

- Exercises can be completed after the lecture.

- Lectures require less preparation time than hands-on sessions.

Disadvantages

Unfortunately, most of us do not retain everything we hear without some kind of repetition and practice. Student retention of knowledge is typically less in a lecture-demonstration session than in a hands-on session. Even when students understand what is being shown or described to them, the challenge is to help them remember pertinent points when they need to use them. Rita Vine offers this warning to lecturers:

I find that instructors try to cram way too much information into a search session. When you think about it, it takes several steps to actually learn something on a computer: First you have to watch it demonstrated, then you have to replicate that demonstration as you saw it to get a feel for it, then you have to learn to deviate from that demonstration and apply the methodology to your own example. This takes time.

Rita's point is worth careful consideration when planning a lecture on Web searching.

Sometimes the available facilities determine the type and size of the session. Unreliable computers, peripheral devices, or Internet connectivity can confound your demonstrations.

In summary, lecture-demonstration sessions involve these disadvantages:

- Students' retention is often lower than their retention in hands-on sessions.

- Time may not be sufficient to cover every step of a topic.

- The size and type of the facility determine the size of the class.

- Equipment, such as computers, peripheral devices, and Internet connectivity, is not always reliable.

Facilities

Even though lectures are subject to the same equipment malfunctions as hands-on sessions are, there is just one computer to worry about. Even so, Internet access is never guaranteed. As Phil Bradley notes, this can be especially problematic in other countries. "Good trainers need to be prepared for this to happen, especially if they're training overseas in a country that doesn't have good electricity supplies or good telecoms."

So it is wise to be prepared with some kind of backup visuals, screen captures, or examples that can be shown offline. Paul Barron notes that in his instruction sessions, he has often run into problems with Internet connection failures or interruptions:

> I am a retired marine who flew helicopters, and my philosophy of planning for the best and expecting the worst has influenced me to develop a detailed presentation using screen shots of actual Web searches to emphasize a teaching point. (The PowerPoint presentation for the 6-hour workshop is 280 slides.) In the event the Internet fails, the screen shots of actual searches enable the presentation to continue while the Internet connection is restored. Since all demonstrated searches are practiced, I also have laminated sheets with the enlarged graphic of the advanced search template so that attendees print their search queries while waiting for the Internet gods to reconnect to earth.

Teaching Web searching in a lecture format with no demonstration is possible, but having a computer, Internet connection, and projection capabilities makes for a better learning experience. The demonstration aspect allows the lecturer to show examples live. Many instructors prefer a canned demonstration, which removes any worry over whether the Internet connection will go down or a search engine will behave unusually, but I prefer to show live examples whenever possible. Web search engines change often; creating a canned session that demonstrates what worked last week doesn't serve your students well. What is the point of teaching how a search engine *used* to behave?

Note that Paul described his approach as a fallback in case the Internet goes down or the facilities fail to work. His laminated sheets incorporate the idea of using offline techniques for getting the students involved and providing some kinesthetic learning. "Screen shots are key to an effective presentation and one item ... that attendees like most." The entire presentation can be too long to print. On the other hand, handouts are necessary "to ensure that attendees can read the search queries when they practice the searches after the workshop and read the URLs of recommended resources."

PowerPoint offers several options for the types of printed handouts it can produce, so Paul is careful to make the result match his purpose. To help participants "see the correct search syntax and read the URL of sites recommended in the final section, the presentation is printed in three sections: six slides per page for the presentation introduction, two slides per page for the demonstrated and practiced searches, and four slides per page for evaluated resources. Two slides per page for the demonstrated and practiced search can be read easily and practiced after the workshop. The evaluated resource URL can also be easily read when four slides per pages are printed." The handouts are additional insurance in the event of facility problems.

Another facilities issue, especially in some corporate settings, is very restrictive firewalls and other security settings. Rita Vine describes the problem of "persistent mechanical problems with labs, projectors, and overzealous system administrators who completely disable most computer functionality."

I have talked with researchers and librarians in government and corporate settings who have no ability to choose the Web browser they use, who are not allowed to install plug-ins, and whose security settings forbid both Java and JavaScript. Shortsighted systems administrators may not realize (or do not care) that such restrictions can completely disable access to certain information sources, on both the free Web and commercial databases.

When faced with teaching in a place that is subject to such overly restrictive security settings, make an effort to give the session off-site. That way you can demonstrate the tools and information resources that your students may not have access to at work and present strategies (such as using a home computer) for accessing that material. If the instruction needs to be on-site, be forewarned that some important Web sites and favorite tools may be unavailable.

Planning

Even though one of the advantages of doing a lecture-demonstration is the ability to teach with little or no planning, that is no excuse for not planning when there is time. Several important points to consider when you plan are the material to cover, the way to get your points across to your audience, and time for questions. Use planning time to prepare several examples to demonstrate a point because any one of them may fail to work during the instruction session.

Furthermore, plan to incorporate some kind of exercises in the session. Of course you can provide exercises for attendees to do later, but my experience has been that people rarely take the time to do them because they feel they just do not have enough time.

I recommend either creating some exercises for students to work on during the session or using no exercises at all. If instructors prepare some brief exercises on paper ahead of time, attendees will have a chance to reinforce the points being taught. Building in a method to check for student retention in this format is important because the instructor can't use hands-on exercises to see how everyone is doing. Checking retention can be as simple as walking around the class and looking over the students' shoulders.

The handouts or workbook can include enlarged screen shots of search pages for the attendees to fill in. Have them circle the buttons that need to be clicked. Rita Vine uses a workbook approach. The workbook includes, for example, a shot of a search results screen; students are asked to identify the ads in the screen shot and the source of advertising. See Appendix B for some excerpts from her workbook.

Semi-Online Tutorials

Since Web searching is an online activity, it seems like a natural topic for online instruction. Self-paced online tutorials or live, interactive online sessions are possibilities that will be explored in more depth in Chapter 4. Here I want to discuss some shortcuts to offering semi-online instruction. These can be one-on-one or one-to-many teaching sessions.

One form of the semi-online approach incorporates screen shots, PowerPoint, and e-mail delivery. I have spoken with several attendees of my workshops on teaching Web searching who use PowerPoint in some interesting ways. Some trainers use PowerPoint for introductory lessons before the live session, and others use it during the live session. Although the same techniques can be used with other presentation software, PowerPoint is a great tool because it allows the target audience to view what's going on.

One corporate librarian uses PowerPoint for remote instruction when he receives a request for assistance with a particular search engine or commercial database. Since the patron is at a remote location rather than in his office, the librarian takes screen shots, pastes them into PowerPoint, circles the search box, adds balloons with explanatory text, and ships the completed presentation to the user. The presentation is designed to be self-paced, and the recipient can phone the librarian with follow-up questions.

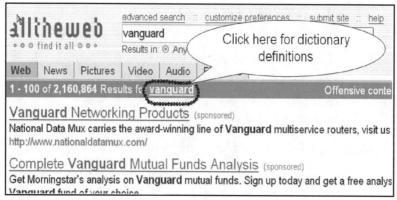

Figure 3.1   Call-out bubble used to show dictionary definition at AlltheWeb

Another librarian uses the same principle but delivers the images via e-mail. It helps to have the whole organization on the same e-mail platform so that you know the recipient can receive graphics in an e-mail message. At the basic level, this kind of instruction can consist of taking screen shots, pasting them into Paint or another readily available graphics program, and circling the buttons to click. Then paste the images into a single e-mail message and include text instructions between the pasted images. If you are not using e-mail, add to the screen shot a call-out text bubble with basic instructions (Figure 3.1).

Capturing a Screen Shot Within PowerPoint

Generally, it should take an instructor about 5 to 10 minutes to add a screen shot to a PowerPoint slide and send it out. With a little practice, most people should find it fairly easy and quick to do. So how does this process of capturing screen shots, circling a box, and adding a text bubble or balloon work? Here is the process using PowerPoint in Windows:

1. Find the Print Screen key (usually in the upper right-hand portion of the keyboard and sometimes labeled PrtSc).

2. Go to the specific search engine page from which you wish to take the screen shot, making sure that all forms and boxes are filled in as you want them to be. Also, maximize the browser window.

3. Press the Print Screen key, which copies the entire screen.

4. Start a new presentation in PowerPoint (and make sure you are in the "Normal" view).

5. To put the screen shot into the first slide, paste by pressing Control-v or using Edit/Paste.

6. To add a highlighting circle around the box or a call-out text bubble, click Insert/Picture/Autoshapes (see Figure 3.2).

7. Type any text into the call-out.

8. Repeat the process as needed and save.

Because of the use of screen shots, the resulting PowerPoint file is likely to be quite large. You can send the PowerPoint presentation as an attachment to an e-mail, but make sure first that the recipient can receive large files. If you are sending the e-mail within your organization, large files will probably be accepted without any problem. Putting the presentation up on a Web or ftp server is an alternative.

Another option is to paste the PowerPoint slides within an e-mail. To do so using Microsoft Paint, save the images as bitmaps (although bitmaps tend to be extremely large files). If using another image program, you can convert the graphic files into a JPEG or GIF format, the standards for Web image display. These are typically much smaller files than bitmaps.

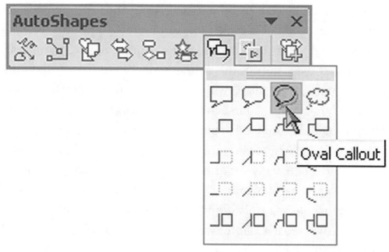

Figure 3.2   AutoShapes toolbar in PowerPoint showing call-out choices

Course Coverage and Distance Education

For people in academic settings, sometimes Web searching can be taught as part of a semester-long course (the length of sessions will be discussed in more detail in Chapter 5). In these cases, the Web searching component can be covered in multiple sessions and in several different formats.

Some instructors may focus an entire course on Web searching, but more commonly, searching is just one component of an information literacy course. In such settings instructors have much more flexibility in structuring the Web searching component. Rita Vine says, "If I could make a perfect instruction environment, I would have a series of 90-minute sessions instead of an entire day. In my experience, 90 minutes is the perfect amount of time to teach one or two major concepts, demonstrate, and have the class replicate and then deviate to apply what they learned using their own examples."

When teaching Web searching in a course, the instructor can get much closer to Rita's ideal. At the same time, the Web searching component needs to be balanced with the other goals of the course.

A further extension of the course model is to move the entire course online. I have talked with a few people teaching information literacy and searching courses online as part of a distance education program. Online courses can include a section on Web searching.

In general, teaching via some kind of interactive distance delivery platform is usually more time consuming for the instructor, requires very careful planning, and may not be as effective in conveying concepts as in-person training sessions. Some of the techniques we will see in Chapter 4, on online tutorials, can be adapted for use in online courses.

In either case, the great advantages of teaching Web searching within a course are time and accountability. Much more time can be spent on the topic throughout a semester course. As for accountability, the pressure of tests and quizzes and the final grade means that many students will do whatever exercises you assign.

A disadvantage of the course approach is that it serves far fewer people. Furthermore, more planning time is needed by the instructor. But even if we instructors can find the time, people who need to search the Web skillfully rarely have time for a multisession course on Web searching.

Sheila Webber, who teaches Web searching as part of a large, college-level course, says, "I feel that Web searching ought to be seen by the students as part of searching in general (or, actually, as part of information literacy) rather than a thing by itself; though of course this doesn't preclude there being separate sessions on it."

Other Settings and Approaches

A great trainer can teach in many other kinds of settings, ranging from one-on-one interactions to social activities to unusual online settings. Although there is no need to limit your teaching approaches to the group sessions described in this chapter, the types of techniques described here are probably the most prevalent and practical. Sometimes the approach is chosen for us, and other times we can choose the best approach ourselves. Any session type we face offers advantages, and all are golden opportunities to teach more about Web searching. With the growth in online library services and online education, one additional approach not covered in detail in this chapter is the online tutorial. Chapter 4 explores issues and challenges with creating online tutorials for Web search training along with a wide variety of examples. So let us move back into the online world.

Chapter 4

Online Tutorials: Friend or Foe?

With the age of the Internet has come a common assumption that almost everything is better online. Newspapers, magazines, journals, books, and radio have gone online. Libraries have pushed their catalogs, collections, and even reference services online. Distance education opportunities have grown tremendously, with lectures, tutorials, workshops, and entire courses being presented via the Internet; you can even earn a degree online.

For a topic like Web searching, most people cannot or will not take the time for an in-depth, multiweek course. Even squeezing a half-day workshop into their schedule seems almost impossible for many. So a self-paced, online Web searching tutorial may seem like a good way to reach a much larger audience.

Advantages

Certainly an online tutorial has the great advantage of being available at any time a student may need it. With 24/7 Internet access, a student can run through a tutorial at 2 A.M., right after dinner, or first thing in the morning.

An online tutorial can be used by hundreds of people at once, allowing an instructor to reach a very wide audience. Because the course is online, the visual learners can see examples and read, while the tactile/kinesthetic learners can do exercises and learn from experience. Audio files can also be incorporated to good effect.

49

Participants can move through the tutorial at their own pace rather than trying to keep up with the instructor and the rest of the class in a classroom environment. Students who already know some of the initial material don't have to wait for the instructor and the rest of the class.

In a hands-on or lecture session, the amount of time available for the class will limit the number of examples used. With an online tutorial, the number of examples provided can be extensive, depending on the amount of time the instructor spends preparing for the course. Some online tutorials rotate examples for different audiences and thus prevent students from copying others' answers.

An addition to online tutorials, called screencasting, started becoming more common in 2004. The term, coined by *InfoWorld* columnist Jon Udell, refers to short, demonstration video files that often incorporate audio commentary. Championed as a better way to demonstrate technology (Udell 2005), screencasts are typically published on the Web in Flash format. One advantage of these short instructional screencasts is that they can be recorded and published very quickly. Even more important, a short screencast with video and audio requires little action from learners, who need only sit back, watch, and listen, just as if they were in a live class. Several companies produce software that can create screencasts: Techsmith's Camtasia, Macromedia's Captivate, Qarbon's ViewletCam and ViewletBuilder, and the free Wink from DebugMode.

In summary, online interactive tutorials have several advantages:

- Assignments can be done at the students' convenience.

- A much wider audience can be reached.

- Students set the pace themselves.

- Instructors can offer many examples.

Disadvantages

For all the advantages, there are also several problems with using online tutorials. One significant difficulty is getting your prospective audience to actually use the tutorial. There are many ways to attract people to a Web page, but keeping them there is another story. In an academic course, students can be required to complete specific tutorials for a class. Yet this sort of requirement can be a challenge for librarians, who may not be able to tie an assignment to a specific course.

Outside an academic audience, the challenges increase. What incentive can be used to get lawyers at a large firm or market researchers in a business setting to take time out of their busy schedules to go through a tutorial? Even if the tutorial can be designed in such a way as to attract members of the target audience, instructors need to constantly entice the audience to continue to the next session. Several very short tutorials work much better for these kinds of students because they can choose the pieces that hold the most interest for them.

A good online tutorial also requires the confluence of exceptional content planning and an appropriate technical delivery mechanism. The technical delivery can be done using basic HyperText Markup Language (HTML) and standard Web pages, but many designers use more sophisticated programs, such as Flash, QuickTime, Java, and others. The entire tutorial may be database generated or managed from within a database program such as ColdFusion or MySQL.

More time is required to create a good tutorial than to deliver a lecture or plan a hands-on session. And once the tutorial is finished, it is equally important to make sure the content continues to be accurate and current. Due to a constantly changing Internet, a tutorial on search engines will need to be updated far more frequently than an information literacy tutorial or some other relatively static topic.

Some tutorial sites provide accurate, up-to-date information and others have excellent design. Few have both. Be sure not to begin developing a tutorial project expecting that it will be easy and quick to do.

In summary, online interactive tutorials have the following disadvantages:

- Instructors need to provide extra motivation to keep students interested.

- Tutorials require considerable planning and sometimes significant technical skills.

- Web searching tutorials need frequent updates.

Issues with Online Tutorials for Web Searching

For Internet topics, online tutorials seem like a natural fit. What better subjects to teach online than Internet search engines and search strategies? Unfortunately, continually changing Web search engines make it notoriously difficult to develop up-to-date and accurate online tutorials. Anyone planning or updating an online tutorial—whether it focuses on Web searching or includes Web searching as a segment of a larger topic—will find that understanding search-engine-specific issues and problems can help improve the product. This section takes a look at some of the challenges, and is followed by reviews of several online tutorials, highlighting what works and what does not.

Search Engine Inconsistencies

Why is it problematic to teach Web search engines through the use of online tutorials? Because Web search engines are changing constantly. There is not necessarily any consistency between the results you might get from a search today and the results you will get tomorrow. I have spoken with many trainers who, in a hands-on instructional setting, have had an entire group do the exact same search on the exact same search engine and still get different results.

While some of the discrepancies may be explained by different preferences or by typographical errors, many times there is absolutely no difference in the settings or the query entered. This discrepancy comes from the search engines themselves. I have seen it firsthand with Google, AltaVista, and others. Because of the massive number of searches that the search engines handle each day and the need to be available at every moment of every day, the search engines have built-in redundancy and load balancing. In other words, they have multiple copies of the database, and they distribute the searches to different computers, depending on the load.

As much as search engine companies might like us to believe that this redundancy creates exact duplicate copies of the database, there are always glitches. There are software and hardware failures. Old records are weeded and new ones added, although this tends to be done on a sudden basis rather than the more gradual approach we might expect.

The bottom line is that search results can and do change on a regular basis, and any online tutorial that uses a specific search and its results to make an instructional point will become less effective as soon as the results change.

Typically, Google updates its entire database about once a month in a process that has become known as the Google Dance. While the "dance" is going on, searches are redirected to various data centers, some of which have the new database and some of which still have the old one. So at any point during the "dance," the same searches could yield very different results (Notess 2003a). While the Dance has changed and Google now uses several update processes, the same kind of problem can still occur at Google and the other search engines.

Search Feature Changes

In addition to the problem of inconsistent search results, search features can change as well. The way a search engine processes a multiword search can change. A unique and useful feature may suddenly disappear or stop working. Even the entire underlying database may change.

Phrase searching is a very powerful technique that is also very easy to teach. I have built several exercises on phrase searching. But a few years ago, it suddenly stopped working for about a month—and naturally I discovered this during a hands-on session! Because I was present in the classroom, I was able to use this as an example of how frequently search engines change, but as part of an online tutorial, such a "live" example would not only fail but would also confuse the students.

Other search features have changed as well. Early on, Google used to include two dates in its cached copy of Web pages—the date it crawled the page and the date stamp reported by the page at the time of that crawl. The dates were removed by Google for a few years, but in the summer of 2004, they reappeared. In the summer of 2003, Google's intitle: and inurl: field searches both stopped working correctly. The problem was fixed by Fall 2003, but any online tutorials incorporating those searches were affected that summer.

Sometimes features disappear altogether and do not come back. Both HotBot and AlltheWeb used to provide a directory depth limit, but that feature disappeared. A while back, Infoseek offered an option to search just the alternative text of images, but the feature disappeared.

A more important change to Web searching instruction in general as well as to online tutorials in particular is the way a multiword query is processed. In the late 1990s, a multiword query was typically treated as an OR search, with ranking preference given to AND matches. Now all of the major search engines default to AND processing of a multiword query. An online tutorial written several years ago, unless it has been updated, may show the older process.

Database Changes

The brand names of Web destinations and well-known search engines do not always match the underlying database. Or if they once did, they may not any longer. Excite, Infoseek, and WebCrawler were all well-known search engines early in the Internet age. Each offered its own database of crawled and indexed Web pages. Today, while all three are still available on the Web, none builds its own database. Infoseek has changed a few times and is now using Yahoo! results. Excite and WebCrawler now provide results from owner InfoSpace's metasearch engine.

Yahoo! is another well-known search site that has made significant changes to its underlying database. Beyond its own directory, Yahoo! has relied on AltaVista, Inktomi, and Google at various times to produce results when no matches occurred in its directory. In early 2004, Yahoo! launched its own search engine database.

When an underlying database changes, especially when a search engine is no longer creating its own database but simply using someone else's, it is definitely time to consider no longer teaching that search engine. At the least, the instruction you provide should include mention of the actual database provider.

Online Tutorial Examples

Let's examine some of the online tutorials available on the Internet. Online tutorials do tend to change, disappear, or be rewritten or updated. For that reason, the reviews that follow include some screen shots to illustrate certain aspects of the version referred to here.

The URL of each is given, as is the authorship when discernible. "Platform" refers to the software technology used to create the tutorial and needed to view it. Plain Web pages are listed as HTML, and tutorials using specialized programs such as Macromedia Flash and Macromedia Authorware are identified by the program used. The plug-ins needed to play these tutorials are always listed and linked from the main tutorial page.

Many useful tutorials are not included in this section. The ones included have noteworthy strengths or weaknesses—at least at the time of this writing.

Web Search Guide Tutorial: Research— Web Searching

By Gwen Harris of Web Search Guide

www.websearchguide.ca/tutorials/tocres.htm

Platform: HTML

Gwen has done an admirable job using basic HTML to create Web tutorials on Internet searching. The tutorials use frames, keeping the table of contents in the left frame so that users can keep track of where they are in the tutorial. The display in Figure 4.1 shows the beginning of the quiz for her Web Searching Research Starter Kit. Other Web Searching tutorials include More Searching, Web Searching, Search Syntax, and Search Engine Comparison.

While the left frame is used for displaying the table of contents, the right frame includes relatively long Web pages containing explanations of the topic and some illustrations. This structure allows a reader to scroll to the bottom of a page (reading the content, of course) and then click on a link to the next topic.

Gwen does a better job than most of keeping all her content up-to-date. However, her effort illustrates a problem inherent in many

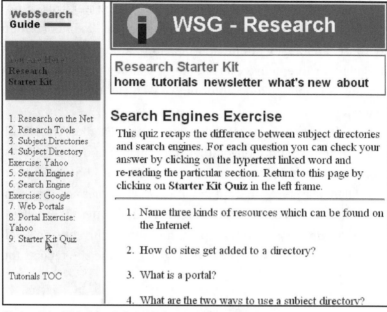

Figure 4.1   Web Search Guide Tutorial: Research—Web Searching

online tutorials: a preponderance of text. Certainly text is an essential tool for conveying information, but many Web users ignore large blocks of text in favor of bullet points or images. The audience of these tutorials will need to have sufficient motivation to read through the text.

Finding Information on the Internet: A Tutorial

By Joe Barker, Teaching Library at the University of California, Berkeley

www.lib.berkeley.edu/TeachingLib/Guides/Internet/FindInfo.html

Platform: HTML and Adobe Portable Document Format (PDF)

Although often listed as a tutorial, Joe's Web pages present "the substance of the Internet Workshops ... offered year round by the Teaching Library at the University of California at Berkeley." These are content-rich pages and quite extensive (Figure 4.2). These tutorials were designed to accompany workshops and to offer content to those unable to attend a workshop, so the pages are not designed for interactive exercises or as a single pathway through the site. It is more like an informative Web site than a tutorial in many ways.

Many pages are in HTML, while others are PDF files. The HTML pages have text and tables rather than images and screen shots. Most of the PDF files are similar. This would not be a very good tutorial for learners who want to see lots of examples and graphics, but for those who can learn from reading, the content is excellent.

Joe also does a great job keeping the content current—no small feat on such a large site. The very large size of the site reflects the

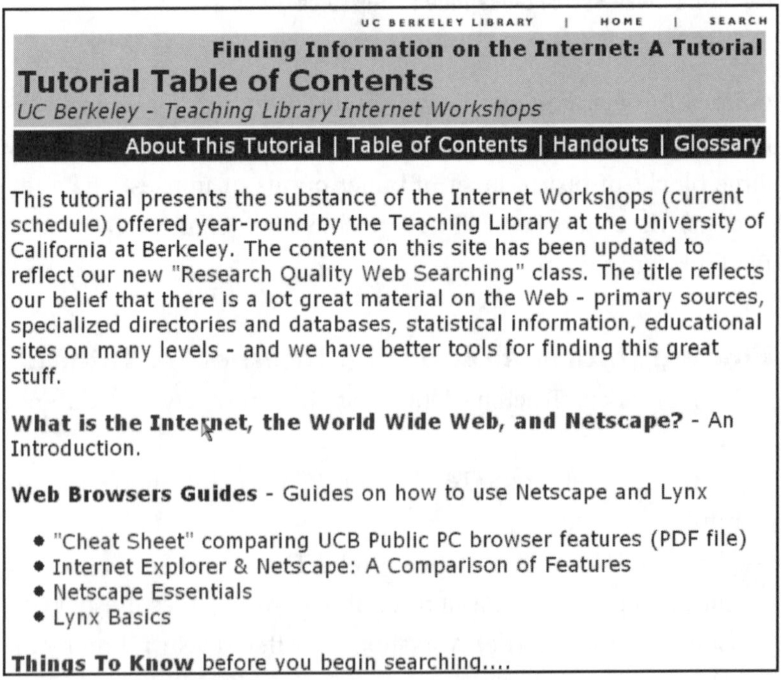

UC BERKELEY LIBRARY | HOME | SEARCH

Finding Information on the Internet: A Tutorial

Tutorial Table of Contents
UC Berkeley - Teaching Library Internet Workshops

About This Tutorial | Table of Contents | Handouts | Glossary

This tutorial presents the substance of the Internet Workshops (current schedule) offered year-round by the Teaching Library at the University of California at Berkeley. The content on this site has been updated to reflect our new "Research Quality Web Searching" class. The title reflects our belief that there is a lot great material on the Web - primary sources, specialized directories and databases, statistical information, educational sites on many levels - and we have better tools for finding this great stuff.

What is the Internet, the World Wide Web, and Netscape? - An Introduction.

Web Browsers Guides - Guides on how to use Netscape and Lynx

- "Cheat Sheet" comparing UCB Public PC browser features (PDF file)
- Internet Explorer & Netscape: A Comparison of Features
- Netscape Essentials
- Lynx Basics

Things To Know before you begin searching....

Figure 4.2   Finding Information on the Internet: A Tutorial

amount of information and advice available, but it can also frustrate efforts to find specific parts of the site or to get an overview of all the information available there. See Appendix B for some specific examples of Joe's work on this site.

Internet Tutorials

By Laura Cohen, University Libraries, University at Albany, State University of New York

library.albany.edu/internet

Platform: HTML

Several search-related tutorials are available on this site; one of the most frequently cited is the "Boolean Searching on the Internet" tutorial. Like the preceding two examples, Laura's tutorials are basic Web pages, with one page per topic. Other topics available include Selecting a Tool for Your Search, The Deep Web, How to Choose a Search Engine or Directory, Recommended Sites and Search Techniques, Second Generation Searching on the Web, and Evaluating Internet Resources. The screen shot in Figure 4.3 shows the beginning of the Boolean Searching on the Internet tutorial.

Built in HTML by a librarian, the material is text heavy. While the text represents good content and Laura keeps it up-to-date, some users will fail to read all of it. More interactivity could increase the appeal of this site to tactile/kinesthetic learners. The sheer number of tutorials available on the site, with no suggested sequence for using them, may also be intimidating to some users. However, text-oriented learners who read through the site will find some excellent information here.

LearnAndGo—Searching the Web

From Learnandgo.com, Internet Tutorials available from customers like Ozline

www.ozline.net/tutor/tutorial.html

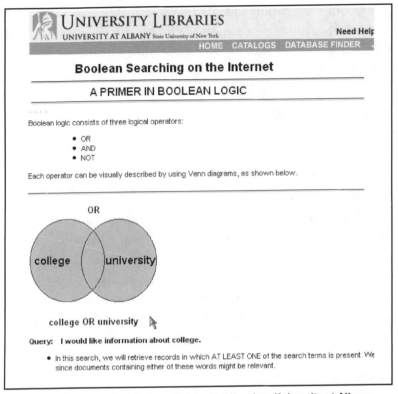

Figure 4.3   Internet Tutorials from University Libraries, University at Albany

Platform: Flash

For a very different approach to a Web searching tutorial, take a look at Learnandgo.com, which produces suites of Internet tutorials for various customers; the example here is a tutorial at Ozline, a Florida Internet service provider. When the link starts up, it first checks for the Flash plug-in; if it finds one, it gives users a with-or-without-audio choice. Then users can choose the Searching the Web component from among other options.

The screen shot in Figure 4.4 shows how this tutorial focuses on the Search button in the Internet Explorer browser. It demonstrates how to use Search directly from the address bar. Then it continues by showing how to browse a directory, with a very dated version of Yahoo! as the example.

This approach is very different from that taught by most information professionals. This tutorial is an important example of the design approach. It is visually pleasing, easy to navigate, and interactive, and the examples include numerous screen shots. Unfortunately, the content is questionable. It does not mention Google or Ask.com. It uses old versions of MSN Search and Yahoo!. It contrasts strikingly with the far more accurate, useful, and information-rich tutorials described previously. This contrast demonstrates one of the problems in creating excellent online tutorials: The people who really understand the content (as in the three previous examples) and the people who possess the sophisticated design and technical skills necessary to create a tutorial like Learnandgo.com's are seldom the same people. Unfortunately, it is

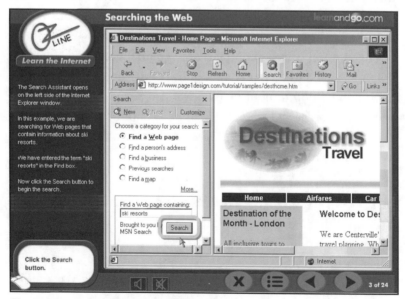

Figure 4.4 LearnAndGo—Searching the Web

not always easy to bring people with these two sets of skills together.

Quick Tutorial on Searching the Internet

By Michael Fosmire, Purdue University Libraries

bigdog.lib.purdue.edu/phys/inst/searchinginternet.html

Platform: Flash

This is also a Flash tutorial, but this time from an academic library. The tutorial demonstrates a middle ground between the fancy, highly designed Flash approach and basic informational Web pages. It is a single, sequential tutorial that covers a bit of background about the Internet, the Web, search engines, and searching. There is no table of contents and no access to sections in the middle of the presentation. It has no audio and its only interactivity consists of clicking to the next section.

Although this tutorial offers much better content than the tutorial from Learnandgo.com, it offers considerably less information than the more content-focused Web pages we have discussed. On the other hand, it may appeal to an audience who will not read the information-rich tutorials.

This tutorial uses a fictional search engine name and a distillation of several search engines' advanced screens to make an instructional point about using advanced search options (Figure 4.5). The "Doogle" advanced search box simplifies how to use the combination capability of an advanced search page and how to use the site limit.

net.TUTOR: Using Web Search Tools

From Ohio State University Libraries

gateway.lib.ohio-state.edu/tutor/les5

Platform: HTML

Here is another approach, back in the realm of an HTML Web site. This tutorial is part of the larger net.TUTOR suite of tutorials.

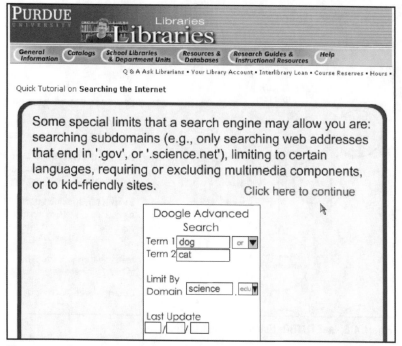

Figure 4.5   Quick Tutorial on Searching the Internet from Purdue University
            Libraries

The design has several strong points. As in the screen shot shown
in Figure 4.6, the graphics are used well and there are efforts to
inspire interactivity. In addition to the flow chart, the tutorial uses
screen shots, suggested activities, and "quick quizzes" at the bottom of most pages to reinforce the learning experience.

The design is well worth a look, though I question some of the
content. For instance, in the metasearch section, users are told that
metasearch should be used "to save time" and that "meta" means
"more comprehensive." Many metasearch engines display fewer
results than some of the larger search engines, so this section
should provide a more detailed and accurate explanation. However,
the design and teaching approach effectively demonstrate some of

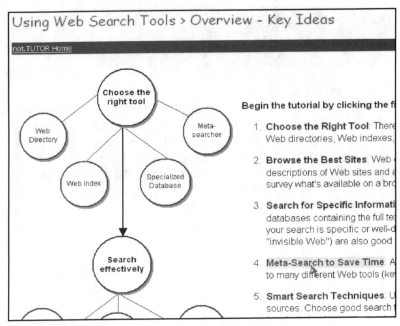

Figure 4.6 net.TUTOR: Using Web Search Tools

what can be done in a Flash application while keeping the site all in HTML.

Interactive Tutorials: Internet Search Tips and Mouse Exercise

From Hennepin County Library

www.hclib.org/pub/training

www.hclib.org/pub/training/SearchTips

www.hclib.org/pub/training/MouseExercise

Platform: Macromedia Authorware

Not only does this tutorial require the Macromedia Authorware plug-in, but the tutorial starts in a pop-up window that some pop-up blockers will kill. Because of their size, these tutorials can take some time to download. Flash is more commonly available than Authorware.

After users set up the plug-in and download the tutorial—two requirements that will keep many people from ever using it—the Internet Search Tips tutorial is a bit of a disappointment. The Authorware platform is a powerful one, but the content on this tutorial consists of just five tips:

1. Use phrase searching

2. Use lowercase letters

3. Use + in front of every term

4. Use the - to take away information

5. Use quotations and the - sign together

The second and third tips are no longer useful and date from about 1997. Even the animation in this tutorial is mostly gratuitous, used for typing text and for some sliding boxes (Figure 4.7). The

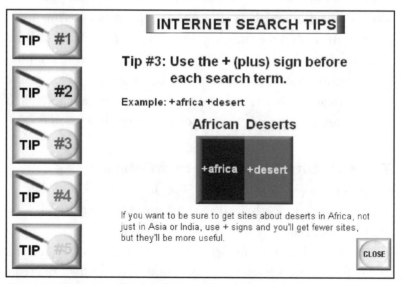

Figure 4.7   Interactive Tutorials: Internet Search Tips

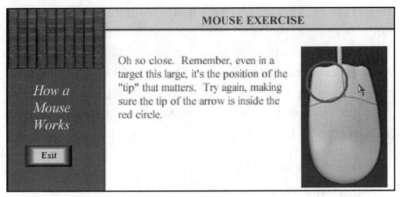

Figure 4.8   Interactive Tutorials: Mouse Exercise

whole lesson could easily have been formatted in HTML, which would make the tutorial easier to update.

In contrast, available on the same site and on the same platform is the Mouse Exercise, a tutorial on the use of a computer mouse (Figure 4.8) that makes great use of the technology, has good content, and uses interactivity appropriately. It starts by asking users to press any key on the keyboard and then offers explanations and interactive exercises for standard mouse functions: using pull-down menus, scrolling in a text box, clicking and dragging, and more. It incorporates humor and the exercises are easy and fun. It is a great example of effective use of technology in a tutorial.

Tutorial: Site Clustering and Filtering

By Greg Notess, Search Engine Showdown
www.searchengineshowdown.com/tutorials/cluster.html
Platform: Flash

This tutorial is an example of a brief screencast with video and audio. It explains one specific aspect of Web searching—the issue of site clustering and near duplicate filtering within search engine results. Then it demonstrates how to uncluster results at several search engines. Compare the screencast approach to others with a predominance of text or an extended interactive approach. Some students will be more willing to sit back, listen, and watch the demonstration than to read an extended textual description.

While no interaction is included in this screencast, the production software (Camtasia Studio 3) includes the capability of adding simple Continue buttons and a quiz. It can also create a menu of several screencasts to create a longer, more extensive tutorial. One important disadvantage of the screencast and video approach is that the resulting files tend to be quite large. The screencast in this example is about 1.5 megabytes. While this size won't pose a problem for many contemporary users on a broadband connection, students who have a dial-up connection will need to wait a while to download large screencasts.

The Information Cycle

From Pennsylvania State University Library

www.libraries.psu.edu/instruction/infocyle.htm

Platform: Flash

The Information Cycle tutorial (Figure 4.9) uses Flash to provide an aural and visual tutorial on the information cycle. This tutorial, one of the better-designed and better-implemented online tutorials in use in academic libraries, does not focus on Web searching. Instead, it covers the information dissemination and publication cycle, using the Columbine tragedy of April 1999 as an example. This is not an interactive tutorial—students are intended to only watch and listen. Its topic—the information cycle—does not change as quickly as does the world of the Internet search engine; thus, this tutorial can be relatively static. It had a "last updated" date of March 3, 2004, when I reviewed it. While a lack of frequent updates is not a disadvantage for this kind of topic, search engine

Figure 4.9   The Information Cycle from Pennsylvania State University Library

tutorials require more frequent updates and, to be most useful, a degree of interactivity.

Note the team credited with creating this tutorial: Two people worked on content, one on design, and one on programming development—an adequate group with an appropriate distribution of roles.

Information Literacy Online Tutorials

While the challenges of development, the need for frequent content updates, and constant changes within search engines plague the creation of useful online tutorials for Web searching, the movement toward information literacy instruction in libraries has provided an alternative. Information literacy tutorials abound. Since the basic sections of an information literacy tutorial usually focus on the research process, developing terminology, and using appropriate information tools, the content and examples used are much more reliable. And the processes taught in many information literacy tutorials are relevant for Web searchers.

In addition, most information literacy tutorials cover some aspects of using Web resources or searching the Internet. It is worthwhile to look at the Web searching sections of some of these tutorials. Following is a short list of some available tutorials, along with brief comments about how they incorporate Web searching.

TILT: The Texas Information Literacy Tutorial
tilt.lib.utsystem.edu

This is one of the best-known information literacy tutorials. One of three sections is on searching, and a small portion of that section covers Web searching.

eManual: Online Information Literacy Learning (University of Winnipeg)
cybrary.uwinnipeg.ca/learn/emanual

In this Canadian information literacy tutorial, one of 12 sections covers Internet searching.

Internet Navigator (University of Utah)
www-navigator.utah.edu

Established to help distance learners and active since 1995 (Hansen 2001), this tutorial has four modules. Some Web searching is covered in module 3, "Information Navigator."

Tales from the MSU Stacks (Michigan State University)
tales.lib.msu.edu
tales.lib.msu.edu/Content/m07/t2/m7t2.html

This online tutorial uses QuickTime and personalizes its nine sections with individual students' names. "Ray Goes Online" covers Web searching and includes a video of Ray talking about his experience searching the Web for his topic. After finding some material on the Web, Ray goes to the library to learn how to use the Web to find library and scholarly resources. There is no instruction on how to use Web search engines.

QuickStudy: Library Research Guide (University of Minnesota)
tutorial.lib.umn.edu

Part 5 of this 8-part tutorial covers finding Web sites. It is text-based and still describes Yahoo! as only a subject directory.

InfoTrekk (Curtin University of Technology, Australia)
library.curtin.edu.au/infotrekk

One of 10 treks, trek 7 covers searching the World Wide Web. It relies on text to discuss search engines, directories, and metasearch engines. The content is dated, mentioning AltaVista and WiseNut.

Mind Mapping (James Cook University, Australia)
www.jcu.edu.au/studying/services/studyskills/mindmap

Although not directly related to Web searching or information literacy, mind mapping is a technique that can be used for many functions. Sheila Webber is teaching its use for research using both Web searching and traditional databases (see Chapter 8 for more details). This tutorial provides one approach to starting the research process.

Finding Tutorials

A great advantage of the Internet is that anyone planning to develop an online tutorial can easily look at what others have done. Many tutorials are freely available online. How can you find them? In any search engine, a search on "library tutorials" can find many, but finding those specific to Web searching is more challenging.

Often, Web searching may be a component of a broader tutorial, such as the information literacy tutorials just covered.

Following are some suggested sources:

Library Instruction Tutorials, Library Instruction Round Table (LIRT)
www3.baylor.edu/LIRT/lirtproj.html
This site provides LIRT Research Committee's list of Web-based library instruction tutorials.

Librarians' Internet Index
www.lii.org/pub/subtopic/5118
This is the Training subsection of the Internet Guides and Search Tools area.

Resource Discovery Network (RDN) Virtual Training Suite
www.vts.rdn.ac.uk
The Resource Discovery Network (RDN) in the U.K. offers dozens of subject-specific tutorials here.

Innovative Internet Applications in Libraries
www.wiltonlibrary.org/innovate.html#tutorials
Find links to many bibliographic instruction tutorials.

Searching the WWW: Tutorials, Techniques, Tips
www.keithstanger.com/search.htm
This site includes a list of tutorials and sites for search engine news.

Peer-Reviewed Instructional Materials Online Database (PRIMO)
cooley.colgate.edu/dbs/acrlprimo/showrec.html
Produced and maintained by the Association of College and Research Libraries (ACRL) Emerging Technologies in Instruction

Committee, PRIMO is a broad database for library training material. Choose the category "Internet Research" to find Internet tutorials.

Learn the Net—Find Information Fast Online from ULiveandLearn
www.uliveandlearn.com/courses/cdetail.cfm?courseid=47

This link finds only one tutorial, but it is an interesting commercial offering in contrast to the primarily academic ones listed thus far. It lasts one hour and is now free (it used to be $6.95). At the end it promises that students will be able to "use Yahoo! and AltaVista" and "perform metasearches."

Tutorials: Worth the Effort?

After careful consideration of all the issues and problems with building online tutorials, an important question to ask is whether creating one will be worth the effort. Without sufficient personnel, skills, and support, it is probably not worthwhile to create an extensive tutorial, but the newer screencasting option is a compelling alternative that can be used by a single teacher with limited time. For organizations with an active information literacy program and the appropriate technological background, design skills, and content knowledge, extensive, sophisticated, interactive options may work best. Study the tutorials listed in this chapter for ideas and approaches, and then customize them for your local situation.

As Scott Brandt wrote back in 1997, "What I hope to see in the next couple of years (or months!) is more tutorials on Internet-related topics on the Internet. I hope that creators give more attention to structure and a systematic learning environment" (Brandt 1997, 46). Certainly many more tutorials are online today than in 1997, but relatively few focus exclusively on Web searching. With the rise of screencasting, more Web search tutorials should become available as well.

Chapter 5

Organization: Focus, Length, and Goals

Most of us involved in teaching Web searching are often called on to teach other topics as well. Web searching is often included in general Internet training, research process instruction, and resource evaluation workshops. What should be taught in a typical training session, and how should Web searching be included? How long should the sessions be? What kinds of goals should each session have? The answers are as varied as the instructors' teaching styles and the audiences' needs.

Primary Session Focus

Many public and academic libraries offer general Internet training sessions, which, depending on their length and focus, may include basic Internet skills, Web searching, and evaluation of Web content. Academic and corporate librarians may combine Web search training with sessions on specific commercial databases. Web searching can certainly be part of an information literacy program.

A training session does not need to focus exclusively on Web searching to cover it effectively. An introductory Internet class or information literacy course can include sections on Web searching, and course-integrated bibliographic instruction sessions may well cover Web searching and resource evaluation. So can market research training and basic business research sessions—the list goes on.

In the 1990s, many of us started off teaching basic Internet workshops. We would cover introductory Internet topics such as Web browsers, e-mail, Usenet, and telnet. Although Web searching was a component of those sessions, it was not usually the primary focus. That was a time when people like Danny Sullivan, the creator of Search Engine Watch and known even then as a search engine specialist, "did briefly do some 'Intro to the Internet' courses, and Web search was part of that." His experience is similar to that of many trainers.

As the Internet-using public finds the basics easier to master, the need for general introductory Internet classes has lessened. There are still novices who can benefit from such classes and public libraries in particular still experience some demand for them, but they are not as popular today as are courses in Internet searching.

This surging interest in Internet training and Web search instruction seemed to peak first in academic circles, then in information-intensive businesses, and then among the general public. So in general, the types of instructional sessions first offered in universities were next offered within companies and then in public libraries, schools, and other public venues.

Internet instructor Joe Barker recalls that from 1996 to 1997, the University of California (UC) at Berkeley offered fairly extensive instruction in Web searching, with courses titled as follows:

- Web Browsers and How the Web Works
- Search Engines
- Beyond General Web Searching (directories, people, listservs, newsgroups, international Web, etc.)

The first two of these sessions were 2-hour classes and the third lasted 3 hours. (Joe remarks, "The 3-hour class was necessary, but it was an endurance test.") Currently Joe teaches a 2-hour Web search workshop and a half-hour resource evaluation workshop that can be taken together or separately.

Internet specialist Jeff Humphrey uses a different combination of course types. "I offer a half-day Search Engines Update and a full-day Reference Strategies and the Internet. I also have a 45-minute-to-1-hour overview of Yahoo! and Google ... for staff in-service days." In his Reference Strategies and the Internet workshop, he spends a considerable amount of time on search strategies but doesn't stop there. "For the full-day workshop, I spend the first 1½ hours talking about applying reference techniques to your search strategies," he says. "I also spend about 20–30 minutes in the same session covering public service tips."

Reference librarian John Ferguson has taught such topics in many ways at the Richland College Library:

> We teach (and have taught) Web searching in several different ways. First, we conduct a hands-on workshop called 'Using the Internet' as part of our Information Literacy Certificate Program. Second, we incorporate Web searching into some of our hands-on, special-topics classes, such as 'News Sources for Busy People' and 'Business Information Sources.' Third, we incorporate Web searching into some of our hands-on, on-request classes, such as 'International Information Sources' for international business and trade classes. Fourth, we currently teach a hands-on workshop entitled 'Searching the Invisible Web.' Fifth, we have (in the past) taught Web searching as part of a three-tiered curriculum: Basic Web Searching, Intermediate Web Searching, and Advanced Web Searching. And sixth, we have taught half-day, hands-on workshops for faculty and staff called 'Internet A to Z.'

Pure Web Searching

Web searching as a separate session or workshop has now come into its own. Numerous studies have shown that searching is one of the most common activities on the Internet and that many people are generally satisfied with their search results. So if this is a common activity with high levels of user satisfaction, why such a demand for training?

Certainly the demand comes from a minority of users. As much as we might like to teach all the Web users out there, many do not have complex search needs. But for those who regularly search for specific, hard-to-find information, search training is a great asset. These searchers recognize that they have run into difficulties finding the information they seek.

Most users don't understand how complex the search process can be and they may not grasp the complexity of the search engine systems, but they seem to be aware of inconsistencies in search results. They know search engines keep changing, and they recognize that they have more to learn about the search process.

For now, at least, workshops and seminars on Web searching may attract audiences when basic Internet sessions, library research workshops, and similar options do not. Many people are willing to devote several hours, if not an entire day, to such training. However, this does not mean that the entire session must be limited to Web searching. Since searching strategies involve such a cross section of Internet knowledge, it is easy to pull in other important, related topics. Even in classes focused tightly on Web searching, other components are often included. As Jeff Humphrey noted earlier in this chapter, he also teaches the application of reference techniques to search strategies.

In beginning or basic Web searching sessions, I usually explain URLs and top-level domains. Many other trainers include resource evaluation in such sessions. Mentioning the kind of information that is unlikely to be found on the Web is another important component. Gary Price, co-author of *The Invisible Web*, believes that "if you're doing a 'Web only' class, it's worth a few minutes ... to focus on what the Web can't deliver and let folks know that libraries can offer many of the materials you can't find on the Web, such as remotely accessible databases and things commonly referred to as books. If you have more time, offering more background on what is not available on the Web provides participants with a range of ideas, concepts, and resources."

Basic Internet Training

If Web searching sessions attract the more sophisticated user, there are still plenty of relatively new Internet users—from members of the older generation who would like to communicate with relatives via e-mail to younger people who may be experts at instant messaging and sharing music files but who may not spend much time using Web search engines. Web search training is certainly appropriate in a basic Internet session aimed at these users. At a minimum, one search engine can be introduced and a sample search can be shown. In this kind of session, providing some context for the topic of Web searching helps novice users. The context can include a description of the type of information that might be available on the Web and the ways that information may differ from other information resources.

Back in the mid- to late 1990s, Joe Barker began his popular workshops at the University of California by explaining the Internet and the Web, along with how to use browsers effectively. Then he would cover how search engines work, how to use them, and how to find information using tools other than search engines. While academic audiences now seem less interested in such basic Internet sessions, some members of the general public now see a need for them.

Keeping that audience in mind, ensure that your students have a basic understanding of the Web, URL syntax, and browser basics before delving deeply into Web searching. Demonstrate key navigation features of the browser first. Then show how to get to a Web search engine, which will probably entail a brief discussion of Web addresses and where to enter them.

Advanced Internet Training

In intermediate and advanced Internet workshops, additional topics can be covered. Web searching can be placed in the broader context of Web use and online research. If Web searching is going to be part of a broader session, Gary Price includes instruction under the following rubrics to demonstrate that "it's not all available from a Web search tool":

- Specialized Web Databases/Invisible Web
- Library Resources
- Searching for Current News
- What's New in Search
- Consider Specialized Tools As You Would Specialized Reference Tools

Diane Kovacs always includes some aspect of Web searching in her sessions. "It is always part of every individual session I teach, but sometimes I do just Web searching training." When doing broader Internet sessions, she also includes the following sections:

- Medical Research
- Genealogy Research
- Business Research

- Homework Research

- Collection Development (on and off the Web)

In the advanced Internet sessions I have taught, I have included the following units to give the audience a broad perspective on both the Internet and the research process:

- Keyboard Shortcuts

- Web Browsers

- News Searching

- Current Awareness Tools and RSS

- Book Searching

Part of Multiple Sessions

Web searching workshops can also be part of a series of broader instructional offerings. Alice Fulbright describes one of the ways in which instructors teach Web searching at the Richland College Library: "It is one part of a five-class program. The other four classes include Introduction to the Library, How to Use the OPAC, How to Use Electronic Databases, and How to Use MLA Format."

Web searching can be combined with other library-related workshops, as at Richland, or incorporated into some other series of courses. It could be one part of a series of professional development workshops for teachers or librarians. It could be added to a series of Internet workshops for the public. It can also be included in a variety of regular classroom courses.

In semester-long courses like the ones Sheila Webber offers in the Department of Information Studies at the University of Sheffield, Web searching is typically a portion of the course. So in her case, it is "part of broader training (information literacy, or search strategy, or business information), but individual sessions might focus on searching Web resources."

Course-Integrated Bibliographic Instruction

Primarily taught in academic library settings and sometimes in school libraries, the course-integrated bibliographic instruction session is common in those settings. As part of some of these sessions, which often focus on commercial databases and local online and print resources, Web searching may be requested or included by default.

Joe Barker says that in UC Berkeley bibliographic instruction sessions, "We are teaching the catalogs, journal index(es), maybe news, and then the instructor wants us to talk about Web searching." So given a limited amount of time, what aspects of Web searching can you cover?

For upper-level bibliographic instruction sessions, I may include just a few notes in the handout about suggested search strategies or search terms. For a recent bibliographic instruction session for engineering doctoral students, I gave the following brief suggestions related to Web searching:

- Find research studies by adding filetype:pdf or filetype:ps to searches at Google.

- Try site limits such as site:ieee.org or site:epa.gov.

- Use more than one word and use technical vocabulary.

- Phrase search with quotes whenever possible (e.g., "deep uv," "chemically amplified").

Even if there is insufficient time in the bibliographic instruction session to give more detailed explanations or exercises, at least the students will leave with a few suggestions to consider.

For undergraduates, such suggestions are probably too advanced. Joe describes the problem with the current generation of students this way: "We are dealing with a population that believes that *everything* worth reading is on the Web, and that anything they find in any search engine is potentially valid research. Their teachers are going crazy with this kind of ignorance about information and scholarship, and we are supposed to work a 15-minute (or less) miracle." How to handle this kind of situation? Joe teaches that "Google is the best search engine indeed (why fight it?), but ... the Google Directory is a pretty good way of getting screened, somewhat selected, and somewhat categorized Web sites—less apt to be embarrassing junk."

Session Length

Next, instructors must consider the length of the session. There can be so much to teach about Web searching that a full-day session, a weeklong course, and even a whole semester class could be created and filled with content. Yet in so many situations, time is limited, as are the attention spans of audience members.

Sheila Webber says, "The more I teach, the more I realize how much time you need for deep learning to take place in the whole class." But sometimes an organization or group may only have 30 minutes for Web search training!

How often is the length really up to the instructor? Much of the time, it seems that the organization or individual requesting the instruction determines the length. The trainer may have little say. Certainly, being flexible in your instructional approach will help.

Variations in Length

During many of the Web searching workshops I have given recently to instructors, I have asked the audience of teachers and trainers what their typical session length was. The answers are incredibly varied, ranging from 10-minute mini-sessions to multiple-day workshops and semester-long courses.

One law librarian talked about preparing a collection of 10-minute sessions: The partners in her law firm would ask for training on Web searching or commercial databases, but she soon learned they never had more than 10 minutes to give her at a time. Recognizing this constraint on her audience, she built the content of her instructional sessions to fit the time available.

Other instructors reported the following session lengths:

- 20–30 minutes

- 60 minutes

- 90 minutes

- 2 hours

- 3 hours for an introductory session

- 3½ hours

The instructor who offers the 3½-hour session describes it as "not enough time."

Paul Barron says the length of a session varies depending on the instructional method:

- Lecture: 1–2 hours

- Interactive with instructor connected to Internet: 2 hours

- Hands-on workshop: 3–6 hours

Jeff Humphrey tends to do sessions for 1, 3, or 6 hours. He says he prefers 3 hours. "It's long enough to go in depth for a couple of search engines and short enough to keep attendees' attention and throw in some practice exercises." Gary Price's sessions range from 60 minutes to all day.

For John Ferguson, 90 minutes is the magic number, although his colleague Alice Fulbright says, "From a teaching perspective, I'd like for the classes to be about 2 hours long, but I truly believe that 90 minutes is the maximum amount of time our students will want to commit or pay attention. ... Ideally, I'd think about three 90-minute sessions would be good, but this would depend on the level of experience of the student."

Phil Bradley offers some of the longer sessions although he teaches "anything from 1 hour to 4 days. Most are usually day-long courses, however." Ran Hock has similar experience, with sessions ranging from 1 hour to 2½ days, although most are either half-day or full-day workshops. Because I teach almost exclusively on contract jobs, most of my own sessions last a full day (6 instruction hours).

In truth, I often give short (1- or 2-minute) lessons at the reference desk. Just the other day, I showed a student how to search for video files using an embedded content filter or searching a separate video database. But for most group instruction, I can fill the time available with lessons in Web searching. My typical sessions on campus have been 1 or 2 hours, but my workshops for librarians are usually a half day or a full day.

Ideal Length

With such a wide divergence in the amount of time we use, what would the ideal time for a session be? Among the experts I interviewed, answers to this question vary widely too. As Ran Hock says, it "depends on the audience and the specificity of the topic."

Danny Sullivan, who usually teaches 3½-hour sessions, "would like to see them expand perhaps by another hour for more 'group hands-on' training." In general, Paul Barron prefers the "longer hands-on workshops of 4 to 6 hours so that attendees can practice searches." Phil Bradley says that the length "depends entirely on what the client wants. A day is fine, though longer is preferable, though I seldom get that! There is a disadvantage in longer sessions since clients can take in only so much information in one go."

Ran Hock also says that the length of the session is determined only after consulting with the organization that is arranging the training. For many sessions he conducts for associations, the workshop length is usually determined by the association's standard time for such workshops or meetings.

Gary Price's preference is "shorter, especially with ... less-advanced searchers. I would rather do several short presentations and focus on a couple of things than get it all in over a period of hours. With shorter sessions, people are more likely to go to their computers, try what they learn, see what it can and can't do, and then come back for more." For him, the ideal length "depends on the audience, experience, etc. Five or more sessions over a period of several weeks" is a general ideal since "people come and learn and then can go back and try it out."

Gary thus echoes the idea Alice Fulbright mentioned earlier—having multiple meetings with the students. Having the time to try exercises, apply the lessons to their own searches, and come back with questions would certainly be a helpful instructional environment, but it seems rarely to be an option. Rita Vine agrees. "If I could make a perfect instruction environment, I would have a series of 90-minute sessions instead of an entire day. In my experience, 90 minutes is the perfect amount of time to teach one or two major concepts, demonstrate, [and] have the class replicate and then deviate to apply what they learned using their own examples."

Rita adds another important point. "I think it really takes a great deal of time to change existing search behavior. I can get to that 'aha!' moment (where students realize the futility of using search engines exclusively) within about an hour, but it can take many more hours for them to successfully *apply* that realization to the practice of Web search. People always defer to what they know, and what they know is 'Plug-n-Pray'—plug in the keyword at Google and hope for the best." If changing searching behavior is one of our goals, then longer sessions and, when possible, a series of sessions are probably the best way to achieve it.

Another significant point Rita makes is that the ideal length depends greatly on the audience. "I find that librarians can absorb a carefully constructed full-day program fairly easily, as long as there is plenty of guided practice and time for exploration. With ... end-users who are not already trained in information retrieval skills, the optimum time is somewhat shorter and the progress slower. Librarians are already so clued in to the world of information and its structure that they can readily apply those skills to Web search. For the end-user, however, the lack of a mental model of the world of information makes teaching and learning a much more challenging experience."

For trainers in schools, the younger the audience, the shorter the attention span. A full-day session for high school students or even for most undergraduate students is probably too long. A series of half-hour sessions may work best for that cohort.

The Burnout Paradox

Most trainers would like to have more time for their sessions, for two reasons. First, with more time, we can cover more material and provide additional examples. Second, more time can allow for hands-on time or other approaches to giving the attendees an opportunity to try their hand at Web searching exercises.

Still, trainers often express concern over how much students can retain in longer sessions. They also point out that there comes a point when burnout starts to set in. Gary Price notes that while "all-day sessions are going to happen, 3 hours is about as much as most people can handle." As Danny Sullivan puts it, "I think after about 3 to 4 hours, people get burned out on anything, regardless of whether they could learn more. They might benefit more from ongoing classes. How long it will take to train them will also vary [depending] on their basic skill sets. For instance, I find many people don't understand how the domain name system works. That's essential for making better use of site-specific searching, so it can be beneficial to take more time to teach Internet basics so they can then do better searching." In high school students, this burnout phase can hit as early as 10 or 20 minutes into a session.

As mentioned earlier, knowing the audience ahead of time, when possible, can help with planning, especially for longer sessions. If librarians, as Rita has argued, can take the full-day workshop more readily than most other audiences, reserve such lengthy sessions for groups with a similar background and sufficient stamina for full-day sessions.

Whenever and whomever you are teaching, the burnout point may vary depending on outside circumstances. If the room is too hot, the lunch too huge, or the background noise too loud, any audience will reach its saturation point sooner than otherwise. So be flexible with break times, and plan for some special activities to lighten up a longer session.

Paul Barron uses door prizes in his longer sessions for teachers. After lunch, he uses "incentives to get them back on time. I pick names out of a hat for a door prize and tell the attendees that if the person(s) who were selected do not return on time, they don't get the prize." The door prize approach helps create some excitement and can serve as one way of postponing student burnout.

Goal Setting

In the length of time we are given to teach Web searching, how many and what kinds of primary goals should we set for ourselves? Certainly the goals are contingent on the audience and their needs and experience. As Rita Vine says, "this depends on the length of the session, the audience level, and audience expectations."

Careful goal setting helps the entire instructional planning process. With so much that can be covered in a Web searching class, choosing a few key goals ensures that the important points get covered.

Establishing goals and objectives is part of the standard instructional planning process. Goals are the broad, general aims, while objectives are the specific behaviors that can be measured and accomplished by students. Yet the two terms are often confused and the line between some goals and objectives is not always clear. The important aspect of this planning is to carefully consider what you want to teach in the session and the main points you expect students to understand at the end of the session.

A Collection of Goals

To help you set your goals, read the following goals provided by our expert trainers. Obviously all these goals focus on teaching search engines, but they reflect a variety of approaches, along with a few novel ideas you may want to consider.

Phil Bradley expects his attendees to leave his session with an understanding of the following:

- What types of search engines exist

- How to use the best type of engine for the job

- How to use two or three specific engines

In teaching community college students, John Ferguson expects to accomplish the following:

- Persuade the audience of the necessity of using Internet search tools

- Acquaint the audience with the types of search tools

- Persuade the audience to use more than one tool and more than one type of tool

John's colleague, Alice Fulbright, expects her students to leave with a broader span of knowledge:

- The variety and different types of search tools
- Ways to analyze and critically evaluate a Web page
- Navigation techniques
- Tools like www.lii.org and similar Web guides
- Ways to focus and narrow searches using Boolean or templates and other features in advanced searches
- The way to cite a Web page in MLA format

Joe Barker has several different lists of goals, depending on his audience. In his current Web searching classes at UC Berkeley, he builds the sessions around these goals:

- Give an overview of Web searching
- Explain what are and how to find the best search engines
- Explain the value of directories and how to use and find them
- Explain that the content of databases on the Web are sometimes not in search engines
- Introduce the skills and methods of evaluating Web pages

In brief sessions for teaching Web searching as part of a course-integrated bibliographic instruction session, Joe has a goal of simply "guiding them to find sufficiently good stuff to be usable in their papers," although he may also "include a few evaluation tips."

For the longer classes Joe gives to librarians through Infopeople, he aims "to equip participants to be and feel competent answering *any* question using the most efficient approach and tools, and to know how to quickly evaluate the reliability of what they find."

From a nonlibrarian with a nonacademic focus, Danny Sullivan's goals still have much in common with the aforementioned. He wants his students to achieve the following:

- Understand how search engine results are typically gathered through crawling, editorial efforts, and paid listings

- Understand top tools for general searching and key features of those tools

- Know a range of specialty search tools and how to locate them

- Search more effectively by following a few basic tips

Danny's first goal, which covers the creation of search engine databases, is one to consider adopting because students can benefit from a better understanding of how search engines work.

Jeff Humphrey's first two goals are familiar ones, while his third is different and worthwhile. He wants his students to

- Be more familiar with the variety of search tools available on the Internet

- Be able to decide which tools, be they Internet or non-Internet, to use for different requests

- Have a more positive attitude about their searching abilities

Giving information to students is one thing. Getting them to feel confident about using their new knowledge is another. Designing exercises so that the students feel they have successfully learned the lessons can help them develop that positive attitude.

Rita Vine explains that her "general, mainly unstated goal is to clarify how information 'happens' on the Web, together with how and why search engines deliver the results they do. I try to move users away from commerce-driven search engines and pay-for-placement search results to less-well-known, high-quality, preselected resources that deliver top starting points for Web research." For students in an intermediate to advanced workshop, Rita breaks this overarching goal down in the following way:

- Understand the nature of search engine indexing and results delivery and make reasoned decisions about when to appropriately use search engines

- Understand how advertising and keyword purchases influence delivery of search engine results and apply this knowledge to decisions about when to use search engines

- Identify, review, and successfully use selected filtered starter sites for resource discovery and quick reference

- Understand the nature of the invisible Web and be able to identify an "invisible" database

- Learn to use search-and-browse capabilities appropriately in resource discovery tools

- Learn and master selected Windows shortcuts to help stay on track during a search

How Many Main Goals?

This collection of goals from a variety of top teachers reveals a degree of overlap, as we would expect. It should also be evident that anyone trying to encompass all these goals in any single session will be overwhelmed. The goals presented here should serve as a starting point to developing your own goals for a session. Combine them with your evaluation of audience needs and take into consideration the time available for instruction How many should you try to include in any one session?

In most sessions, I tend to focus on just two to four main goals. Among the other trainers, two to four was a common response. Phil Bradley tries to have "no more than four major goals in a day session," and Jeff Humphrey "believes in the rule of three." John Ferguson splits the difference: "No more than three or four."

Fewer goals make a great deal of sense for both less-experienced audiences and those with broader experience. Instructors with 10 or more goals tend to have very specific goals, or what might better be termed objectives. In keeping with standard pedagogical advice, keep to just a few goals. Diane Kovacs sums up this approach: "Two to three goals can be covered in a day-long session, with only one per half-day session."

Certainly, as several trainers have said, the number of goals depends, to a large degree, on what the audience wants and expects and on the type of session. For Gary Price, the number "is completely determined by who the audience is." Or as Rita Vine says, "I think that the goals and number of goals must vary [in consideration] of the things you can't change—which are the skill sets of the learners, the type of instruction space, and the learner expectations of the event. You can't take anyone on a learning journey unless you can start at the place where they are now, today."

Specific Objectives

From any one goal, dozens of objectives can be generated. Objectives also depend to a large degree on the audience. This section includes just a few objectives as examples of the many that may be appropriate for you and your students.

In my own sessions, goals and objectives vary depending on the focus and style of the course and the level of the audience. In a basic session, I usually have at least two main objectives that all students should be able to put into practice by the time we finish: (1) know how to go directly to the Web site of an organization likely to have answers to a specific question and (2) know how to use phrase searching. I achieve both objectives through explanations and hands-on exercises.

Another way to look at objectives is to focus on what your students have learned at the end of the session. As Gary Price says, "I hope that each person who attends one of my presentations leaves the room knowing and understanding a few [more] concepts than when they entered." Gary focuses on objectives that some call the "take-aways"—the new skills that attendees should gain from the session. In particular, he wants them to take away the following knowledge:

- Places to go to learn more

- Places to go to keep current

- An understanding that the Web doesn't have it all

- The ability to use the right tool at the right time

For each objective, Gary provides instruction in actual sites or skills. Spending planning time identifying some key points or take-aways will help you determine how to emphasize those points to be sure students remember them. Simply stating an objective and mentioning it once in a lecture will not usually achieve the objective. Reinforcement is essential.

How can you reinforce key objectives? First, introduce and explain the concept you want to illustrate. Demonstrate it with an example; then give the students an exercise to use it in. Some concepts take more work than others. Teaching phrase searching, for example, is relatively easy. Teaching question analysis or the difference between search engines and directories is more complex.

For the more difficult concepts, add more reinforcement. Reword the explanation and give additional examples. In the exercises for the next objective, try to incorporate an aspect of the earlier one so that students have another opportunity to use it.

Of his sessions, Paul Barron says, "The primary objective of the training is to enable the attendee to progress beyond keyword searching by learning to use the advanced search features of search engines. ... The secondary objective is that the attendees take what they have learned and teach their peers."

Having attendees turn around and teach their peers—whether in the instruction session or later on—certainly reinforces the techniques Paul teaches, especially since he often works with teachers. Having your attendees teach someone else what they have just learned is definitely one of the best ways to reinforce and accomplish your instructional objectives.

Paul prefers just one "teaching point" per section, although in a longer workshop he may have several sections. He gives a search demonstration and then provides time for practice. In support of his goal of teaching advanced searching techniques, he starts by "teaching a search process that begins with a phrase search, progresses to using Boolean and proximity operators with field to top-level and geographic domain limiters, and culminates with link checking of a selected result. Link checks are further limited using the Boolean AND operator with a keyword/phrase and a top-level domain."

Bringing It All Together

Using a pure Web searching session of sufficient length as an example, let's take a look at Paul's process of moving from goal to specific objectives, incorporating hands-on exercises. He takes the following steps:

- Define a title search

- Demonstrate a title search

- View the document source to show the HTML title tags and explain that the search engine searches for keywords/phrases in that title, not in what may be displayed in the Web document

- Highlight the Web document title in the browser window

- Have the attendees develop a title search query or use a predetermined title search query

- Select and review a result and compare the title on the Web document, HTML source, and browser window

- After reviewing that process, explain, demonstrate, and practice:

  ° Title search with AND Boolean operator

  ° Title search with a top level or geographic domain limiter

  ° Title search with AND Boolean operator and top level or geographic domain limiter

With this sequence, Paul provides many opportunities for his attendees to achieve his goal and to practice and reinforce his objectives.

The focus of the instructional session and its length are not always in the teacher's complete control, as we have noted several times. But goals and objectives, which are guided by the organizer's requests and the audience's abilities, are ultimately determined by the instructor. Rita Vine says, "I think that goal-setting and understanding learner skills and expectations are critical to success of any type of training." So in the planning stage, consider the audience, session focus, and length of time, and then carefully plan appropriate goals and the achievable objectives that will lead to them.

Chapter 6

Terminology

In any new discipline, commonly accepted terminology is a key to communication in the community as well as in instructional settings. But although the Internet has been around for well over a decade, the terminology related to Web searching and search engines has remained remarkably ill defined. Few frequently used words have commonly accepted meanings.

Many students of Web searching will have heard a number of these terms but will not necessarily have a good sense of their meaning. A student's understanding of a given term may be quite different from the instructor's.

Terminology is an important instructional issue. It is the basis for communication between teacher and student, and different interpretations of terms can lead to communication problems and confusion. To understand the potential difficulties, consider how you define the following terms:

- search engine
- directory
- portal
- meta
- database
- index

The meanings of many of these terms are evolving. Some are used by various groups to describe drastically different functions, and even among teachers of Web searching, there is often significant disagreement regarding their usage and meanings. Over time, as general usage changes and some previously used terminology no longer seems appropriate, our own word choices change.

For example, consider search engines that do not have their own databases but instead search a combination of other search engines and combine the results: I used to refer to these as *multiple search engines*, but *metasearch engines* has emerged as the term of choice.

While this chapter could have appeared as a back-of-the-book glossary, I believe that definitions and terminology are too important to the instructional endeavor to so relegate them. Also, devoting a chapter to terminology offers a greater opportunity to consider the varied meanings of the terms and the potential instructional problems with some.

Importance of Terminology

In teaching, defining terminology is critical to effective communication. Regardless of the discipline, a teacher is presumed to have greater knowledge of the subject area than the students, and part of that knowledge is an understanding of terms, concepts, and background in the field. Sharing that knowledge helps place commonly accepted definitions in context within the field. Take the time to explain and define important terms to the group near the outset of the session (or at the latest, when you get to a point where confusion is likely).

Students sometimes have very surprising interpretations of words and terms that you have long taken for granted. I have seen students sign up for a class advertised as "Basic Web Searching" and say they have come to learn how to find research materials in library databases. Other students, asked which search engine they use, have answered "Windows."

Getting everyone to speak the same language need not require that the class memorize an entire page of definitions; it can be as simple as starting out by explaining what you mean by *search engine*. As you provide an overview of what will be covered in the session, you can easily include definitions of some of the basic terms you will be using.

Unfortunately, most of the commonly accepted meanings of words relevant to Web searching do not yet appear in standard dictionaries and some dictionary definitions can be misleading. For example, the *American Heritage Dictionary of the English Language*, Fourth Edition (2000), provides the following definition of search engine: "A website whose primary function is providing a search engine for gathering and reporting information available on the Internet or a portion of the Internet." The definition not only commits the faux pas of defining a word in terms of itself, but it also focuses on the Internet rather than just the Web, creating a rather fuzzy and misleading definition. While some dictionaries are beginning to catch up, Internet terminology is too new and too much in flux for students to rely completely on dictionary definitions.

Many trainers will include a basic glossary in their handout packets. This can provide a reference for students who may have forgotten the definitions given at the beginning of a session or who encounter terminology confusion. As a handout or a Web page, a glossary also has the advantage of being available to the students long after the session has ended. When instructors themselves compose the definitions in the glossary, definitions can be targeted at the appropriate level and provide the appropriate detail for the specific audience.

Definitions

I offer the following definitions for the key terms we use in teaching Web searching. After each definition I list some examples, followed by some alternative terms. If one of my interviewees provided a particular alternative, his or her name appears beside it in parentheses. This is followed by a discussion of issues associated with the term. Some of the discussion sections include information about other trainers' definitions, along with their comments about a given term.

Search Engine

A search engine is an Internet-based search box that provides text-match searching of its own crawler-built database of text-indexed Web pages. Search results are ranked according to internal relevance-ranking algorithms. It is a tool providing searchable access to the text of millions of freely accessible Web pages.

Examples

Google, MSN Search, Ask.com

Alternate Terms

crawler-based search engines (Danny Sullivan)

crawlers (Danny Sullivan)

free text search engines (Phil Bradley)

search index (Jeff Humphrey)

Discussion

I use *search box* to emphasize the visual appearance that so many people connect with the concept of search engine. I also emphasize concepts of text matching and text indexing rather than the commonly used concept of keyword matching. I do that to emphasize that search engines often do not work well for subject searching and that the results retrieved contain a text match for the search query. In other words, the results may not have the query terms as "key" words.

Although *search engine* generally refers to Web search tools, the term has several other usages. Certainly, search engines were around long before the Web came on the scene. In the older and more general context, a search engine was any technological approach used to search some data set. Only since the advent of the Web has the term come to specifically refer to software used to search for terms on Web pages. I still remember Scott Brandt saying at a Computers in Libraries conference during the late 1990s that the search engine was a dead technology because the name was wrong and common sense would lead to better terms. Alas, the search engine label has stuck, and thus the confusion continues.

A broader definition, by which *search engine* refers to any Internet searching interface, continues to be common. One way I talk about this meaning is to ask how many people in the audience have received spam e-mail touting search engine submissions to hundreds if not thousands of search engines. In this context, a search engine seems to be any kind of searchable database on the Web. (Never mind that the vast majority of these "search engines" are rarely used and may rely on one of the primary search engine databases.)

Jeff Humphrey accepts that *search engine* is often used in this general sense and says, "I try to use *search directory* and *search index,* now that *search engine* has become a more generic term."

Even though Web search engines have been around since the mid-1990s, the terminology is still not stable. For example, the venerable *Oxford English Dictionary* handles the term *search engine* in a draft entry from the OED Online service dated June 2001: "*Computing,* a piece of hardware or software designed for searching, *esp.* a program that searches for and identifies items in a database that correspond to one or more keywords specified by the user; *spec.* such a program used to search for information available over the Internet, using its own previously compiled database of Internet files and documents." This definition gives usage examples as far back as 1984 and demonstrates how the usage has changed from a broader meaning to one more specifically focused on Internet searching.

Directory

On the Web, a directory is a classified listing of Web sites, in which brief records for sites are placed within an appropriate hierarchical taxonomy. The classification of sites is typically done by human editors, and the sites are searchable by the category names, site titles, and brief site descriptions. A directory is a tool for browsing selected sites or getting started in a new subject area. Note that directories usually include only one main page per Web site.

Examples

Open Directory, Librarians' Internet Index (LII), Yahoo! Directory

Alternate Terms

categorical directories (John Ferguson)
directory search engines (Phil Bradley)
gateway pages (Joe Barker)
human-powered search engines (Danny Sullivan)
search directory (Jeff Humphrey)
search starters (Rita Vine)

Discussion

This concept is extremely important for Web search trainers, but there is great diversity in the way we refer to it. Although *directory* is the most common term, many trainers express concern over how best to describe and teach it. Certainly, the difference between the search engine function and the directory function receives substantial attention from many trainers, as will be seen in Chapter 7.

Rita Vine remarks on the problem with the term and gives her current approach to addressing the issue. "I've modified the language over the years—we call subject directories *subject starters* rather than directories—partly because the word *directory* often means 'phone book,' and only librarians think of the words *directory* and *catalog* to describe tools like Yahoo! and LII. I find the term *subject starters* far more descriptive of what you're trying to do with these tools, which is to identify good starting points for finding information on the Web." Sometimes, as Rita points out, it can be more effective to develop your own terminology for use in your classes.

Ran Hock uses *directory* but in a slightly broader sense. He says he generally refers to "... Yahoo!, Open Directory, and LookSmart as general Web directories and sometimes also includes in that category sites such as LII. I separate these from specialized directories (e.g., metasites, cyberguides, or resource guides) and in this category often discuss the portal concept."

Given the amount of public confusion over the terms *search engine* and *directory*, Danny Sullivan has taken a different approach. He says, "I no longer try to use *search engines* to mean crawler-based search engines. Instead, I've given up and use *search engines* generically to mean either. When being specific, I'll say *directories* or *human-powered search engines* versus *crawlers* and *crawler-based search engines*. I prefer the longer terms and use them initially to keep emphasizing the different methods of gathering listings." By using *crawler*, Danny differentiates the two functions based on how they populate their databases.

Such is the dilemma with choosing terminology in instruction. Longer terms, as in Danny's examples, provide for greater differentiation but can be difficult for students to remember. Both instructors and attendees may tend to use shorter versions.

While I personally continue to use the term *directory*, it has become more difficult to clearly define now that so many directory sites include a search engine and often add portal content as well.

Portal

Originally designed as gateways to other Internet resources, portals have become destination sites with popular information such as news, shopping, and entertainment, along with Internet services such as e-mail, messaging, personalization, home page creation, and more. Portals may, and often do, include a directory and search engine as well. A portal is a tool for quick access to popular information and basic directories and search engines.

Examples

Yahoo!, MSN, Lycos

Alternate Terms

gateway

hybrids (John Ferguson)

specialized directories (Ran Hock)

Web portals (John Ferguson)

Discussion

Portal is one of the most ambiguous of a family of slippery terms. There seem to be several competing meanings for the phrase. One common service of portals is the personalization capability, with which individuals can establish a "My Yahoo!" or "My Lycos" page and select items to appear on that page. A common alternate meaning, especially in the library, university, and corporate communities, is that a portal is a specialized software package that provides users in an organization with personalization abilities and community-building tools—in other words, software that will create a local portal mimicking the functions of a general portal, as defined previously.

In either meaning, a portal is designed to be a Web starting point for users. The term is used less now than it was a few years ago, when the idea of a portal was all the rage in many Internet circles. At the time, many subject-oriented portals, industry-specific portals (sometimes called *vertical portals* or *vortals*), and corporate portals were created.

With usage of the term on the decline, is it important to even teach it? Certainly at this point, Yahoo!, MSN, and AOL continue to receive a huge volume of traffic. And as they combine the directory and search engine functions, along with lots of additional popular information and Internet services, it helps to have some terminology to describe them.

John Ferguson teaches portals by talking about "Web portals or hybrids, which combine categorical directories with search engines," using Yahoo! as an example. Ran Hock talks about *specialized directories* as distinct from general directories, and "in this category [will] often discuss the portal concept."

Devoting some time to this group of sites—especially when teaching a general audience, which may have great interest in the popular services offered by portals—will benefit your students. When teaching courses for organizations that have their own portal, certainly the organization, services, and functions of the internal portal should be covered, as appropriate to the session.

Metasearch Engine

A metasearch engine is a finding tool that does not have its own database. Instead, it sends a query to several other search engines and then compiles the results on a single screen or in multiple frames or windows.

Examples
Clusty, ixquick, Dogpile, Copernic

Alternate Terms
desktop metasearch engine
federated search engine
meta crawler
metasearch engine
multiple search engine
multisearch engine (Phil Bradley)

Discussion
While the metasearch engine concept has been around for some time, the terminology has varied. Current usage seems to favor *metasearch engine* (also seen as meta search engine). Some metasearch engines offer interesting and useful features while others have little to recommend them. These tools can be useful for post-processing of results, such as clustering, or for getting a quick sense of what various search engines are finding, but better results are typically obtained by using any one of the large search engines.

When explaining metasearch engines to my students, I point out that while it seems they should deliver more results than a single search engine, they often deliver less. I also note that many of these tools deliver an overabundance of results from ad bidding engines (see the definition in the section that follows) and that relatively few of them include results from Google or any of the other major search engines. More advantages and disadvantages of metasearch engines are discussed in Chapter 7.

For most Web searching sessions, it is important to define metasearch engines and make it clear how tools like Copernic and Vivisimo differ from search engines like Google and Ask.com.

While *search engine, directory, portal,* and *metasearch engine* are the four most important terms to define for students today, many others may also be useful, depending on the scope of the class. I use the following terms in instruction sessions; some I coined and some were provided by other trainers.

Ad Bidding Engine

An ad bidding engine is a special kind of search engine with a database of paid ads. The ranking of results is determined by which company is willing to pay the most per click. The top bidders for any particular search term are listed in the top spot, followed by those that bid lesser amounts. The ads may be followed by results from a general search engine.

Examples

Google AdWords, Yahoo! Search Marketing (formerly Overture), Kanoodle, Miva

Alternate Terms

pay-per-click engine

sponsored listings

text ads

Discussion

I coined the term *ad bidding engine*, but *ad engine* might serve just as well. By giving this group of search engines a specific label, it is easier to talk about and teach them. In some cases, results from ad bidding engines are not available on their own Web sites. Instead, their results show up only at their customers' search engines.

The oldest ad bidding engine is Yahoo! Search Marketing (formerly known as Overture and before that as GoTo), yet most users are not aware of the Yahoo! Search Marketing site. Google's sponsored links all come from its own ad bidding engine, but even though they are listed separately on the right side of a page, some users do not recognize these results as advertising.

Kanoodle, Miva, and the old Overture site all run searches and display just the ad results. The old Overture site also has the ability to display the price each advertiser has bid. Unfortunately, Google does not provide a separate search box for its AdWords database, let alone show users the prices bid for ads.

For advanced searchers and online marketers, ad bidding engines can provide useful information about how much advertisers will pay for particular search terms. These tools can also identify potential advertisers on the basis of specific keywords. By clearly explaining and identifying ad bidding engines and then demonstrating how to check bid prices, you will help students recognize search engine advertising wherever and whenever it appears.

Answer Engine

An answer engine is a specialized search engine that builds a database of questions and matching answers. It typically provides just one answer for each question. A search query is matched with one or more of the question-and-answer pairs and presented to the searcher.

Examples

Ask.com, Fact City (now defunct), Shortcuts

Alternate Terms

natural language search engine

Discussion

I coined the term *answer engine* since Ask.com did not fit neatly into any other search engine category. Although the answer engine aspect of Ask.com has diminished (it now relies more on results from its own database) and attempts to compete in this industry space have been unsuccessful (as the experience of the now defunct Fact City, for example, illustrates), Ask.com continues to enjoy substantial user traffic.

By first defining this unique type of search engine, I find it much easier to describe the shortcuts available at Ask.com, Google, Yahoo!, and MSN. Although the question-and-answer matches are no longer very prominent at Ask.com, they still appear under the label of Smart Search. Try a search such as "boston flight delays" to see an example. These shortcuts (see sp.ask.com/en/docs/about/site_features.shtml for more) come from a distinct database and continue to be placed above more common search results that come from the Teoma database. When you are teaching, you can describe the question-and-answer results as coming from the answer engine, in contrast to the search results, which are derived from the regular search engine.

Answer engine results also appear at Yahoo! (see help.yahoo. com/help/us/ysearch/tips/tips-01.html for a detailed list), Google (see www.google.com/help/features.html), and MSN Search from the Encarta encyclopedia. All these sites aim to provide quick answers to popular and frequently asked questions.

While many articles have described Ask.com and the other search engines' shortcuts as natural language searching, in fact the site has never incorporated natural language searching techniques. The technical details of natural language searching, which uses quite different techniques and algorithms, are beyond the scope of training in Web searching. Answer engines simply match specific popular search queries to specific records within their own question-and-answer database.

Metasite

A metasite is a Web site that includes a collection of links to unaffiliated Web pages, Web sites, and other online resources on a particular topic. The best ones include annotations to the listed resources.

Examples

About.com

Alternate Terms

finding aids
Internet resource guides
resource guides (Ran Hock)

Discussion

Metasites can be extremely useful tools for finding information on the Web. The Argus Clearinghouse (at www.clearinghouse.net) was a notable collection of these Internet resource guides compiled mostly by library school students. But such endeavors are difficult to maintain, and the Argus Clearinghouse shut down around the end of 2001. Fortunately, similar sites are available.

At the former Teoma, metasites were listed separately from other search results under "Resources: Link collections from experts and enthusiasts." This description emphasized an important point: Metasite creators may indeed be experts in their field, but oftentimes they are enthusiasts—people who are keenly interested in a topic but whose true knowledge and credentials are unknown.

At one time, the Yahoo! Directory tagged retrieved metasites as indexes. Yahoo! ceased the practice several years ago, possibly because few users understood what the tags meant.

About.com is an information-rich (although advertising-heavy) site that has always been a bit difficult to classify. It is primarily a collection of metasites, created by various enthusiasts who work as About.com guides. Some people refer to About.com as a directory because it provides a hierarchical listing of its metasites.

For searchers, a well-researched metasite can save much time. Unfortunately, many metasites are neither well done nor kept up-to-date. Therefore, when you are teaching metasites, it is important both to point out their potential advantages and to raise a flag cautioning that not all will be useful, accurate, or up-to-date.

News Search Engine

A news search engine indexes only pages from news-oriented Web sites. Some cover only the Web sites of established news outlets, while others have a broader news focus or specialize in blogs and RSS feeds.

Examples

Yahoo! News, Google News, Feedster, Daypop

Alternate Terms

blog search engine

headline search engine

RSS search engine

Discussion

An important resource, the news search engine offers access to unique content and very recent articles that are often not available from the regular (or Web) database of a general search engine. Some trainers include a brief mention of news search engines in their regular courses while others offer separate sessions specifically devoted to news searching.

One pedagogical advantage of introducing the news search engine to students is to show that the general Web databases of search engines often do not have the most current news items available on the Web. Compare results from a general search engine to results from a search in a separate news search engine.

This demonstration reinforces the lesson that the general search engine databases are often dated.

I include blog search engines under the news search engine heading, but these might just as easily fit under Opinion Engines (see next term). Since Daypop indexes both news sites and blogs, it certainly can fall under both terms. A blog search engine can be an extremely helpful source for locating current news, especially individual reports of events.

Opinion Engine

An opinion engine is a specialized search engine that indexes a collection of discussion forums, Usenet newsgroups, or other content based on individual opinion.

Examples

Google Groups, Epinions

Alternate Terms

Usenet search engine

Discussion

While there used to be a number of Usenet newsgroup search engines, today there is only one: Google Groups. That said, there are several other kinds of search engines and sites that offer similar kinds of information. Usenet postings certainly consist of more than just opinions, but they can be searched for individuals' opinions. As online discussions have moved away from Usenet to Web-based forums and blogs, the general search engines have become another good place to search for this kind of information. Although in the past, search engines like MessageKing and Forum One existed exclusively for Web forums, they are now defunct.

Another category of opinion engines is individual consumer review sites. Amazon and other e-commerce operations encourage users to submit their own reviews of books and other products. Epinions is another example of a searchable site offering individuals' opinions about a wide range of products. While shopping is rarely a focus of Web searching sessions, the information provided by these opinion engines can be an excellent source of information. When teaching this concept, compare it to asking friends, family, or neighbors about a product.

Blog search engines like Feedster and Daypop can also be included in this category since many blog postings consist of opinion combined with reporting or commenting on news items.

Site Search Engine

A site search engine searches content within a specific Web site or a small group of sites.

Examples

Most major Web sites, such as CNN, eBay, and CNet, have one.

Alternate Terms

enterprise search engine
internal search (Rita Vine)
intranet search engine

Discussion

All kinds of software packages are available that will create and run an internal or site search engine. Most have many options that can be configured differently at each installation. Some work fairly well, and others may not work at all. The search syntax may be similar to that of general Web search engines, or it may be idiosyncratic or counterintuitive.

Many people use site search engines to navigate a site, so teaching the basic ways they differ from general search engines can be an important component of a training session in Web searching. In particular, you should point out that they are not always the best way to find information on a site.

When Rita Vine teaches site search engines, she points out their difficulties this way: "Many Web sites offer an 'internal search'—a search box that lets you search the internal contents of that site alone. ... They usually offer very basic search options. Recent research has shown that most internal search options do not work as stated. The solution? Try to browse instead of search. Do not rely on internal searches alone to find what you are looking for."

Invisible Web

The invisible Web consists of Web sites, pages, and other sources of Internet-accessible content that are not indexed by search engines or included in their databases.

Examples

Clinton-era State Department documents
Citations from Agricola (hidden in a database)

Alternate Terms

dark matter
deep Web
hidden Web

Discussion

Some people still believe search engines cover the entire Web. Pointing out that a substantial portion of information available on the Web is not directly available from search engines is a good attention grabber. Students may pay more attention to the rest of the class once they realize the limitations of search engines.

There are many ways to address the topic. Paul Barron contrasts the surface Web and the deep Web to help clarify the difference between what is indexed by search engines and what is not.

Content may be invisible for several reasons. It may be due to the use of a robots.txt file, which Web site owners create to block search engine crawlers, as in the case of the Clinton-era State Department documents. Or the information may exist within a database (such as a catalog or a bibliographic database Agricola) or a database-generated Web site that is rarely crawled by search engines. For more information, I recommend *The Invisible Web: Uncovering Information Sources Search Engines Can't See,* by Chris Sherman and Gary Price (Information Today, Inc., 2001).

Other Terminology Distinctions

The list could go on since so many terms used in the search engine world are not used in common parlance. The terms I have defined here are the most important ones, but you shouldn't view this as a comprehensive glossary.

Some terms may be interchangeable, and the instructor needs to decide which is most appropriate in the context at hand. For example, I like to refer to the underlying information content provided by a search engine as being in its *database*, but search engine programmers tend to prefer the term *index*. Because librarians hold a rather different interpretation of *index* than programmers do, I consistently use *database* when addressing library-oriented groups, but when talking to search engine programmers or engineers, I use *index*.

URL and *address* are another set of terms often mixed-up. *Uniform resource locator (URL)* can be unwieldy. In addition, the usage is not common in all groups. Thus, I will often refer to the URL as the address, explaining the URL acronym if I accidentally use it (which happens often) or if someone asks. In recognition of this, Microsoft uses the term *address* right before the URL box in Internet Explorer and calls the whole bar an Address Bar.

The distinction between a Web site and a Web page is another common point of confusion. I usually explain that a Web page is a single document with its own URL (oops!—make that address), whereas a site includes a collection of pages located at the same domain or host. This distinction can be made when you are explaining how addresses are constructed, how to read top-level domains, and what parts of the address identify the host (see Chapter 8).

You will likely come across many terms used in different ways by different search trainers, and sometimes it may seem there is little agreement. For instance, Alice Fulbright and John Ferguson use *unified search tool* to describe sites or tools that provide listings of other search engines; however, one such site, Search Engine Colossus, bills itself as an "international directory of search engines." Which descriptor is more accurate? In this case, the site's own phrase is a little misleading because Search Engine Colossus includes entries for Web directories, such as the Open Directory, as well as search engines. If you make up your own term, it is unlikely to be used elsewhere. Even so, as the instructor, you may encounter a need or an opportunity to define your own terminology in order to clarify concepts for your students.

Final Thoughts on Terminology

The words related to Web searching are a messy lot, with definitions shifting and usage overlapping freely. This lack of standard terminology creates instructional and communication difficulties and leads to some ambivalence on the part of teachers.

There was a time when I avoided using the term *search engine* in the context of Web searching because it had previously been used in a broader context. Eventually, though, certain terms earn wide acceptance, and it doesn't make sense to fight the tide. Diane Kovacs expresses a similar sentiment: "I hate *portal, invisible Web,* etc. I use plain functional language." I had a similar reaction to *portal*, but as with *search engine*, it has become widely used and understood, so I decided to use it.

Sheila Webber captures the difficulties and problems perfectly: "I call all the things that index a wide variety of Web pages *search engines* and try to get people to focus on thinking about what it is these search engines might be searching and what's in them. With many of them having both a directory bit and a full text search bit (and Yahoo! making the full text search prominent), I feel that talking about Web directories versus search engines is possibly confusing. I do talk about directories and directory-type information, mostly in relation to directories that have a specialist type of information (for example, business directories)."

Sheila also offers some insights into the causes of the confusion and the remedies:

> Actually I think the whole terminology thing is problematic [because]
>
> (A) different people and texts use the terms in different ways;
>
> (B) *search engine* is often used by non-LIS people to mean anything that has a search function; and
>
> (C) possibly library and information people ought to rethink how we label these things, for example, *databases, catalogs, directories, search engines*. Some of the labels identify distinctions of function and content that *used* to exist (for example, when the library catalog just used to have items physically possessed by the library).

Indeed, we as instructors need to constantly reassess and reconsider the terms we use. We need to adjust them for our audiences' changing perceptions of these terms as well as for evolving meanings. There may never be a consensus on all these terms. As long as we clearly teach our students the meaning we intend, maybe we can remove some of the clutter and confusion.

Chapter 7

Content: Web Search Features

With one or two industries having sprung up around Web searching, there is plenty of material for a Web searching instructional session. For example, take a look at some of the conferences related to Web searching. For Web searchers, the rotating Web Search University conferences (www.websearchu.com) offer 2-day information-packed sessions. On the search engine optimization and marketing side, Search Engine Strategies (www.search enginestrategies.com) offers 2- to 3-day sessions, in multiple tracks.

So what is an instructor to do when asked to present a 1-hour workshop covering all aspects of searching? This chapter as well as Chapters 8 and 9 will address content issues. The constantly changing nature of search engine features makes teaching them a particular challenge. This chapter addresses key points to teach about specific search engine features and capabilities. Chapter 8 covers the broader concepts and search strategies, such as question analysis, directory uses, and evaluation of Web sites, that can be included in an instructional session. Chapter 9 discusses additional and tangential aspects of Web searching, such as news searching and the invisible Web, that might be included for specific audiences.

We start with search features such as phrase searching, limits, Boolean searching, and truncation because these features are exactly what many students hope to learn. While some instructors start with the more general topics that are covered in the next chapter, all instructors include at least some of the features discussed here.

Search Features

In much of the history of bibliographic instruction, one constant seems to be coverage of specific search features, from using headings in print indexes to combined author and title searching in an online catalog. Today, teaching Web searching often also includes instruction on search features of the search engines.

One reason for the success of search engines is that they make searching as easy as possible. Many searches require just one or two words. Relatively few searchers use advanced search pages. Yet knowledge of just a few such features can make searching even easier, and it is often these features that excite students the most. Librarian Paul Barron says he covers advanced search features in his presentations and workshops "because they give the searcher more control of the search process and, hopefully, the results returned by the search engine."

Audience and content will determine how much time to devote to advanced search features. In her university classes, Sheila Webber starts with an emphasis on overall strategy rather than on search features—an approach that is covered in more depth in Chapter 8. However, Sheila makes an exception when she is teaching Dialog, for which she has "a specific sustained focus on using Dialog's commands and syntax." Likewise, when teaching a business information class, she covers advanced features since "the students have all had some previous education in searching and are ready to absorb more detail."

The pages that follow delve into issues related to teaching a variety of advanced search features, but I do not explain in detail how these features are employed in a given search engine because the topic is too dynamic to cover in any book. For current, in-depth information about search engine features and how they work, see my Web site for reviews of various search engines (searchengineshowdown.com/reviews) and the regularly updated Search Engine Features Chart (www.searchengineshowdown.com/features).

Phrase Searching

Joe Barker calls phrase searching "the single most powerful search trick in existence," and he notes that it is "accepted almost everywhere." Telling a search engine to do a phrase search is as simple as putting quotation marks around the precise phrase for which you are looking. The search engine should then match only pages that have the exact phrase with the words exactly in the order specified. For example, when a philosophical concept known as the difference principle is searched by simply entering the two words without quotation marks, results will include variations like *difference in principle* and *difference of principle.* Entering these same two words with quotation marks forces a search engine to match only that exact phrase.

Alice Fulbright says, "I always teach phrase searching because it is a sure-fire way to return focused results," while Jeff Humphrey reports teaching the technique "to demonstrate obtaining more exact results and to emphasize the value of proximity searching." According to Ran Hock, "For many searches, it is one of the best ways to achieve higher precision." Danny Sullivan calls it "an incredibly useful way for people to get better results."

When I am teaching beginners, phrase searching is one of the main points I hope all attendees will grasp, use, and take away from the class. If it is the only point students remember, they will become better searchers. Gary Price also emphasizes phrase searching and notes that the technique is one that most searchers do not know, especially beginners. He adds that it is "a great way to show the 'power' that a little limiting can do."

Web search engines made phrase searching easy to do through the simple command of using quotation marks, and now other search systems are starting to adopt it as well, including some library bibliographic and full-text databases. According to John Ferguson, phrase searching is "increasingly useful [with] Internet search engines, like Google, and in using proprietary search interfaces, like EBSCO*host*. In some cases, phrase searching is approaching natural language searching in effectiveness."

All of the trainers I spoke with agreed that teaching phrase searching is essential. Rita Vine says, "Phrase searching is particularly useful in finding things that you know are on the Web already, like organizations, names, institutions, and companies." But Rita also points out the difficulty some users have with phrase searching. "The problem we find in phrase searching is that most searchers use phrase searching improperly. For example, if we were to ask searchers to look for information on water quality, they would put the words *water quality* inside quotation marks. It's perfectly possible that good information on water quality may use variations on the term—for example, *quality of water* [or] *water safety and quality*."

Diane Kovacs offers a variation on teaching phrase searching. Instead of simply telling her students how to use specific tools to search for an exact phrase match, she explains "how a given tool will respond to a phrase search." This is an important point because while all the major Web search engines return a fairly accurate match when a phrase is entered within quotation marks, this is not true of all search tools or Web sites. It is also useful to explain how search engines respond to phrases entered without quotations marks or the use of special syntax.

Boolean Searching

Venn diagrams, Boolean operators, nested Boolean statements, and in-depth discussions of the various ways words can be combined in a search were standard components of online searching instruction in the 1980s and early 1990s. Certainly, with the command line commercial online systems, complex Boolean searching was essential for quality information retrieval. Today, Web searching presents a very different situation.

During the rise of Web search engines in the 1990s, some pundits argued for getting rid of Boolean searching altogether, painting glowing pictures of the day when Boolean concepts could be abandoned by all searchers. Others, especially long-time commercial online searchers, have bemoaned the lack of accurate and functional Boolean capabilities (in some cases *any* Boolean capabilities) among the Web search engines. Although some search engines have claimed to support Boolean searching, it has never worked as accurately and reliably as it does on the commercial online search services.

Some search engines support one Boolean operator and not others. Some use a special box on the advanced search page. In some engines, but not all, Boolean operators have to be typed in uppercase. Engines support different versions of the NOT operator. Considering all the variations, what can we teach users about Boolean searching on the Web?

Alice Fulbright teaches Boolean "because students need to know how to broaden and narrow their searches." Her colleague John Ferguson concurs, pointing out that Boolean operators are still used to search both subscription databases and online catalogs. However, he acknowledges that the situation is changing. "We still teach basic Boolean searching, but less and less when it comes to using Web search engines. Advanced Boolean searching—such as nesting—is no longer taught."

Phil Bradley differentiates his instruction based on his audience. With librarians, he will teach traditional Boolean logic "if required, and sometimes it is." For students who are not information professionals, he will teach the search engines' advanced search forms.

Danny Sullivan does not teach Boolean operators but instead will explain that "search engines typically look for all of your search words." He directs those who want more control to the advanced search pages. But he goes into more depth about the

+ and - operators under a heading he coined "search engine math," in which he also explains how quotation marks work for phrase searching.

Although behind the scenes, all the search engines use Boolean combinations of the search terms, they do not handle many Boolean commands or nested Boolean searches effectively. Full Boolean nested searching is supported by Yahoo!, MSN Search, Exalead, and Gigablast. Yet when advanced queries such as full Boolean nested searches are used, the search engines' relevance ranking algorithms will not work very effectively. Some trainers emphasize using just a basic search and making the most of the relevance-ranked results before trying a Boolean search.

At one time Joe Barker taught Boolean searching because he felt that "people had to know this to survive." Today he teaches it only in his advanced Web searching classes. Even then, Joe says, "I teach that you need it only about 10 percent of the time and can live happily without it." With so many people unable to construct an effective Boolean query, Joe feels it is "better not [to] use it than to make a mess of it." Still, Joe does teach how and when to use the OR operator and offers a handout for those who want to learn how search engines support Boolean.

Rita Vine offers a more extreme view. "I know that I'm probably the only one out there who doesn't teach Boolean, not even to expert searchers. We used to in the old days (mid-'90s) but then stopped." It seems that many instructors are backing away from teaching Boolean, at least when they teach Web searching. What has changed for Rita? "First, I think that teaching Boolean in search engines simply reinforces the misuse of search engines for resource discovery. If you are picking around with keywords and combinations and synonyms, trying to find that needle in a haystack, chances are you shouldn't be using a search engine anyhow, and you are better off with a resource discovery tool."

Rita is certainly not the only trainer who has stopped teaching Boolean. Indeed, most of us agree that sophisticated Boolean abilities are rarely needed for Web searching. An understanding of Boolean searching is helpful for advanced searchers at many levels, especially in commercial and specialized databases, but the world of Web searching is rather different. Rita says, "Search engines should be used, paradoxically, only for things that you know are on the Web already. Using Boolean presupposes that you're hopeful but not confident that something is on the Web. Second, in the free Web, even those search engines like HotBot that boast full Boolean don't actually work properly when Boolean is applied." This last comment makes a particularly important point.

Indeed, for most audiences, learning how to do Boolean searches on Web search engines will be more distracting than helpful. But, as always, it depends on the people getting the training. As Ran Hock says, "My audience usually is doing the kind of research that at least occasionally requires the advantages of full Boolean. ... The concept of Boolean, even if AND, OR, and NOT are not used, is still essential to effective serious research. Also, many individual Web sites use Boolean." Ran even teaches the + and - operators since they are necessary "in order to understand the full capabilities of certain tools."

In my own training sessions, I often find advanced users who are frustrated that search engines do not process Boolean operators accurately. They say there are times when they want to be able to use Boolean commands. For these users, I continue to teach how and when to use Boolean searching and which search engines support it.

For the majority of Web searching students, should Boolean be tossed out the window? Not completely. The concept of Boolean combinations remains important. In particular, students should understand how a search engine responds to a multiple word query. In the late 1990s, many search engines would do an automatic OR operation. Today, thankfully, all the major search engines default to an AND search, but this default too may change. Consequently, I explain that search engines can respond to a multiple-word query in different ways. This is a concept I can teach without ever discussing Boolean operators or syntax. In those cases where my audience is already aware of Boolean syntax—perhaps through the use of commercial databases or in computer programming—I will translate from Boolean to search engine language.

At a very basic level, to teach the automatic default AND used by most search engines, I instruct students to add more words to find fewer results. My motto here is "More words equals less results." (While it would be more accurate grammatically to say "More words equal fewer results," something seems to be lost in the way of instructional impact.) Most students want relevant results more than they want a large number of results, and my motto usually makes the point effectively.

Even so, I like to point out that other search systems (library catalogs, bibliographic databases, directories, or site search engines) may behave differently and find more results as more query terms are added. Here is a simple technique students can use to check a given search tool: First, search on one word and note the number of results. Next, add a second word and search again. If the number goes down, the search system is performing like a Web search engine (and hence using Boolean AND). If the number increases, then it is finding more results and thus doing a Boolean OR operation.

The + and - Dilemma

A subset of Boolean searching is the so-called simplified form, which involves using the + and - operators. This "+ - system," as I refer to it, or "search engine math," as Danny Sullivan calls it, was first employed by the search engines of the late 1990s (Infoseek was its earliest exponent). The use of the + and - worked better as a simplified Boolean when the search engines defaulted to OR. In those days, the + was used to require a term and the - was used to exclude a word, so that the + functioned as an AND while the - functioned as a NOT. Using neither the + nor the - meant the term was processed as an OR.

When it eventually became clear that most searchers entering more than one word really wanted an AND operation, the search engines changed the default operator to AND. So, you might ask, with a default AND operation, what function does the + serve today? The fact is, it is no longer required; without it, all entered words will be included in the search.

On top of the change in the default operator, the + began to be used for other functions. Google was the first to use it to force the inclusion of stop words (frequently occurring words such as *of, the,* and *is,* which are usually ignored by the search engine), with other search engines following suit. So, depending on the search engine being used, the functionality of the + has changed. It may require a term to be present, make a stop word searchable, or have no effect at all. Also keep in mind that some specialized search engines, including site search tools, still use the + - system and default to OR.

Until the late 1990s, many Web trainers considered the + - system a convenient way to teach Boolean, but some absolutely hated it. When I asked my fellow trainers if they taught the + - system, I was surprised at the vehemence of some of the responses. Joe Barker says, "Never! Useless unless the default is OR. I wish + had never been invented, and I teach it as 'Baby Boolean' that does not work very well." Rita Vine gives it a "Ptooie!"

The one remnant of the + - system that warrants further consideration is the minus operator. The minus operator is fairly consistent among search engines in its function of excluding specific words from a query. Despite his feelings about the +, Joe does teach the minus operator as a way to exclude words or phrases, though he recommends that it be used only rarely. The minus is useful when search results have a large number of irrelevant results that all contain the same term. Rerunning the search while excluding that term with the minus operator can improve precision.

Truncation

Beyond phrase searching and some aspect of Boolean searching, the other search features that may be covered vary depending on the instructor and the class. Choose the ones that make the most sense for your audience.

Even though it is rarely available now on general Web search engines, truncation is frequently requested by librarians and other advanced searchers. Truncation is the ability to search just a portion of a word, typically using a symbol such as the asterisk to represent the rest of the term. The symbol is also often called a wild card. For example, searching with colleg* may find college, colleges, collegium, and collegial. At the time of this writing, Exalead is the only search engine supporting truncation. Google does some automatic word variant searching, which can create similar results, but its variant searching is not the same as truncation.

Truncation is not a feature most searchers would use every day, but it can be very useful for some searches. Ran Hock says that although the availability of truncation "is not that widespread, when it is available, it is extremely useful for dealing with alternative word forms."

John Ferguson teaches truncation and wild cards in part because they are useful in online library catalogs. His colleague Alice Fulbright says, "I always teach truncation because otherwise too many hits would be eliminated."

Even if a search engine does not support truncation, pointing out the differences in results from searching the singular and then the plural form of a word can make a forceful point. (Try *research methodology* and *research methodologies*.) Diane Kovacs says about the value of mentioning truncation, "Searchers need to be aware of why they get certain results with one search and not another."

Field Searching

Field searching allows the searcher to designate where a specific search term will appear. Rather than searching for words anywhere on a Web page, fields define specific structural units of a document. The title, the URL, an image tag, and a hypertext link are common fields on a Web page. Field searching is an option on the advanced search pages of some Web search engines and frequently can also be accomplished through the use of a prefix. For example, title:tarsier will look for the word *tarsier* in the title of a Web page. Unfortunately, the command syntax for title search varies among search engines. Older search engines such as AltaVista used just the title: prefix, but when Google started using the intitle: prefix, both Teoma and Yahoo! adopted it. Check the search engine help files or see my Search Engine Features Chart (www.searchengine showdown.com/features) for current syntax.

Ran Hock teaches field searching in general "because of the precision it can provide." But which field searches should we teach? A fair number of field search options are available at different search engines. In general, title, link, and URL field searches are taught. I often introduce title searching as a way to get a more accurate subject focus. Paul Barron spends substantial time on field searching in his workshops, focusing in particular on title searches and link checking using the link: field search. "Title searches usually provide the most relevant results for teachers and librarians," says Paul. He uses link searches to help find related sites. "The objective with link checking is to review the Web sites that link to a great Web site as a way of expanding the number of relevant resources. Since like attracts like, and other Web sites will link to a great resource, why run another search query? Check the links to a relevant resource as a method of expanding the resources." In other words, he has his students run a link search on the URL of a site to find additional, similar sites.

Joe Barker, among others, teaches field searching only in his advanced classes. He explains title searching because "it helps find pages primarily about your word(s)." He teaches URL field searches as a means of limiting a search to certain top-level domains or sites such as .edu or .nasa.gov. Joe shows how to do a link field search because when evaluating a page, it is useful "to see what other pages link to it and what they say."

Beyond the use of the link search for evaluation purposes, I demonstrate it as a tool for competitive intelligence and recommend its use by Webmasters during site redesigns. They can use a link search to see which other sites have linked to their old URLs. Gary Price says link searching is "a great thing to show business researchers" for doing competitive intelligence research and for seeing which organizations link to each other.

Limits

Limits provide a searcher with the means of narrowing search results by adding a specific restriction to the search. On Web search engines, the most common limits are date, site, and language. Language restricts a search to Web pages in a specified language. Some limits are more accurate than others. The language limits, for example, use word matching against dictionary files from various languages. Since not all languages are covered, and since multiple languages can appear on the same page, the language limit is not always accurate.

Limits are most easily accessible on the search engines' advanced search pages. They are usually located in various drop-down menu choices. Of the many limits available on the various search engines, site searching is the most commonly taught. Danny Sullivan teaches the site limit "as a means of filtering searches," and finds it "a good way to drop out sites dominating your results or to narrow into what you want (information from educational sites, for example)."

Of the other limits, when teaching Google, Danny will cover language and date and how to use them from the advanced search page. However, he always explains that "dates generally don't mean much" and that "often when people want to do a date search, they really want news content, so it's better to go to a news search engine."

Ran Hock teaches limits, but he warns about "the accuracy and advisability" of date searching. He says he teaches limits in part "to point out that they usually should not be primary criteria, except in cases such as news."

Several other trainers agree that date limiting is problematic. We all would welcome a date limit that could consistently identify Web pages whose content was created or updated within a specified date range. Unfortunately, the date listed for a retrieved Web page may simply reflect the last time an advertisement was changed or the date when the search engine last visited it. In other words, the date may have no connection with the production date of the information content. Joe Barker is well aware of this, and he demonstrates date limiting specifically to show that results reflect "the date last visited and not the real date of the page." Gary Price, among others, recommends against teaching the technique at all. Still, I have found that a date limit can be useful for excluding some (but by no means all) older content from a search. It can also be used to find Web pages that have not changed in several years, which is useful for Webmasters searching for pages on their site that might need updating.

Language limits help when searching terms that appear in Web pages written in various languages (for instance, names of businesses, people, products, and places), but the trainers I interviewed do not spend much time teaching the technique—largely, I suspect, because so many of them teach in the U.S. For many searches, the results will tend to be in the same language as the search. As Joe Barker notes, "Language searches are not as important ... as teaching that you are searching full text, and [that] foreign language pages require searches in that language." The exception is such things as names of businesses, people, products, and places as well as common terms that appear in multiple languages. In other countries, language limits are of far more interest since searchers there may often search (and speak) in several languages.

Stop Words and Case Sensitivity

Stop words are frequently occurring words that may not be searchable. Common stop words include *the, a, is, of,* and *be.* Numbers and recurrent URL strings (such as *html* and *com*) can also be treated as stop words. They are called stop words because they are so common that a search engine may stop processing them when indexing or running a search. Some search engines will search stop words only if they are part of a phrase search or if they are the only search terms in a query or have a + in front of them.

In the past, both the treatment of stop words and the differences in processing uppercase and lowercase characters were more varied among search engines than they are today. Thus, today's teacher will often pass over these topics in favor of more critical advanced features, such as phrase searching, truncation, field searching, and limits.

Case sensitivity refers to how the case of letters within search query terms affects search results. Most search engines are case insensitive: They will ignore uppercase, lowercase, and mixed case when searching for a given term. On any search engine, entering a search term in lowercase will usually find all case matches, though with a case-sensitive engine (such as AltaVista used to be), entering any single uppercase letter in a search term will invoke only exact case matches. So, for example, while a search on *next* will typically bring up *next, Next, NeXT,* and *neXT,* searching on *NeXT* in a case-sensitive engine will find only pages that contain *NeXT.*

For advanced classes, both stop word and case sensitivity issues may be taught. Paul Barron has attendees do a search for "to be or not to be" in different search engines so that they learn which search on all of these small words and which do not. To show the value of a case-sensitive search feature, he used to have his class do a search for the software company AI in case-sensitive AltaVista, then compare the results with those from a case-insensitive engine.

Ran Hock notes that with changes in how the search engines handle stop words and case, his teaching has changed. "With the (fortunate) decrease in stop words in search engines and the (unfortunate) rarity of case sensitivity, teaching these is less relevant than it used to be."

For John Ferguson, "Case sensitivity isn't a big issue, but using stop words in a phrase search is. The most important search engines, like Google, allow stop words to be retrieved if included in a bound phrase (enclosed within quotation marks)."

Knowing such details can help you achieve other instructional goals. Jeff Humphrey finds these features are "a good way to demonstrate flaws and special features of search engines." Have your students try a search for the music group The The or the aforementioned line from *Hamlet* to better understand stop words. For case sensitivity, searching on acronyms that are also common words—for example, *IT* for *information technology* and *PIPES* for *Piperazine-N, N'-bis* (ethanesulfonic acid)—can provide effective illustrations.

Sorting

Search engines can order search results in various ways, such as alphabetically, chronologically, or randomly. Sorting is the ability to change that order. Most search engines give no options beyond the default, which sorts results according to the search engine's relevance algorithms. The idea is that the most relevant results will appear before the less relevant ones. Sometimes this works. For navigational queries such as finding the Web site for a company or organization, relevance ranking tends to work well. For other types of queries, relevance ranking has mixed success (Notess 2000).

The problem for instructors is that no one knows precisely how search engine relevance algorithms are determined. (The search engines do not make the details public, partly to prevent unscrupulous Web marketers from manipulating search results in their favor.) In addition, the relevance algorithms change frequently. Thus, we cannot know with any degree of confidence what makes certain results rise to the top. The algorithms are based at least in part on link patterns on the Web and in part on the location of the text on the page, but these concepts are difficult to explain to novice searchers.

As of 2005, only Exalead and MSN Search provide some additional sorting options. MSN Search's Search Builder has sliders for results ranking that can change the order based on date and popularity, while Exalead offers a chronological and reverse chronological date sort.

At the beginning level, sorting can be explained to students by pointing out that the search engines are trying to list relevant results first but that automatic sorting does not always work well. Next, have them try a few search words to see what comes up first, then ask them to think of ways to add more words to get more relevant results. Sheila Webber says, "getting them thinking about getting the best out of a relevance-ranked search is very important."

The Teaching Choice

So which of the search features should you teach, and what proportion of a session should be dedicated to covering them? First of all, note that the various features can fit into a wide variety of sessions, though it is not necessarily a good idea to try to teach them all at once. Teaching them together may make sense when working with advanced searchers, especially those familiar with comparable features on commercial online systems. Paul Barron teaches "a search process that begins with a phrase search and progresses to using Boolean and proximity operators with field, top level, and geographic domain limiters and culminates with link checking of a selected result. Links checks are further limited using the Boolean AND operator with a keyword/phrase and a top-level domain."

In sessions for novices, explaining just one or two of these features may be enough. Phrase searching should certainly be one of the two. It is such a powerful tool that I cover it in every session. Advanced search features can be a strong draw for training sessions. The key is to teach the features that are most relevant to your audience and instructional goals. Provide the students with a few solid advanced tricks using these features, and they should see dramatic improvement in their searching success.

Chapter 8

Content: Primary Concepts

Specific search features and advanced techniques such as those covered in Chapter 7 are exactly what some attendees hope to learn in a Web searching session. Yet for many searchers, it is the conceptual background of search behavior and a broader picture of search engine issues that is essential to becoming better Web searchers. Some primary concepts about Web searching should be included in most sessions.

Different trainers emphasize different concepts. Some trainers start with a focus on one specific search engine. Others prefer to begin by teaching searching concepts first. This chapter outlines some of the most frequently taught searching concepts, and then tells you what primary concepts individual trainers emphasize. Then a look at the way we taught Web searching in the past sets the stage for the new conceptual topics we teach. As a final idea generator, we will look at several additional concepts that may be worth adding to the content of a Web searching class.

Research Process

As in so much other information literacy and bibliographic instruction, teaching the research process is an important component of instruction in Web searching. While especially pertinent in academia for students who may be learning how to do research, an understanding of the research process is also helpful to many other groups.

Sheila Webber, who teaches information management and business information classes, prefers to start with a focus on strategy and question analysis. "I try to get them to concentrate on thinking about overall strategy ... so I tend to prioritize that over talking about particular sources at length." For the strategy section, she tries to get them to postpone choosing an answer source until they have thought about questions such as, what is it I'm looking for, what's the best source, how does this source work, and what's it got in it?

Some audiences, instructors, and organizations sponsoring a training session will want the training to focus on specific tools, whether it be the current favorite like Google or new and exciting tools that will attract an audience. Yet it is often the research process that people really need to learn. Sheila concentrates on "helping [her students] learn the underlying concepts, rather than specific tools." However, she also notes that teaching specific search engines and specific tools "can be a selling point to the students."

One important reason to focus on the research process is the constantly changing nature of search engines. Sheila says, "With services changing (and disappearing and appearing) so rapidly still, I think it is vitally important that citizens have the flexibility— that an understanding of the research process fosters—so that when they come across a new search engine, they are information literate enough to work out what it's best for and how to get the best out of it."

Rita Vine has also begun emphasizing "the four stages of research, pre- and post-Web." As she describes it:

> Research has always followed four basic stages:
>   1. Gathering information
>   2. Selecting from what you have gathered
>   3. Processing the information into knowledge

4. Communicating that knowledge in some way

> Until the advent of the Web, we gathered information by physically going and getting it and dropping it on a table until we had enough. Only then did we begin to sift through the information and select the stuff we thought might be best. And after that selection process, we began to read information and absorb it thoroughly.

How does Rita explain the research process in today's Web world? "The problem with the Web is that because we don't have to physically go and get something, we become disorganized in our searching. In the middle of our gathering phase, we move directly to information processing. When we try to return to our gathering phase, we can't remember what we've done or where to pick up the process. The Web makes results retrieval so easy that we become sloppy researchers."

To prevent this slide into sloppy research, Rita proposes the following approach: "Replicate the traditional gathering processes of the pre-Web research world." In particular, "The process consists of putting a folder on your Windows desktop to 'catch' your gatherings. All you need to do is drop a URL shortcut into the folder, then continue your gathering. Eventually your folder, which is the virtual equivalent of a table in a library, will have enough to make you stop gathering. At this point you can sit at your virtual folder, review the Web sites you gathered, and decide which ones make the cut. This simply recreates the selection process that traditionally follows the information gathering phase and enables the searcher to stay on track."

Question Analysis

Question analysis is a related conceptual approach, a narrower aspect of the research process that teaches searchers how to think and expand their question. Diane Kovacs starts by introducing "the concept of analyzing the question and then selecting the appropriate search engine, directory, e-library, or subject-specific database."

One approach I use in basic sessions is what I call "go to the source." I ask students to try to think of an organization or type of Web site that would likely provide them with an answer to their research question. I compare this to what reference librarians do when asked a question. We start with the source (book or online) that is most likely to have the answer. For Web searching, I suggest the students consider searching for a government agency, a non-profit organization, or a company that would likely provide the answer to their question. For example, I ask the class what organization can provide information about the current population of whatever U.S. town I am presenting in. While some suggest the local Chamber of Commerce, there are usually others who say the Census Bureau. Then we will discuss strategies for finding the Census Bureau's Web site.

One reason for this approach is to bypass some of the concerns with evaluating the quality of Web information sources. By starting a population question at the U.S. Census Bureau's site, we are already starting with a source of commonly accepted authority rather than using a Web site that provides no information about the source of its data or the publisher of the site.

Using More Than One Search Tool

While many attendees at Web searching workshops would like to go away knowing the one perfect tool that answers all questions, none of the highly experienced and educated trainers I consulted know what that tool is. Instead, we trainers unanimously endorse the importance of using more than one search tool.

John Ferguson says, "We always stress that no one search tool will retrieve everything you want to find on the Internet," and he goes on to emphasize that even "all search tools *combined* will not retrieve everything." Ultimately John wants his students to realize that "most of the information stored in libraries today can't be found on the Internet."

Rita Vine also impresses on her students the value of using more than one search tool. She says, "I can prove, using several search examples, that you will acquire more, better, and a greater variety of resources in the same amount of time by conducting your search in several resource discovery tools rather than just searching and checking results from a search engine."

Paul Barron calls using more than one tool "a must if a searcher is going to thoroughly search the Web." At his workshops, he underscores the point by demonstrating "the wide variation in results of a title search in thirteen different search tools." Alice Fulbright shows students one metasearch tool and a unified search tool index. Danny Sullivan promotes "the idea that different search engines give different results or 'opinions' of the Web, so consulting more than one is useful."

Ran Hock adds, "Every tool and category of tool has its unique advantages," and Jeff Humphrey "emphasizes this in every session, usually by searching the same terms across different tools." Indeed, we all agree that one purpose of Web searching instruction is to make the students aware of the wide range of Web information resources.

Search Engines Versus Directories

Because search engines seem to get the majority of attention in the press, searchers often overlook a very important resource: directories. Joe Barker feels they are so valuable that "students should learn to use directories for about 50 percent of their searches." Joe also notes that "people have a lot of bad habits, ranging from always using Google to always using Yahoo! ... I have to unteach as much as I teach sometimes. I find my job is often 'selling' directories."

Like search engines, directories have changed greatly over the years. Yahoo! has greatly de-emphasized its directory portion; other directories have vanished. The Open Directory project was quite successful around 2000–2002, but it then grew unwieldy, and many question whether its updates can be sustained. Meanwhile, library-oriented directories, such as the Librarians' Internet Index (LII; www.lii.org) and the Resource Discovery Network (RDN; www.rdn.ac.uk), have expanded and improved greatly. Even so, use of search engines is much higher than that of directories, and most directories are unfamiliar to our typical students.

Why insist on teaching students about directories? Because, as Alice Fulbright puts it, "Web pages found in a directory have been selected by humans whereas search engines are crawling the Web without regard to human selection criteria." Her colleague John Ferguson expresses similar sentiments. "It's the difference between humans and robots. Humans are capable of making discriminations, both categorical and evaluative, that robots can't."

One difficulty in teaching about directories is the way directories have changed over time. When Yahoo! de-emphasized its directory in favor of general search engine results, many trainers changed their view of Yahoo!. Danny Sullivan used to differentiate between directories and search engines. Now, "Given the change at Yahoo!," he says, "I'm having to change this. I expect that I'll still point out that results are gathered by humans in some cases and available at 'link lists' or categories, showing how to access these. That's because in some cases, it remains very useful to get a long list of Web sites on a particular topic."

Asked whether he differentiates between search engines and directories, Ran Hock says, "Absolutely and imperatively because the difference embodies the classic information retrieval problems of recall and precision, exhaustivity and selectivity, finding the best answer versus finding 'any answer,' ... though I don't necessarily couch the situation in those terms. I do express it in terms of 'Every tool has its unique advantages.'"

Joe Barker also emphasizes the difference. "I divide the universe of Web searching tools into two parts: search engines and directories. They are totally different, built differently, and should be used and evaluated differently. I teach search engines as striving for comprehensiveness, totally unevaluated, and built by brainless computers. I teach good directories as collections of sometimes searchable links on a topic ... human-selected, organized by subject." Directories like LII and RDN are an important component of Joe's instruction. "I teach the value of finding subject-focused directories even more than the big general directories like Yahoo!."

Gary Price is well known for presentations that cover many tools and a wide variety of information resources. He also emphasizes directories. "A good session, unless resource specific, focuses on a variety of tools. This is crucial in this Google-centric period. Variety and options are what make the Web such a valuable tool." And while Gary notes that he does not differentiate between directories and search engines as much as he used to, due to the common availability of the directories at search engines and search engines at directories, he will "always spend time talking about non-commercial directories" and mentions Infomine, the RDN, and the LII in particular.

Explaining the differences in the ways directories and search engines gather and index their records can help students understand when it's best to use each. Jeff Humphrey will "include an example of each, usually Yahoo! and Google" and discuss "why you may choose one over the other." Paul Barron adds, "The way the databases are indexed differs, and the human indexing of a directory influences database size."

As discussed in Chapter 6, directories are often considered to be a subtype of search engines. With Yahoo! being a portal, a directory, and a search engine, the lines are blurred even further. The confusion of terminology with directories and search engines makes teaching them somewhat problematic, but most audiences seem to pick up on the difference in function once they see a few examples.

Evaluation

Does the Web have high-quality, accurate, and reliable information? This question was frequently repeated in the Web's early days and is still heard today. The answer is certainly yes ... and no. The Web includes some very accurate and reliable resources, along with many inaccurate, unreliable, misleading, and outright false ones.

Most teachers include a section on evaluation when discussing Web searching. As Gary Price puts it, "No Web search session is complete ... without spending a few minutes on quality and authority issues." Often, evaluation of results pervades all the examples in a workshop. Some teachers incorporate evaluation throughout the whole session while others present it as a specific topic.

Many articles and books address the issue of evaluating Web information. Robert Berkman's *The Skeptical Business Searcher: The Information Advisor's Guide to Evaluating Web Data, Sites, and Sources* (CyberAge, 2004) is an excellent resource for evaluating business sites. Many other sources are listed in the "Bibliography on Evaluating Web Information" at www.lib.vt.edu/help/instruct/evaluate/evalbiblio.html (Auer 2004).

Joe Barker includes evaluation even during his course-integrated bibliographic instruction sessions, when he has only a brief amount of time to cover Web searching. Joe emphasizes that "Google is *not* evaluated, and the Google Directory is a little bit better. ... You need to evaluate what you find. I teach spotting personal pages, looking at the top level domain carefully, asking who wrote the page and what their credentials are, and finding and reading the 'About' section of any page you do not know the source of." In his 2½-hour classes dedicated to Web searching, Joe devotes 30 minutes to evaluation.

More recently Joe has also been trying to teach evaluation in a new way. He picks three or four very ambiguous sites. Then he introduces techniques for evaluating the pages, such as how to use a link: search and how to recognize personal pages. Then he has the class "work in teams to try to evaluate these difficult pages. And we talk about the ranges of possibilities for evaluating and realistic expectations."

Which Primary Concepts to Teach

The research process, question analysis, the value of using more than one search tool, search engines versus directories, and evaluation are all primary topics for many trainers. However, it is not possible to cover all these concepts in one course. Trainers must pick and choose what primary topics they will cover and in what order to cover them.

John Ferguson puts most of his emphasis on "subject indexes and categorical directories, a little less time on search engines, and even less time on unified search tool indexes, metasearch tools, and Web rings." Why this order? "Subject indexes (like Digital Librarian) and categorical directories (like Open Directory) are covered first, because these tools are most appropriate for general searching at the beginning of the research process. Then search engines are covered second because this type of tool is appropriate for finding very specific sources later in the research process." Ran Hock spends most of his time on search engines, then resource guides, and then directories. The difference in emphasis and order of topics covered is due to their audiences: John is teaching community college students while Ran's audience tends to be older or at least more experienced.

Diane Kovacs offers three main points for her workshops:

- Analyze the question

- Choose the best tool whether it is a Web source or offline or commercial database

- Evaluate information sources

In community college settings, Alice Fulbright presents three featured concepts for her Web searching sessions:

- How to analyze a Web page for authority

- Why LII is an excellent search tool for limited, yet highly credible results

- How to continue to refine a search again and again to get more focused results

Gary Price offers these two primary concepts: the limitations of Web search and the need to use a variety of tools. When teaching librarians, Gary says, "It's important to emphasize the need to 'know' a variety of tools to be ready to assist all patrons."

Joe Barker offers two different sets of primary concepts for two different audiences. In his workshops aimed at librarians, he offers three key concepts:

- The best approach to use always arises from skillfully analyzing the question before you start searching.

- You should use search engines no more than half the time and directories half the time. And remember that the invisible Web is also out there.

- Learn from your searches ("search with peripheral vision") and vary your approach as you learn.

In Joe's University of California, Berkeley, workshops, the emphasis is on two concepts:

- Search engines work with full-text matching of what is in the pages in an unevaluated database.

- Directories allow you to take advantage of research and subject organization that others, sometimes experts, have already done.

In her daylong workshops, Rita Vine says that sessions are built around these two primary concepts:

- Limit your use of search engines to things you know are already on the Web

- Use resource discovery tools to identify high-quality resources on subjects when you don't know where to start

Phil Bradley spends the most time on search engines since they are the "most complex (and interesting!), and they provide the basis for further coverage." His two primary subjects are phrase searching and exploring advanced search concepts.

Ran Hock covers many specific sources in his sessions. His two main concepts are using multiple tools and knowing the full capabilities of any tool.

Jeff Humphrey also emphasizes moving beyond a single tool with his two primary concepts:

- Google is not the alpha and the omega.

- Subject-specific resources are often a better choice than a general search engine.

The advice from search engine expert Danny Sullivan might be surprising to some; he emphasizes moving beyond search engines with these four points:

- It's not always on the Web, so if you don't find what you want after looking for about 10 minutes, you might want to consider non-Web search methods of obtaining it.

- Search engines might get you part of the way, such as to a page where someone may seem to know the answer you want; contacting the person might get you the answer even though it isn't published.

- Using more than one search engine is essential because they have different views of the Web. Your query might "fail" at one, not because the engine isn't useful, but because a good answer to your query is not available at that particular search engine.

- Think like the author of the material you seek. Want "cheap floor tiles?" The merchant selling them probably will describe them more attractively, such as "discount floor tiles." Want to see how others are dealing with a medical ailment? Searching for the common name rather than the medical or scientific one will probably bring back better listings.

For my own basic Internet searching sessions in the academic environment, I emphasize two specific concepts:

- Go to the source by searching for an organization that is likely to have an authoritative answer to your question

- Use phrase searching to target both organizational Web sites and topics

Recent Changes in Teaching Topics

It is important to remember how quickly search favorites can change, even in today's era of Google dominance. Google is now included in all workshops, but it was not always so. Over the past decade, my colleagues and I have covered—and subsequently no longer cover—an astonishing number of search engines in our courses, including:

- AltaVista
- AOL Search
- BUBL
- Debriefing
- Dogpile
- Excite
- FAST
- FastSearch
- Go Guides
- HotBot
- Inference Find
- Infoseek
- LookSmart
- Lycos
- Mirago
- Netscape Search
- Northern Light
- Open Directory
- Profusion
- SearchUK
- Snap
- UKMax
- WebCrawler

Beyond the many search engines dropped from training sessions, trainers are also less likely to cover such topics as:

- Bookmarking
- Case sensitivity
- Gopher use
- How to use Web browsers
- Truncation or wildcards

These lists should make us all stop and consider how much things may change (and what may vanish) in the next decade. Rita Vine sums up our recent experience well:

Until about 1998, when Web pages were rarely database driven and the typical search engine included all 56-million-odd pages out there, we could focus on search engines and Boolean searching. We stopped focusing on search engines with three events: (1) Google's appearance in the marketplace and the billion-page world in late 1999; (2) the great increase in the late '90s of searchable (and invisible) Web databases like PubMed; (3) the utter ubiquitousness of the Internet on practically every desktop around 1998, which brought about a massive amount of incorrect search mythology and rampant search malpractice. These events demanded that we markedly adjust our teaching methodology.

Even as we abandon teaching dead search engines, little used search features, and less effective methods, trainers have started teaching some new concepts. I now spend more time teaching search methodology and include more examples of effective use of advanced features. I also focus more on teaching ways to identify advertisements on search engine results pages.

When Rita Vine stopped focusing on the search engines themselves, she began emphasizing subject-specific resources. More recently, she has been covering the stages of the research process (see her description under "Research Process" earlier in this chapter) and teaching students how to open links in new windows. "This is the most important skill I can teach to keep you from losing your place in a Web search," she says. "If you see a page that has more than one possible link that you want to click on, learn to open that link in a new window in order not to lose your original page. Your original page remains on the desktop, ready for you to right-mouse-click on the remaining links of interest, in order to methodically maintain your search intent." Remember to show students using alternate browsers like Mozilla, Firefox, and Opera how to do the same thing in a new tab.

Diane Kovacs has begun teaching "how to work with patrons who insist on using the Web without critical thinking." Alice Fulbright has started putting "more emphasis on using title field searches and searches for specific domains." Paul Barron has been showing more "results clustering with search tools like Teoma, WiseNut, and Vivisimo." Phil Bradley has focused more on advanced search functionality.

Danny Sullivan has added newsgroup searching "since it became more dependable at Google" and covers invisible Web resources in more depth. John Ferguson says, "With the improvement in the relevancy ranking of search engine results, we have been teaching the importance of submitting multiple search terms and entering natural language phrases and questions."

Jeff Humphrey has started teaching more multimedia searching. "With the explosion of audio and video on the Internet, I've tried to emphasize learning a non-text search engine. Unfortunately, these types of sites seem to have a short shelf life or quickly become unsuitable for all ages. Luckily, most major search engines are incorporating such capabilities."

In addition to teaching SurfWax and Teoma for the unique power features they have, Joe Barker also has begun teaching that "simpler is best. Several simple searches (with OR maybe, and possibly with title limiting) are faster than advanced searching."

I have been moving in the same direction, emphasizing that a simple search may be all that is needed. While I often teach expert searchers about advanced features, I also emphasize that the effective use of such advanced features depends on knowing when to use them. Case-sensitive searching, truncation, and full Boolean can be combined to achieve some great results, but I emphasize that I use some of those features only once or twice a year.

Recently, Sheila Webber has been focusing more on a technique called mindmapping, using diagrams to explore a specific question. More details about the technique as applied to information literacy in a variety of settings can be found in Dale, Johnston, Webber, & O'Flynn (2003). Essentially mindmapping involves brainstorming and refining a topic by using branches to build a graph structure from a central concept or keyword. The technique has many applications and is promoted at several sites, including www.mind-mapping.co.uk.

Mindmapping is just one of the techniques that Sheila has been exploring recently. "I'm also trying to rethink the whole business of 'concepts' (as in 'how many concepts are there in this query'), because if I follow up on the mind maps, trying to get students to think of combining different bits of the mind map, that actually might be more effective in ... encouraging [students] to have more than one shot at a search. ... I encourage them to think about different models of searching and the search process and to think about it as an iterative and learning process, not a linear process."

Additional Concepts to Consider

Many other concepts can be covered in a Web searching clinic. Sometimes only a few minutes may be spent on any one of these. Some fit perfectly for one audience while another might match a different group. Each concept is worth considering as a portion of a training session in Web searching; at the least, we should be prepared to answer questions about these topics.

Identifying Ads

In the late 1990s, the identification of ads did not take long to teach. We could simply point out flashing graphics of a certain size and say, "these are advertisements." With the rise in text advertising and the greater emphasis on search engine marketing and optimization, it is more difficult to understand which results are ads and which are not. Now we can teach the identification of graphic ads, text ads surrounding search results, and optimized search results.

Google and Yahoo! Search Marketing Solutions (which started as Overture) are the most prominent search engine text ad sources for "sponsored" links. (The search engine industry seems to have settled on the terms *sponsor* and *sponsored* to refer to advertisers and advertisements, but those labels may well change.)

Overture was the original ad bidding engine. Now called Yahoo! Search Marketing Solutions, it is the only one that still provides easy access to the sums advertisers are bidding for certain words. Just go to www.overture.com and run a search. Due to problems with automated bid comparison robots, Yahoo! Search Marketing Solutions removed the bid price from the regular Yahoo! Search Marketing Solutions search results page. Now it is accessible only via the "View Advertisers' Max Bids" link in the upper right-hand corner. Click that and a new window pops up in which the user must enter a code contained in a graphic (this technique stops the robots). Then run the same search and the results include the bid price (Figure 8.1).

Demonstrating this in a class is a great technique to get the students' attention, as they are quite interested in the prices paid per click for certain search words. Google now also has a similar tool at adwords.google.com/select/KeywordToolExternal. While it will provide an estimate of the advertising cost if you use the "Cost and ad position estimates" option to make a high estimated bid, it does not report how much particular advertisers are paying.

Far more difficult is the issue of identifying optimized pages. Search engine optimization companies are paid to advise and manage other companies' Web pages so that they will rank higher

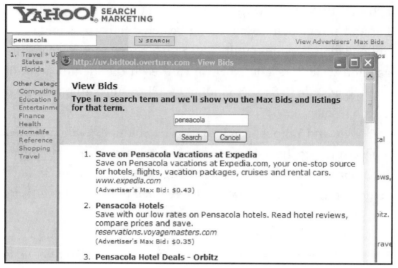

Figure 8.1   Viewing Yahoo! ad-bidding prices

in search engines. Say that Joe's Tire Pump shop wants to rank first, or at least in the top 10, when someone searches for "tire pumps." Over several months a good search engine optimization company may be able to increase the shop's ranking by making changes to its Web site, such as getting links from other sites, improving the quantity of textual content on the site, adding significant informational content, putting the keywords in the URL, and many other techniques. Some less-reputable search engine optimization companies also use tricks such as small text sizes, font colors that match the background, keyword loading, cloaking, and running link farms.

If the optimization company is successful, Joe's will have paid it (but not the search engine) to get better ranking. But how does the searcher identify these optimized results? Since the search engine engineers themselves cannot always detect these optimized results (called "spam" if they are deceptive), there is no definitive way. Stay alert for an obvious example that can be used in your class.

Unfortunately for us trainers, the most egregious examples rarely continue to work for long. I have used the search phrase "origin bubonic plague ships" in the past at Google. Since several of the top 10 results were from term paper mills, they were obvious examples of optimized pages.

One exercise for teaching the identification of ads can be done even when the students do not have access to a computer. Just print off a search results page that contains several ads. I try to find one with text banners at the top, text ads on the right, and some obvious optimized pages in the regular results. Then ask the attendees to circle the ads. In the course of the discussion after the exercise, be sure to point out the "sponsored" labels if and when they appear.

Understanding Web Addresses (or URLs)

In connection with teaching students to analyze their question and then go to an authoritative source for an answer, I teach the basics of reading URLs—explaining some of the basic top-level domains and the structure of site domains and URL paths. Teaching students to understand Web addresses also helps them evaluate Web documents.

Trainers say that many students, especially younger ones, do not have any sense of the difference between the .gov, .com, and .edu top-level domains. Certainly some less-sophisticated users do not even fully understand that a URL is the Web address for one specific Web page. Understanding domains and top-level domains is essential for effectively using site limits and top-level domain limits.

To help students understand how Web addresses are put together and to give them more confidence in their knowledge of the URL syntax, I suggest bypassing search engines at times by simply guessing the address. Following up on my Census Bureau example discussed earlier in this chapter, and after explaining the major top-level domains, I ask the class to guess what the URL for the Census Bureau might be. Most students can guess www.census.gov fairly easily. For a more detailed look at my guessing exercise, see Chapter 11.

Understanding Databases

Search engines and directories all store their information in some kind of database. For an audience that has a basic understanding of databases (such as librarians), a discussion of the underlying databases helps students understand search engine results better. The search engines themselves usually refer to their underlying database as their *index*, but since librarians often use *index* to refer to other kinds of tools, I find the term *database* better conveys the point. Even for an audience not used to thinking about databases, explaining some of the concepts involved with search engine databases, such as datedness, differences, and scope, can help explain why search engines can give such unexpected results.

Database Datedness

I frequently teach that search engines are searching a picture of the past. That is why they may find dated information. Since the search engine crawler visited the page sometime in the past (from a day ago to several months ago), indexed the words on the page at that time, and then put that information into a database, we can search only the results from the crawler's visit. Some students have the misconception that search engines search the Web live, as it exists in the present. They simply assume that the crawling of all those billions of Web pages occurs after the query is submitted. A demonstration of the datedness of the underlying database helps students understand why some results are dead links or have content completely different from what the search results indicate. It also reinforces the point that news search engines are more appropriate when searching for news stories.

Database Differences

Because the search engines are always adding to their databases, we can also teach about the multiplicity of databases that supply search engine results. On many search engines, the various links on the results page can come from several distinct databases, such as a news database, a shortcuts database, an ads database, and the regular Web database. We can teach this using Google as an example. The ads come from one database. Several news headlines may display, all of which come from another database. The link in the blue bar from the search words leads to definitions from Answers.com. The page-top links go to separate database results from Images, Groups, News, Froogle (shopping), and Local.

The issue of multiple databases can be presented within an ad identification unit or when contrasting directories and search engines. It also fits well with some of the additional content discussed in Chapter 9.

When teaching about this multiplicity of databases (Notess 1999), we can also introduce students to changes in the sources of underlying databases. For example, over the years Yahoo! has switched from AltaVista to Inktomi to Google as the provider of its search engine results, and now to its own search engine database. MSN Search dropped LookSmart and has now replaced Inktomi with a Microsoft-developed database.

Database Scope

When we talk to our students about the underlying Web database, we can compare the search engines to one another. Some users still think that search engines are comprehensive and that they all cover every single page on the Web. Explaining the limitations of the databases and how much material on the Web is *not* included segues nicely into a discussion of the invisible Web.

Providing examples of the lack of duplication between search engines gives students another reason for using more than just one. Each of the major Web search engines finds pages that others do not. Demonstrate an example on a very narrow search. Then point out that when searchers get zero hits at one search engine, they may find results if they try the same search at another search engine.

Teaching Change

One additional concept to consider teaching is change. The Web search engines have been changing frequently since their incarnation. The pace of change has continued to be rapid, sometimes with several new announcements a month. Search engine results can change from day to day. Within a classroom, a dozen people searching the same exact words at Google or another search engine may very well get different results.

It is certainly frustrating to build the perfect lesson plan around a feature or specific search that then changes right before the class, but this constant search engine flux has a positive side. Start out a session by commenting on how often things change at search engines and say, "Something is likely to have changed today." Then if you come across an unusual result or something that changed since you prepared the lesson, say, "See, I told you something would change." It is an easy way to make the instructor appear prescient—and to emphasize an important point.

The continuing change within search engines can also help promote your training sessions. Encourage people to attend sessions once every year since so much can change from one year to the next. Market the workshops as Search Engine Updates or New Features of Search Engines. Look at the constant change as reason to offer updated workshops and to build more traffic to your classes!

Chapter 9

Additional Content: Image Searching, News, Usenet, and More

Web searching encompasses a variety of techniques, strategic approaches, search engines, and databases. While the main focus of this book and most training sessions in Web searching is the major Web search engines and related search strategies, content-specific searches work wonderfully for certain questions. Sources for pictures, opinions, current news, phone numbers, and audio files used to be completely separate search engines, distinct from the major Web search engines. Now the major search engines often include separate databases for searching just these types of content.

Each search engine has its own collection of additional content. Some stand-alone, content-specific search engines are more comprehensive than those connected to a major player. This chapter covers some of the alternative content search tools that are worth considering as an addition to a Web search training session.

News

Since breaking news is rarely indexed in time to be included in the regular Web page databases from the search engines, it is important to show students where to find that kind of frequently requested information. Google, Yahoo!, Ask, and MSN Search all have their own separate news databases, but these are not always the best places to start. Instead, many instructors suggest starting with major news media Web sites. Ran Hock will often introduce news searching with some news resource guides, and then he will acquaint students with "the big news network sites, such as BBC, MSNBC, newspapers, news alerting resources," and more.

A common approach among trainers is to offer a separate class for news searching. Alice Fulbright teaches a special News Sources class and, as would be expected in academe, she covers both Internet news resources and the local subscription database resources for news. For Web sources, she covers Google News and will "sometimes show students Internet Public Library Newspapers."

Where the members of the class live is very important in determining what news sources to teach. Those who teach outside the U.S. tend to cover more international sources. Within the U.S., some locations are better covered than others in certain news search engines.

Most news search engines are similar to Web search engines in that they crawl news Web sites to create their database. Instead of refreshing their databases once per month or even less frequently, however, the news search engines revisit their sources very frequently—some every few minutes. They also tend to cover far fewer Web sites, say thousands, compared to the millions indexed in a Web search engine.

Note that the source of news is different from the commercial news databases that get direct wire feeds. Most Web news search engines just find what they can get for free on the Web. The Northern Light News search used to give access to different news content since it had direct feeds from dozens of news wires rather than just from news Web sites. Unfortunately, Northern Light News ceased operation in early 2003.

Of the many news search engines available, some commonly taught ones include the following:

- Google News (news.google.com)

- Yahoo! News (news.yahoo.com)

- NewsNow (newsnow.co.uk)

- Rocketinfo (www.rocketnews.com)

- Daypop (www.daypop.com)

- Feedster (www.feedster.com)

Most of these cover only news from the past week or month, although Yahoo! News sometimes goes back further. Feedster, Daypop, and Rocketinfo cover blogs as well as news sites.

Usenet Newsgroups and Opinions

Back in the 1980s, long before the Web even existed, wide-ranging online discussions took place within Usenet newsgroups. With the rise of the Web, many people today are completely unaware of the old Usenet newsgroups, even though they live on under the Google Groups name. DejaNews, an early Usenet search engine and newsreader, brought the discussions, advice, and vehement opinions of Usenet users to a wider audience. With Google's acquisition of DejaNews and its conversion into Google Groups, this database of opinions is searchable from 1981 to the present. Some users still participate in Usenet.

Ran Hock mentions teaching Usenet searching at Google Groups, along with "non-Usenet" groups searching within a site like Yahoo! Groups (groups.yahoo.com). While Usenet is still an important location to look for online discussions, Web-based forums like the various Yahoo! groups are increasingly important.

Joe Barker goes a step further, saying he "used to teach [Usenet searching] as a way of finding some information, but now I find many useful threads in routine Google results." With more Web-based discussion forums, search engines cover more of that kind of information in regular searches than they did in the late 1990s.

Specialized opinion search sites have become more common with the rise of e-commerce and the solicitation of user reviews by sites such as Amazon. Epinions (www.epinions.com), now owned by Shopping.com, includes product specifications, professional reviews, and personal evaluations. E-commerce opinion sites are well worth teaching to an audience interested in shopping searches.

Pictures and Images

The ability of graphic browsers to display text with embedded images was one of the great attractions of the early Web. If the rise of digital photography has not expanded the interest in online images, it has certainly expanded the number of pictures available online. Add in all the graphic buttons, logos, screen captures, and graphic design elements on the Web, and it is easy to see how image search engines can include more than one billion images.

Searching images is popular, but the issues involved with image search are complex. With Web searching, the text of the query is matched with text on a Web page. With image searching, the text of the query has to be matched with a picture. Fortunately, images on the Web have some text associated with them: text within the file name, including the site name and directory; any text surrounding the image on a page; or an alternative text tag designed for non-image browsers. But the quality of all this connected text depends on the site creator. Diane Kovacs offers a separate workshop devoted just to finding graphics on the Web. She has plenty of issues to cover and notes that image search engines are not nearly as effective as text search engines. (Diane's workshop also covers copyright awareness as it pertains to images found on the Web—a very important issue related to image searching.)

Picture search engines are available at Yahoo!, Google, Ask, and MSN Search. Paul Barron also teaches image-only search engines Ditto (www.ditto.com) and Picsearch (www.picsearch.com).

Rita Vine offers another approach to teaching image searching. Instead of showing the image search engines, she advocates using "resource discovery tools like LII, which link to browseable image libraries." Indeed, search engines do not necessarily index many of the image collections that can be found via a directory like LII. The directory approach helps find the collection by a broader topic word.

With all picture search engines, instructors should be wary of potential display problems when demonstrating an image search. Even if you use seemingly innocuous words or enable family filters, pornographic images may show up in the search results. Check the searches before the session or use a pre-recorded search for demonstration if you want to be especially safe.

Multimedia

Searching for multimedia on the Internet is a very popular search activity, especially among iPod users and other music fans. Yet this category is not frequently taught in Web searching classes. Ran Hock says that he will occasionally teach audio or video searching but not in much detail. Jeff Humphrey shows MediaChannel (www.mediachannel.com) and Yahoo!'s Launch for multimedia content.

Paul Barron combines image and multimedia searching. He starts by showing the image search engine Picsearch in his workshops. He shows the advanced search, which limits searches to animated images, and then has attendees find animated images of Winston Churchill. Next Paul asks his attendees to use AltaVista's

MP3/audio search to locate an audio file of Churchill's "finest hour" speech.

When teaching a younger audience, you should certainly consider multimedia search issues. The hard-core music fan may know all about how to search the various quasi-legal peer-to-peer MP3 search engines (such as BitTorrent or Gnutella), but those search skills may not translate well to basic Web searching. Even so, knowing if some attendees have that experience should help the instructor target the Web search training better.

Of the Web search engines, Yahoo! and Exalead have audio databases. Yahoo!, Google, and Exalead have video databases. Singingfish (singingfish.com), now owned by AOL, is exclusively an audio and video search engine. While few use it directly from its Web site, Singingfish powers the search feature within multimedia software players like Real and the Windows Media player.

Phone Numbers

Traditional telephone directories, both white and yellow, make very effective classroom examples of databases: Compare the phone book to a database and an individual listing to a search engine result record. In addition to their suitability as an analogy, phone numbers are a frequently requested information item. There are numerous online telephone search engines, often based on third-party databases from vendors such as Acxiom or InfoUSA, which compile phone numbers from scanned phone books and direct marketing lists. Due to the source, there may be some errors in the data, but telephone search engines are quite useful nonetheless.

Google, InfoSpace, and Yahoo! all have U.S. phone number databases. There are also specialized phone search engines like Switchboard. As with the news, where the students live influences which phone number search engines the instructor should discuss.

For Ran Hock, "If there is an international aspect, as there is in many of my courses, I start with a resource guide such as Wayp (www.wayp.com), and for the U.S., I usually look at two or three directories, such as AnyWho (anywho.com) and Switchboard (switchboard.com)." Phil Bradley, from the U.K., teaches 192.com. In Indiana, Jeff Humphrey features Switchboard and The Ultimates (theultimates.com), both U.S.-centric directories.

Rita Vine does not spend much time on phone number databases, although she does show a phone number portal or two. She uses an exercise to teach students how to fill out searchable forms. "For example, a phone directory lookup tool may offer search boxes for any or all of last name, first name, address, city, state. We use this opportunity to train end users to *avoid* filling out all the boxes, because filling out every box can rule out relevant search results. Most users never think of this on their own."

Bibliographic Databases

Two types of bibliographic databases can be taught in Web searching: the freely available databases on the Web (such as PubMed) and the commercially available databases purchased by a library, employer, or other affiliated organization. Bibliographic database searching has traditionally been the major focus of library instruction sessions and may be taught by the same people who teach Web searching. Yet few Web searching trainers include bibliographic databases in their Web searching course. It is far more typical to offer separate sessions—one for general Web searching and one or more for using the library's commercial resources. In academia, course-integrated bibliographic instruction and information literacy courses may include Web searching and bibliographic databases.

Web searchers outside the academic and public library environment may not have access to commercial databases. For those audiences, free bibliographic databases can be very valuable. In his sessions, Ran Hock will sometimes include resources ranging from "general ones like Ingenta and the Library of Congress, to bigger subject-specific ones like ERIC, USPTO [the U.S. Patent and Trademark Office], and PubMed, to more specific ones such as SSRN [the Social Science Research Network], Population Index, CORDIS, and Integrum [World Wide]."

With some search engines entering into this arena—recent examples include Google Scholar (scholar.google.com) and Windows Live Academic (academic.live.com)—teaching databases may become a more significant part of search engine training. I have taught both Google Scholar and Scirus (Elsevier's scientific Web and full-text journal article search engine at scirus.com) in workshops for audiences that include scientists who are not affiliated with a major company or academic institution.

The Web has also provided free access to many small, niche bibliographic databases. Because they can be so small and subject focused, they are covered in the following section.

Subject-Specific Sites

Many workshops that trainers are called upon to teach may have a subject focus: They are designed for an audience that works in the same industry or at the same company or research institute. In such a focused workshop, part of the teaching should cover relevant, high-quality, subject-specific Web sites. For example, a pharmaceutical session might focus on the U.S. Food and Drug Administration (FDA) site, while a business workshop could include Web sources for market research reports. The Web has thousands, if not millions, of excellent subject-specific sites for everything from manufacturing to hobbies to scholarly research. One difficulty for trainers is identifying the common subject interests of the audience and then tracking down the top sites in that subject area. This is even more difficult if the subject area is completely unfamiliar to the instructor. Yet subject-specific sites may be appreciated above anything else you teach in the session.

Ran Hock says he almost always covers subject sites, "from a few examples to dozens, depending on the course." Jeff Humphrey mentions some of the ones he includes: Corporateinformation. com; Allmusic.com, to hunt down songs and recording artists; Infoplease, to locate, among other things, winners of awards and major sporting events; and the Internet Movie Database (IMDb) for all things movie related. Gary Price gathers all kinds of specialized subject sites, targeted bibliographic databases, and pertinent government agencies and reports for students in his sessions.

Since many subject-specific sites are easy to find within a good directory, the inclusion of a collection of subject sites might appropriately be tied into a section on using Web directories or even the invisible Web. By digging deeply into a subject-specific site, students may well find specific resources, records, and whole databases that are not included in the search engines.

Invisible Web

Explaining the limitations of search engines reinforces the need to use a variety of sources and to use appropriate strategies. The concept of the invisible (or hidden or deep) Web makes one of the limitations clearly evident: Not everything on the Web is indexed by search engines. The invisible Web consists of those resources that are not found by search engines. In addition to his emphasis on quality directories, Joe Barker stresses the importance of invisible Web resources: "I also teach about the many fabulous databases accessible through the Web and whose content is not to be found in either [search engines or directories]. And I teach using search engines and directories to locate databases on all kinds of things. I teach the invisible Web as something that searchers must remember exists thanks to the Web's making remote databases searchable."

An example I have used comes from an Economics 101 assignment at Montana State University. The students were asked to find the unemployment rate for the past 10 years in Montana—a fairly basic question. A search on "unemployment rate montana" finds all kinds of sites that include those words. Some actually have the latest unemployment rate or the monthly (but not annual) unemployment rates for Montana or explain how the unemployment rate is calculated. But the search gets frustrating when page after page is examined and not one gives the exact answer. Yet the answer is freely available on the Web. The Bureau of Labor Statistics gathers that data and is an authoritative source. Its site offers several ways to access the data, but most require a search form. Using the form to request the unemployment rate in Montana for the past 10 years will bring up a table with exactly the numbers needed.

Explaining to students that the form prevents search engines from finding and indexing the Bureau of Labor Statistics illustrates the important and often-repeated point that information that may very well be available on the Web is not always directly accessible via a search engine. Many more examples and a much more in-depth description of the invisible Web is available in Sherman and Price (2001).

The Lost Obvious

Although not a separate database, the second page of search results is a major blind spot for far too many searchers. This obvious expansion of search results is lost to many users, and without it, they may miss a great deal of information. Most search engines default to displaying 10 results and cluster their results so that only one or two records per Web site will be included in those first 10.

Unfortunately, most users never look beyond the clustered top 10. Blame David Letterman and his Top 10 lists or blame the search engines for giving so few results by default, but take this opportunity to teach something else about Web searching. Gary Price considers results beyond the first 10 to be part of the invisible Web since so few users ever look that far.

Teaching students how to reach these other results can be as simple as showing them how to click on the Next button to get the next 10 hits. It can be taught as a reason to explore the advanced search page, from which searchers can get up to 100 results, depending on the search engine. In addition, the frequent neglect of the second page can be used as an introduction to personalization capabilities, which, like the advanced search, can allow up to 100 results to be set as the default.

To find the third or fourth results from a single Web site, students need to learn another strategy. Most search engines cluster the results and provide access to the other hits from the same site under a link labeled "More Results from." Unfortunately, that link is usually at the bottom of the record and in a different (often lighter) color, so it mostly goes unseen. Simply pointing it out makes a difference for many searchers. In a hands-on class, incorporate clicking on that link into one of the exercises so that students get experience actually using it.

Each group of students may benefit from the inclusion of one or more of the content types discussed in this chapter. But the main Web search engines remain the focus of Web search training. They have changed over time, so let us now explore the current crop of major Web search engines, along with a few important minor ones.

Chapter 10

The Search Engines

Which search engines should we teach, and why? What unique instructional points can we make about each one? What particular instructional difficulties do they present? After a brief survey of the search engines various trainers cover, we will compare basic information about some of the major and minor search engines, including key instructional points to teach and some of the engines' specific advantages and disadvantages that may interest your students.

As I have noted several times, search engines change. While many of the teaching issues, audience characteristics, unique instructional problems, session types, technical approaches, and search concepts remain somewhat static, search engines develop new features, fail in different ways, merge, die, find new names, and acquire each other. Much of the content in this section will change from year to year, while other parts will remain constant for several years.

The Starting Point

First you must decide which search engines to teach. For the past few years, Google has predominated as the most popular and frequently used search engine. All the trainers surveyed cover Google to some degree, yet none of them focus on it exclusively. Instead, they were unanimous in teaching more than one search tool. Beyond the big three search engines—Google, Yahoo!, and MSN Search—what else do they teach? Ran Hock says that he will "usually divide search tools into general Web directories, resource guides (metasites), and search engines, spending successively more time on each category. I often cover Yahoo! first because people know it already and can use it to relate to other tools."

In addition to the primary search engines, Alice Fulbright teaches Dogpile, Librarians' Internet Index (LII), About.com (sometimes), and a "unified search tool index, like Proteus" (www.thrall.org/proteus.html). Paul Barron teaches Vivisimo, a metasearch engine with clustering, and the visual searching approach of KartOO, as well as Guidebeam. Phil Bradley covers metasearch engines ixquick, ez2Find, KartOO, and Ask.com, and the U.K. directory BUBL.

Jeff Humphrey adds Firstgov and Vivisimo to his mix. Sheila Webber also focuses on Vivisimo, as well as ixquick and LookSmart.

With so many choices, which do you teach first? With Google's popularity, it should be no surprise that many start with Google, but the rationale varies.

Alice Fulbright teaches Google first "because I think it is fantastic for returning relevant results, and the students are usually already somewhat familiar with its basic functions, as we have it on all the toolbars for our public workstations and also on our library home page." In addition, Alice spends "the most time covering Google, because it has so many useful features that I want to share with the students."

Phil Bradley also starts with Google. He finds that since attendees are familiar with it, they "are keen to learn more. Once they've got some new material and usage from Google, they're generally keen to broaden ... their understanding."

In a similar vein, Danny Sullivan starts out with Google "because it remains probably the best general tool out there, with lots of interesting, helpful features that aren't always evident to new users. Plus, when you've explained some features at Google, it's then easy to explain similar features at other tools."

Jeff Humphrey points out that he spends more time on Google than on any search engine and that "it seems to be the engine of choice, but most users don't understand its limitations."

Ran Hock takes a different approach. "For search engines, which [one] I introduce first depends upon the audience and the purpose of the course. As strange as it may seem, alphabetically often works well in providing immediate contrasts between capabilities and features. I usually cover metasearch sites last, if at all, and then mainly to point out the degree to which users should be aware of their weaknesses."

In this brief overview of the major search engines (and some minor ones), let's follow Ran's example and take an alphabetical approach.

Ask (www.ask.com)

Since 2001, when Ask (www.ask.com) bought Teoma (www.teoma.com), these search engines have shared the same underlying database, that is, until Teoma was retired in 2006. Ask is often included as one of the four major search engines, along with Google, Yahoo!, and MSN Search.

Ask has several unique features worth mentioning in an instruction session:

- It includes many search shortcuts and gives answers to many popular questions above the regular search results.

- The relevance-ranking algorithm is based on link patterns, with a focus on link communities. The algorithm is different enough from that of other search engines that the results are likely to have a different ranking order from those found at Google or Yahoo!. The rankings are better on some searches and worse on others, but either way, it provides a different view of Web results.

- The Narrow/Expand Your Search option provides useful suggestions on revising a search.

Unfortunately, Ask has far fewer advanced search features than the others. For example, there are fewer cached copies of pages and inconsistent support for the OR operator.

Exalead (www.exalead.com)

Exalead (www.exalead.com) is a newer search engine from France that is unknown to many Internet users. One instructional advantage of its relative obscurity is that it provides something new with which to impress an audience. In addition, it has some advanced features unavailable from other search engines.

Exalead has both unique search features and a unique display of search results that is well worth teaching:

- The display features thumbnail screenshots, suggestions for related search terms, directory categories, Web site location limits, and file-type limits.

- It has special limits for pages with audio or video files.

- It is the only search engine that supports truncation and proximity.

- The advanced search page allows more sophisticated options, such as a phonetic search and approximate spelling.

- Date sorting is available.

Unfortunately, some of these advanced features work most effectively with larger databases. Exalead's database size is somewhat smaller than those at Google, Yahoo!, and MSN Search. In addition, Exalead does not refresh its database quite as often as the main search engines.

Gigablast (www.gigablast.com)

Gigablast (www.gigablast.com) is another lesser-known search engine that has some interesting and unique features. Smaller than Google, Yahoo!, and MSN Search, it had just over 2 billion records as of mid-2005. In addition, it is basically run by one person.

Then why teach Gigablast? Remember, it was not that many years ago that Google covered only about 500 million URLs. Most important, though, Gigablast can be used to teach how search engines index the dates for Web pages. On its search results page, at the end of each record, Gigablast lists the date it last crawled that page and the reported last modification date of the page, if any is given. With both dates visible, it is much easier to explain how dated a search engine database can be. Gigablast deserves credit for being honest about these dates.

Gigablast offers other reasons to include it in a Web searching session:

- It includes both cached copies of pages and links to the Wayback Machine for older copies.

- It is the only search engine that indexes the content of many metatags. Most other search engines ignore everything but the meta description and meta keywords tag, if they even cover those. Anyone looking for pages with Dublin Core metatags may find this useful.

But Gigablast has a down side. Its database is not only smaller but also refreshed less often than Google's, MSN's, or Yahoo!'s.

Google (www.google.com)

Google (www.google.com) rose from relative obscurity in 1999 to become the most prominent search engine today. Many reasons have been given for its popularity, including the simple design of its main page and the success of its relevance ranking algorithms. It is essential in a Web search training session. Many people are now aware of Google, and it has become the point of reference for many people when they are searching the Web.

Google's prominence brings with it a set of instructional difficulties. Some will question the need for training in searching the Web when they have been able to find what they want so easily in the past with Google. Others will question the reason for learning any tool other than Google. Given Google's self-proclaimed mission to organize the world's information by making it universally accessible and useful, it is easy to see how some users get this impression.

Still, most users are unaware of many of Google's capabilities and features, and few truly understand the scope of the information and search resources it offers. When teaching Google, consider including the following aspects:

- The link to Google's cached archive of the page as it looked when Google crawled it

- The file types available—including Adobe Portable Document Format (PDF), PostScript, Microsoft Word, and others with high content value—along with the HTML version of the files that Google indexes

- Additional databases, including Google Scholar, Google Book Search, Google Groups, Google News, Google Directory (from the Open Directory Project), Images, Definitions, Phone Numbers, the Froogle shopping engine, Maps, Satellite Images, and Local Search

- Ad placement and naming

- The Advanced Search page

- The Preferences page

Even if Google retains the crown as the largest and most popular search engine, it has several faults to point out. It still lacks many advanced search features and has no truncation. Advertising is becoming increasingly heavy, and Google-run text ads are now appearing all over the Web. Spammers are ever more successful at getting inappropriately high rankings on some terms. Not only does Google lack full Boolean searching, but even the OR operator, which it does support, does not always work correctly. Google usually indexes only the first 110 KB of text on a Web page. Another shortcoming is an inability to accurately report the total number of search results it finds. (More inconsistencies are documented at searchengineshowdown.com/features/google/inconsistent.shtml.)

For many audiences, the major point a trainer should emphasize is that Google is neither comprehensive nor always the best starting point for searches. Other search engines and specialized information resources may give a quicker and more authoritative answer. On the other hand, instructors should admit that for many searches, Google performs quite well. An instructional focus on strategies, tools, and engines "beyond Google" is often effective at attracting an audience.

MSN Search (search.msn.com)

For years, MSN Search (search.msn.com) used databases from other search companies. With the launch of its own database in 2005, MSN Search became an important search engine to teach. In addition, it is the default search engine used by the Internet Explorer search button, and when a non-functioning URL is entered into the Internet Explorer address box, the resulting page usually links to MSN Search.

Despite its heavy use by the general public, few trainers or librarians seem to talk much about MSN Search. MSN Search should be taught because of its popularity and the likelihood that users will stumble across it via the Internet Explorer search button or as a result of entering a non-existent URL, in addition to the following reasons:

- The search builder does a better job than the other search engines do at showing how to translate advanced capabilities into command line searching. It provides free access to much of the content in the Microsoft Encarta encyclopedia.

- It uses Encarta and other sources to provide shortcut answers above the search results.

- It can do full Boolean searching.

On the down side, MSN Search can sometimes produce overly commercial search results and does not always find some of the obvious pages that should rank high. In addition, its estimated number of results is sometimes wildly inflated.

Windows Live (www.live.com)

Microsoft is experimenting with new branding for its search engine and several other products: Windows Live. The beta version live.com site provides access to the same database available at MSN Search (as of mid-2006), but it offers some unique search and display features along with some databases that are not available at MSN Search. Consider teaching it for the following reasons:

- Ability to scroll the first 250 results without clicking for another page

- Ability to add searches as an RSS feed to the live.com home page

- Search macros for creating specialized searches or limits to a hand-chosen group of sites

- Academic and product search databases

As with any search engine in beta form, there are several glitches and problems with Windows Live. It can be slower to load and respond than other search engines, and it may not work at all on older browsers. As of mid-2006, it has no advanced search form and does not provide access to Encarta like MSN Search does.

Yahoo! (search.yahoo.com)

Still one of the most popular sites on the Web, Yahoo! (search.yahoo.com) is a search engine, directory, and portal and has many popular subject sections with unique content, such as Yahoo! Finance. The Yahoo! Directory is available only from Yahoo!. Even though the directory's prominence has been diminished in search results and on the front page, it remains one of the most comprehensive general directories on the Web.

While Yahoo! formerly used Google search results, in early 2004 it launched its own search engine that has become a compelling alternative to Google. It is similar in size and scope and has become, along with MSN Search, one of Google's primary competitors. Even before that happened, the unique content and directory at Yahoo! made it worth teaching. The search engine is available directly at search.yahoo.com as well as on Yahoo!'s front page. The following features should be pointed out to students:

- Cached copies of pages

- Links to the directory content

- Ability to do full Boolean searching

Other features and sections of Yahoo! can also be included in a Web searching workshop:

- The ease of getting to the Yahoo! Directory (from the Directory tab or direct at dir.yahoo.com)

- Yahoo! News and Finance sections that have some unique content (sources not available elsewhere)

- Personalization available in My Yahoo! and in MyWeb

One difficulty in teaching Yahoo! over the years has been its constantly changing search defaults. Fortunately, it now consistently defaults to an AND search like the rest of the search engines do.

Directories

Many specialized subject directories are useful to include but will vary from session to session, depending on audience interests. The major large general commercial directories include the Yahoo! Directory (dir.yahoo.com) and the Open Directory Project (dmoz.org). Since it is freely available to any takers, the Open Directory Project is reproduced on many sites. The Google Directory is Google's implementation of the Open Directory, and it is one of the major versions to consider teaching when discussing the Open Directory.

For more directories with a stronger information focus and little or no commercial content, trainers cover the LII (lii.org) and the Resource Discovery Network (RDN; www.rdn.ac.uk). The LII is the product of collaboration among many U.S. librarians and focuses on resources that would serve a public library clientele. With around 17,000 records, the LII database is significantly smaller than even the smallest of search engines mentioned in this chapter; however, the records in LII are professionally chosen and reviewed resources classified by subject. The RDN has a more international focus and is composed of a collection of U.K.-run subject directories. The RDN aims at university-level interests. Although it too is quite small compared with the search engines, it has tens of thousands of records chosen specifically for a scholarly audience and classified by subject.

When you teach the LII, RDN, and similar directories, it is important to emphasize that with smaller databases, broad search terms are most effective. Instruct students not to use unusual terms, as they might to find very specific Web pages via large search engines, but to browse these directories to find Web sites and online resources.

Now that we have taken a look at specific search engines and directories, we will turn to a specific approach to hands-on classroom sessions that uses a framed Web page to keep the class together.

Chapter 11

Creating a Framed
Workshop Web Page

In a hands-on classroom, keeping the whole group together can be problematic. Some students may not be comfortable using the back button in the browser. Others will come across sites that put new pages into a pop-up window, which has no back button. Some will get interested in certain search results and browse away from the class Web page or the specific search engine being taught. An exercise as simple as running one search and then looking at a few results can frustrate some students when the time comes to get back to the search engine and continue with the next example.

After encountering these problems several times, I found a solution that works in most situations. By creating a course Web page that uses frames, shown in Figure 11.1, the trainer can keep a table of contents for the workshop visible on the screen at all times. Students can wander where they wish in the right-hand side, but when the class is ready to move to the next lesson, the students can just click on the appropriate table of contents link on the left to get to the same page as everyone else.

Two workshop pages that use framing are available online: the Basic Internet Searching tutorial (www.searchengineshowdown. com/strat/basicsearch.html) and the Advanced Internet Searching tutorial (www.searchengineshowdown.com/strat/advancedsearch. shtml). Both are designed for use during a hands-on workshop rather than as stand-alone online tutorials.

While the page in Figure 11.1 does not show an obvious use of frame sets, it is made up of two frames. The left frame holds the

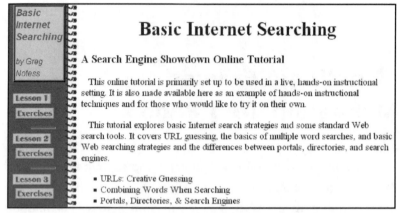

Figure 11.1 Basic Internet Searching workshop home page in frames

table of contents. Clicking on the icon for Lesson 1 changes the content on the right side by bringing up the information for the first lesson. After students have read that information, clicking the Exercises icon brings up the exercises in the right frame.

Figure 11.2 shows the exercises for Lesson 1. In the figure, the frames are highlighted with a border and numbered for reference. Frame 1 is the table of contents, listed in the code (discussed later in this chapter) as the named target frame of "contents" (the right-side frame is "rmain" for "right main"). The right main frame actually uses another framed page, by the name of exer1.html, which has a top frame (labeled 2 in the figure) for questions and a bottom frame (labeled 3 in the figure) for answers.

Once the class has finished those exercises, everyone can click on "Lesson 2" in the contents frame to get to the next lesson.

Advantages and Disadvantages of Frames

This framing approach works quite well for keeping the class together. During time set aside for doing class exercises, some

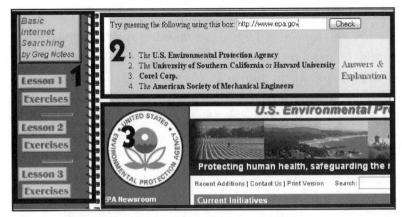

Figure 11.2   Exercise for Lesson 1 with each frame labeled

students will finish quicker than others. Often these students start browsing on the Web, and while doing so, some make mistakes and get lost. The table of contents frame displayed on the left side serves as an easy tool for either moving on to the next lesson or, for those who wander and get lost, finding their way back and starting the exercises again.

The contents frame has an additional advantage. It provides a constant visual reminder of the organization of the session. When descriptive labels are used instead of "Lesson 1," "Lesson 2," and so on, it can offer an outline of the course content as well.

Another advantage of the framing approach is that once the initial lesson has been set up and all the necessary pages are in place, it is much easier to create a second lesson. Just copy all the files to a new directory and change the content portions.

While using a framed page in hands-on workshops helps students' navigation greatly and keeps the group together, it is far from foolproof. Some Web sites you may want students to view as part of an exercise are designed to break out of frames. A solution for frame breakers is provided at the end of this chapter.

Frames also require careful planning. They take more work to create than simple Web pages do. You need sufficient time to create, test, and troubleshoot the workshop pages, and that time is not always available. Also, frames are not intuitive to everyone. Some students have difficulty knowing which link to click on. That is why I chose graphic navigation links when I made the version shown in Figure 11.1. Even graphics do not always work, and students occasionally get confused about which lesson to choose. Although different colors, shapes, and labels for each link may not look polished, students identify them more easily.

Frames Code and Explanation

Here is a simplification of the HTML code used to create a framed page for a hands-on instructional session. This example, based on my Basic Internet Searching workshop (available online at www.searchengineshowdown.com/strat/basicsearch.html), uses a navigation frame on the left.

The HTML code that follows is numbered by line, but the numbers should not be included in the code. They are included simply for ease of reference in the comments that follow. The HTML code here is a simplified version, without the colors, fonts, and other style elements that are in the full code on the live page. This simplified version can be used as a basic starting point. To see all the style elements I use, look at the underlying code at the Basic Internet Searching tutorial (www.searchengineshowdown.com/strat/basicsearch.html) and the Advanced Internet Searching tutorial (www.searchengineshowdown.com/strat/advancedsearch.shtml)

Top Page with Frameset (index.html)

The first page is relatively brief and simply gives the links to the two framed pages—the table of contents frame on the left and the main frame on the right.

```
1.   <html><head><title>

2.   Basic Internet Searching Seminar

3.   </title></head>

4.   <frameset cols="141,*">

5.   <frame src="toc.html" name="contents"
     noresize>

6.   <frame src="top.html" name="rmain">

7.   <noframes><body>These pages are designed
     for classroom use and need support for
     frames and JavaScript.</body></noframes>

8.   </frameset></html>
```

Comments

Lines 1–3 contain the typical header tags and title.

Line 4 has the frameset element, which specifies the size of the left frame—in this case 141 pixels wide. The * means that the right frame does not have specified size and will fill up the remainder of the window.

Line 5 gives the file name, toc.html, for the table of contents file and names the frame as "contents." The term "noresize" keeps the students from accidentally dragging the frame border and obscuring the right frame.

Line 6 shows the file name, main.html, for the content file on the right and names that frame "rmain."

Line 7 is not necessary and is only displayed in a browser that does not display frames. This way users are told when they reach this site that the page will not work on their browsers.

Line 8 includes the various closing tags needed.

Left Frame Table of Contents (toc.html)

The next list of code is needed to create the table of contents frame on the left. I named this file in the Top Page as toc.html. This file lists (and links to) three lessons with exercises for each lesson.

```
1.   <html><head><title>Contents</title></head>

2.   <a href="index.html" target="_top">Basic
     Internet Searching</a><p>

3.   <a href="lesson1.html" target="rmain">Lesson
     1</a><br>

4.   <a href="exer1.html"
     target="rmain"> Exercises</a><p>

5.   <a href="lesson2.html"
     target="rmain">Lesson 2</a><br>

6.   <a href="exer2.html"
     target="rmain">Exercises</a><p>

7.   <a href="lesson3.html"
     target="rmain">Lesson 3</a><br>

8.   <a href="exer3.html"
     target="rmain">Exercises</a>

9.   </body></html>
```

Comments

Most of this can be standard HTML. For those not used to working with frames, the href links with the target elements are the important tags. Every link should specify where the new content will appear by using the target element. On this two-frame design with the table of contents on the left, clicking the links in the table of contents will change the content in the main frame. The target portion of the href tag determines where the link opens. So clicking a menu link on the left opens new content in the main frame on the right (rmain) and does not change the content of the left frame.

Line 1 contains the typical header tags and a title (which will not be visible since it is part of a frame set).

Line 2 gives the apparent title (the one a student will see at the top of the frame) and serves as a link back to the first page. The target="_top" means that the whole page is replaced rather than just one frame.

Lines 3, 5, and 7 link to the three lesson files, but the rmain target means that the change will take place in the right (or main) frame.

Lines 4, 6, and 8 link to the three exercise files, with rmain changing the right frame.

Line 9 includes the various closing tags needed.

Content Pages

Note that for three lessons, four content pages need to be created for the right frame: the introductory page plus one page for each of the three lessons. The first of these, top.html, displays when the framed site is first loaded and is a good location for the title, instructor information, and some introductory comments, bullet points, or a quotation.

Each of the three lesson pages can be a regular HTML page including whatever content is desired. Using the syntax from the table of contents frame, name them lesson1.html, lesson2.html, and lesson3.html. Make sure they are located in the same directory as the table of contents files (toc.html).

If each lesson simply contains explanatory text and examples, no special linking syntax is needed. The one obvious link that could be placed within each of the lesson files, at the end, is a link to the related exercises. This link can be a simple Next icon or just a text link. Since the link would bring up the exercises in the same frame (the right main or rmain frame), no target attribute of the href tag is needed. Omit the target attribute so that only the content in the right frame changes, leaving the table of contents always available on the left.

Exercise Pages Frame Set (exer1.html)

The pages for the exercises add another layer of frames. For each of the exercise pages, two more frames appear in the "rmain" frame. The questions are in a small top frame, and the bottom frame displays a search engine or specific Web page. In Figure 11.2, the top frame is labeled 2 and the bottom frame is labeled 3.

The file that produces this kind of exercise page is small and fairly simple. Here is the frameset exer1.html file, which simply gives the height of the top frame, the links to the two files, and the names for the frames. It specifies only parts 2 and 3 of Figure 11.2.

```
1. <html><frameset rows="140,*">
2. <frame src="topexer.html" name="topexer">
3. <frame src="blank.html" name="botexer">
4. </frameset></html>
```

Comments

Line 1 contains the typical frameset header tags and gives the height of the top frame in pixels; the * specifies that the bottom frame will fill the remainder of the window.

Line 2 designates the top frame target as "topexer" and tells the site to load the file named topexer.html.

Line 3 designates the bottom frame target as 'botexer' and instructs the site to load the file named blank.html (which is just an empty file). Loading this blank file allows the lower frame to look empty while it waits for the student to try one of the exercises in the top frame.

Line 4 includes the closing tags.

Exercise One Top Frame: JavaScript and a Form (topexer.html)

This particular frame is the most complex one used in these framed workshop pages. This is the section labeled 2 in Figure 11.2

and incorporates JavaScript and a form. It asks students to guess the URL for a series of organizations and supplies a box into which they enter their guess for each one. Clicking the Check button after each guess will retrieve in the lower window the Web site (or error message) that corresponds to the URL they enter.

```
1.  <html><head><title>Exercises for Lesson
    1</title>
```

```
2.  <script language="JavaScript"><!--
```

```
3.  function functionName()
    {parent.botexer.location.href =
    window.document.formName.textName.value;
    return false;}//-->
```

```
4.  </script></head><body>
```

```
5.  <form name="formName" onSubmit="return
    functionName()">
```

```
6.  Guess the following, using this box:
```

```
7.  <input type=text name="textName"
    value="http://" size=25 maxlength=100>
```

```
8.  <input type=submit value="Check"
    onClick="return functionName()">
```

```
9.  </form>
```

```
10. <ol type="1">
```

```
11. <li>The U.S. Environmental Protection
    Agency
```

```
12. <li>The University of Southern California
    or Harvard University
```

```
13. <li>Corel Corp.
```

```
14. <li>The American Society of Mechanical
    Engineers
```

```
15. </ol></body></html>
```

Comments

Line 1 shows the typical header tags and a title (which will not be visible).

Lines 2–4 contain the JavaScript used to make the form send a submitted URL to the lower frame. It is a fairly short script but confusing to most non-programmers. The important part is the pointer to the bottom frame, where it says "botexer" after "parent." Just change that name if you choose a different name for the bottom frame.

Lines 5–9 have the form elements for the box, button, JavaScript link, and text before the box. The onClick part calls up the JavaScript.

Lines 10–14 are a numbered list of the organizations whose URLs the students are to guess.

Line 15 contains the closing tags.

Other Exercise Pages

Once the basics just discussed are mastered, the rest of the site simply requires more of the same. The other lesson pages can contain simple explanatory text. The exercise pages for the second and third lessons can be based on the exer1.html double frame model. The questions can go in the top frame. The bottom can start as a blank frame (as in the first exercise) or it could contain the first search engine to be used in the exercise.

For example, if the first question uses Google, start with Google in the lower frame. The second question might use Yahoo!. Just place a link in the question to Yahoo! that uses a target of 'botexer' (the name given to the bottom exercise frame).

Solutions for Frame Breakers

One potential problem with the framing technique, mentioned earlier in this chapter, occurs with Web sites that break out of frames. A site can use a small snippet of JavaScript to keep other sites from putting it within a frame. Sites do this to prevent others from stealing their intellectual content and making it appear to be part of a completely different site. Fortunately, a couple of tricks can help you use Web sites that break out of frames.

To identify which search engines and sites may break out of frames, be sure to try them out in the full exercise. Both Yahoo! and AltaVista will break out of frames but not necessarily on their first screen. Sometimes they break out of the frames after doing one search or sometimes after several searches (in other words, the contents frame on the left and the exercises on the right, as in Figure 11.2, will disappear, and the search site will fill up the whole frame).

One approach is to put the frame breakers in a pop-up window rather than in a frame. Then be sure to teach the students, either by demonstration or by noting it in the exercises, to close the pop-up window when done with that exercise. To get a basic pop-up, simply add a target attribute using a Window name that is not already in use. Something like `<a href="http://www.loc.gov/" target="pop">Library of Congress</a>` will work.

Adapting that approach, you can use JavaScript to position a pop-up window directly over the frame where it should appear. The JavaScript can also remove all surrounding toolbars so that it looks more like a frame. With careful positioning (be sure to check on the actual computers to be used by the class), the window can appear directly above the frame it should have appeared in. That way, once the student is done with that part of the exercise, clicking on the contents or another exercise will bring the main window back to the forefront and the pop-up will then be hidden behind it. The intent of this approach is to keep the flow of the instruction unimpeded by the technology so the focus can remain on the instructional point.

Figure 11.3 shows what this looks like. The link coding is more complex than for a standard link. Instead of a plain `<a href= "">` link, the JavaScript tidbit is inserted as follows:

Figure 11.3 Pop-up window positioned with JavaScript

```
<a onclick="window.open('http://dir.yahoo.
com',','width=628,height=371,top=172,left=
200')"href="#">Yahoo!</a>
```

Here, the pop-up is for the Yahoo! directory, in a window that is 628 pixels wide by 371 pixels tall and positioned 172 pixels from the top of the screen and 200 pixels from the left margin. Since no toolbars, menu bars, location bars, or status bars are specified in the JavaScript, they are not displayed, leaving a cleaner looking window that looks almost like a frame.

This frame set approach takes careful planning, and it will take some time to create all the necessary Web pages. For anyone with a bit of Web site design background, it should not take too much effort. By reading the explanations in this chapter and copying the code from my pages, even a novice should not find it too difficult. Just adapt the content to your local situation and the topics you wish to teach.

Chapter 12

Presentation Tips, Tricks, and Shortcuts

When you are conducting an instructional session, whether a lecture-demonstration or a hands-on session, technology can get in the way of instruction. Computers, projectors, or the Internet can crash. Programs can fail to work correctly. Anytime a teacher uses a computer to demonstrate something or to just run a PowerPoint presentation, technological problems may occur.

Ever been to a conference presentation at which the presenter spends the first few minutes trying to get the computer to do what it should? Watching people try to go from the PowerPoint window to full presentation mode can be painful. Often presenters are trying to use equipment that is not their own and that may be set up quite differently from the equipment they are used to. Instead of a mouse, the computer may have a touch pad or track point, which can be difficult to master quickly if you are unfamiliar with it.

Whatever the cause of the problem, any delay due to equipment problems means less time for teaching and the risk of quickly losing the audience's interest and respect. So with that in mind, here is a collection of presentation tips, tricks, and shortcuts that can minimize disruptions, help demonstrate examples more quickly, and be passed on to students to help expedite their own searching process.

Keyboard Shortcuts

While the mouse is a useful pointing device, it is not always the quickest way to navigate on the Web or through a presentation.

Many standard browser functions can be performed on a keyboard as well. These keyboard shortcuts can be used when you are faced with an unfamiliar mouse and are especially useful if the mouse freezes or stops functioning inexplicably. (Most of these suggestions are designed for use on a Windows computer. Users of other operating systems often have similar capabilities with slightly different key strokes. For Macintosh users, most keyboard shortcuts are available using the Command [or Apple] key rather than the Control key.)

Keyboard shortcuts typically use a combination of keys. Whether you are combining two or three keys, all need to be pressed simultaneously. The easy way to do this is to hold down the first key, which is usually Control, Alt, or Shift, and then press the other key(s). Only a few shortcuts are single keys, such as the function keys like F1 or F3. Here is an example to help at conference presentations, especially when you are using an unfamiliar computer: PowerPoint can be set to automatically begin in show mode (in which the slides are full screen) just by a single keystroke. Once the PowerPoint presentation is open, just press the F5 key. Or if you are comfortable with the mouse or other pointing device, select the file, right click the mouse, and choose Show. That maneuver takes PowerPoint directly to show mode from a desktop shortcut or the file even more quickly.

A note about syntax: To designate keys that are to be pressed simultaneously, a hyphen is used to connect the two key designations. In addition, the letter keys are shown as uppercase letters because that is how they look on the keyboard, but you should press the shift key only if it is part of the combination. For example, Control-S means to hold down the Control key and press the s key.

General Windows Shortcuts

When I get a question after a presentation about something other than the content, it is usually about how I did something during the presentation, like copying and pasting a URL. Many standard Windows shortcuts are unknown to many users. Some are very useful in many programs beyond Web browsers. For example, Control-S saves a file (and should be used frequently while word processing). For printing, Control-P is handy in most programs that include a print option.

Selecting text, copying, and pasting are also useful in most programs, including Web browsing and searching. The standard Windows key combinations are well worth memorizing: Control-C copies marked text, Control-X cuts marked text, and Control-V pastes the copied or cut text. One less-familiar shortcut is Control-A, which selects an entire page of text and can also be used to improve readability of text on a Web page and expose unintentionally hidden words that use the same color font as the background color.

Browser Shortcut Keys

Whether you use Internet Explorer or some other browser, such as Mozilla, Firefox, or Netscape, there are many shortcut keys. Table 12.1 provides a fairly extensive list, but even more possibilities exist. For instruction, the browser's back and forward buttons make navigating between examples easy. Begin with a search engine, enter a search, present the results list, and click on a result. When a student has a question about a previous step, just click the back button. You may find it even faster, if you have your hands on the keyboard, to use the shortcuts: Just hold down the Alt key and press the left arrow to move back or the right arrow to move forward.

The stop button also has a keyboard shortcut: the escape key. If you come across a page with questionable images during a presentation, just press Esc to stop the remainder of the page from loading. If a page is stopped too soon or does not load properly, or if you wish to show how the frequently updated content has changed, use the Reload button or the keyboard shortcut Control-R. It is possible, however, depending on the browser's settings, that pressing Reload may just reload the same page from the cache. To force the browser to go back out to the remote server and reload the page from there, use Control-F5 for Internet Explorer or the three-key combination of Shift-Control-R for Mozilla, Firefox, or Netscape.

Table 12.1   Browser Keyboard Shortcuts (in alphabetical order)

Command	Internet Explorer 6	Mozilla /Netscape 7	Firefox
Add Page to Favorites/Bookmarks	Control-D	Control-D	Control-D
Check/Uncheck Checkbox (toggle)	Space	Space	Space
Close Window or Tab	Control-W	Control-W	Control-W
Copy	Control-C	Control-C	Control-C
Cut	Control-X	Control-X	Control-X
Display Shortcut Menu for Link or Page	Shift F10 or Right Click	Shift F10 or Right Click	Shift F10 or Right Click
Edit Page		Control-E	
Exit	Alt F4	Control-Q	Control-Q
Find Again		Control-G or F3	Control-G or F3
Find in Page	Control-F	Control-F	Control-F
Force Reload (not from cache)	Control-F5	Control-Shift R	Control-Shift R
Go Back to Previous Page	Alt-Left Arrow or Backspace	Alt-Left Arrow or Backspace	Alt-Left Arrow or Backspace
Go Down One Screen on Page	Page Down or Space	Page Down or Space	Page Down or Space
Go Forward One Page	Alt-Right Arrow Key	Alt-Right Arrow Key	Alt-Right Arrow Key
Go Full Screen (toggle)	F11	F11	F11
Go Home	Alt-Home	Alt-Home	Alt-Home
Go to Bottom of Page	End	End	End
Go to Top of Page	Home	Home	Home
Go to URL/Address Box	Alt-D	Alt-D	Alt-D
Go Up One Screen on Page	Page Up	Page Up	Page Up
Manage Favorites/Bookmarks	Control-B	Control-B	Control-B or Control-I

Command	Internet Explorer 6	Mozilla /Netscape 7	Firefox
Move to End of Line (in a text editing field)	End	End	End
Move to Next Item in Form	Tab	Tab	Tab
Move to Next Link in Web Page	Tab	Tab	Tab
Move to Previous Item in Form	Shift Tab	Shift Tab	Shift Tab
Move to Previous Link in a Web Page	Shift Tab	Shift Tab	Shift Tab
No Zoom (back to normal/100%)		Control-0	Control-0
Open a Drop-Down Menu	Alt-Down Arrow	Alt-Down Arrow	Alt-Down Arrow
Open Favorites	Control-I		
Open File		Control-O	Control-O
Open File or URL	Control-O or Control-L		
Open Help	F1	F1	F1
Open History	Control-H	Control-H	Control-H
Open Main Menu	Alt or F10	Alt or F10	Alt or F10
Open New Tab Within Same Window		Control-T	Control-T
Open New Window	Control-N	Control-N	Control-N
Open Search in Explorer Bar	Control-E		
Open Selected Link in a Web Page	Enter	Enter	Enter
Paste	Control-V	Control-V	Control-V
Press Selected Button / Select Radio Button	Space	Space	Space
Print Page	Control-P	Control-P	Control-P
Redo	Control-Shift-Z	Control-Shift-Z	Control-Shift-Z
Reload	Control-R or F5	Control-R or F5	Control-R or F5
Save Page	Control-S	Control-S	Control-S
Select All	Control-A	Control-A	Control-A
Stop	Esc	Esc	Esc
Submit Form	Enter	Enter	Enter
Undo	Control-Z	Control-Z	Control-Z
View Page Information		Control-I	
View Page Source	Right Click V	Control-U	Control-U
Zoom Text Larger	Control Scroll Wheel	Control = (or Control keypad plus sign)	Control = (or Control keypad plus sign)
Zoom Text Smaller	Control Scroll Wheel	Control - (minus sign)	Control - (minus sign)

For navigation within a page, using the mouse to move the scroll bars is only one way of moving around. The arrows, Page Down, and Page Up keys can make quick work of intrapage navigation. If these do not seem to work, be sure to either click somewhere on the page or use the Tab key to move onto the page from the toolbars. To show where search terms actually appear on a page, the find-within-a-page function is a great way to demonstrate a term's location. Press Control-F, enter the word, and press the enter key. In Mozilla, Firefox, or Netscape, use Control-G to find the same term further down the page.

If Control-F fails to find the search term, it may still be available somewhere in the HTML code (in Mozilla, Firefox, and Netscape only). For example, sometimes I come across pages that have the search term in a dropdown list. Control-F does not find those. Instead, I use the keyboard shortcut of Control-U to display the underlying HTML source code. Then I use Control-G to find my term since I have entered it previously. In Internet Explorer, right click the mouse, press V to view the source file, and then try a find function.

Another very useful function when presenting is the ability to increase the font size on Web pages so that the audience can actually see the words on the screen. Mozilla makes this easy with Control = (or Control keypad plus sign) to increase and Control - to decrease the font size. Sometimes Internet Explorer can change the font size, but it has only five size settings and they won't work on all pages because some pages have a hard-coded font size within the HTML. To quickly change the font in Internet Explorer when it is possible to do so, press Control and scroll the wheel on the mouse. If no scroll wheel is available, use Alt-V, then X, and then the arrow keys to choose one of the five settings.

Shortcuts for Filling Out Forms

Multipart forms (for example, advanced search screens in search engines) can become quite tedious to fill out if you have to click on each box before entering data. Fortunately, there are easy keyboard shortcuts to use when filling out a form. The Tab key is the easiest and most essential. To move from one data entry box on a form to the next, simply press the Tab key. Tab again to get to the next. Shift-Tab moves the cursor back to the previous box.

What about forms with check boxes and radio buttons? These can be managed as well. Continue to use the Tab key to move to the buttons or select boxes. Then use the space bar to select or des-elect specific options. Tab into dropdown boxes and use the arrow keys to select an item. Once you are in a dropdown box, you can also move to a particular item on the dropdown list by simply pressing the first letter of the item For example, if the dropdown box is a list of all the states in the U.S. and you want to select Montana, then press M and use the down arrow to get to Montana (or press N and then the up arrow since Montana is alphabetically the last of the M states).

Once you have finished filling out the form, use the Tab button to submit it. The submit button can be reached with the Tab key and then "clicked" by pressing the space bar unless it is a graphic, which may require a mouse click. The Tab key also moves from hyperlink to hyperlink on a Web page and even to the address box, as mentioned earlier. Thus, the Tab key can be used for filling out forms as well as navigating within a Web page. After using the Tab key to move to a specific link, pressing the Enter key will work the same as clicking on the link and will open the new page.

Other Shortcuts

Knowing some of these keystroke shortcuts can be invaluable in an online presentation when the technology starts to fail. If the mouse pointer disappears on the projection unit, locks up, or responds extremely slowly, using the keyboard may be the only option. When you are assisting a user, teaching a hands-on class, or giving an online presentation, many of these tricks can be invaluable in getting quickly to the appropriate screen.

If the mouse fails, an important shortcut is the Alt key. Press that to open the Main Menu bar, which in most Windows programs and browsers is a dropdown menu bar at the top of the window. Usually, pressing Alt will select the File heading. Then press either the down arrow or Enter to choose one of the dropdown options under that menu. If you need a menu other than File, use Alt combined with the underlined letter of the menu you want (Alt-V for the View menu, for example).

Quick Links and the Personal Toolbar

Bookmarks (or Favorites as Internet Explorer calls them) can be used to show examples during a session quickly. The keyboard shortcut Control-B brings up the Organize Favorites (or Manage Bookmarks) window. Use the Links bar (the Personal Toolbar in Mozilla, Firefox, or Netscape) to provide quick access to examples and sites to be used in the presentation.

Figure 12.1 shows Firefox's personal toolbar, bordered in black to emphasize its location. To make sure your personal toolbar is displayed, look under View/Toolbars/Bookmarks Toolbar in Firefox (View/Toolbars/Links in Internet Explorer or View/Show-Hide/Personal Toolbar in Mozilla). Once the personal toolbar is displayed, just drag links or URLs to the toolbar to add a bookmark for that page. To change the name, just right click and select Properties to change the bookmark name to something meaningful.

For Firefox, Mozilla, and Netscape users, the ability to display multiple tabs within the same window is very handy for browsing. It is even more useful for instruction and online demonstrations and presentations. The tabs are all quickly available within one window. In addition, a single bookmark can open a whole set of tabs at once.

Figure 12.1   Firefox personal toolbar and multiple tabs

In Figure12.1, the folder bookmark labeled Demo includes multiple bookmarks set up in advance for a specific class. Clicking this folder lists the bookmarks and gives the option at the bottom to Open in Tabs. In this example, one tab will open my Search Engine Showdown site, the next opens Ask, and the third gives search results from MSN Search for a specific term. By using this technique, I can quickly open all the Web pages that I want to use for the next portion of a class.

To create a bookmark for a set of tabs in Firefox, just add all the desired pages to a specific bookmark folder. I find it works best to have from 3 to 10 pages per folder. If I plan on using more than 10 pages, I create a folder for each segment of the class. To get directly to search engine results for a specific search, just run that search and then bookmark the results page.

Bookmarklets

While bookmarks and favorites in the links bar or personal toolbar can be very useful to presenters, bookmarklets provide yet another level of capabilities. Bookmarklets are a special, interactive kind of a bookmark. A standard bookmark consists of two parts: a URL and a bookmark name. A bookmarklet (sometimes called favelet) uses JavaScript instead of a URL. Thus a bookmarklet is a mini-program that can do a variety of actions instead of just linking to another page. For example, a bookmarklet can remove all images on a page, extract the URLs on a page, or send selected text directly to a search engine.

What use are bookmarklets in teaching Web searching? Frequent searchers can use bookmarklets to very quickly search more than one search engine. Second, bookmarklets can aid in presentations by removing extraneous and distracting content on pages, improving readability, and quickly showing certain search differences.

Bookmarklets work in most browsers. The good news is that even though they are written in JavaScript, you don't need programming skills to use them. With many collections of bookmarklets available on the Web, just choose one, drag, and click. Choose a useful bookmarklet from a collection like Jesse Ruderman's Bookmarklets (www.squarefree.com/bookmarklets), then drag it to the personal toolbar or drop. When you are ready to try it, click on the bookmarklet or select some text and then click.

Zapping Images, Animations, and More

Some Web sites could be very useful from an information perspective, but their graphics, ads, or colors make them too distracting to use when teaching. A zapping bookmarklet may be just the thing. At the Jesse Ruderman's Bookmarklets site, you will find many different kinds under the Zap category. For example, one will replace all images on the page with their alternate text, which is useful for showing the page more as a search engine spider might see it. Another will remove all plug-ins such as Flash, background music, and third-party iframes (which usually have graphic ads). The Zap Colors bookmarklet converts a page to black text on white, which greatly helps the readability of pages that have a distracting background image.

Not sure which one to use? Try the plain Zap (Firefox, Mozilla, or Netscape only), which gets rid of most plug-ins, colors, cheap effects, event handlers, and timers. (Note that zapping book-marklets work on only one page at a time.)

Bookmarklets for Web Searching

Another way to use a bookmarklet is to highlight some text on a Web page and then click the bookmarklet to search for that text at a specific search engine. Google calls its search bookmarklet Google Browser Buttons. Available at www.google.com/options/ buttons.html, the Google search bookmarklet will directly search highlighted text at Google.

More bookmarklets are available from third-party lists. Bookmarklets.com has a Search Bookmarklets section at book marklets.com/tools/search/srchbook.phtml that includes many other search engines and directories and subject-specific search tools. Bookmarklets.com even offers a Make Search Bookmarklet Tool at bookmarklets.com/mk.phtml. This tool, a bookmarklet itself, lets you create your own bookmarklet for many search engines. I also have a list of helpful bookmarklets at searchengine showdown.com/bmlets.

As useful as these search bookmarklets can be for searchers, and as interesting as they might be to demonstrate in a workshop, they are less useful for instructors. I would rather show the search engine itself in a workshop than show a shortcut to it. Far more useful for Web search instructors are the transfer search engine bookmarklets. After you have run a search at one search engine, these bookmarklets will run the same search at another search engine. Jesse Ruderman's Bookmarklets has some of these in its Search Engine Optimization Bookmarklets category (their names start with the @ symbol). Using these, you need only one click to hop from search results at Google to search results at Yahoo! and only another click to hop to MSN Search results. These book-marklets are one of the easiest ways I know to compare search results from one search engine to another.

More bookmarklets of interest may be found in the Search Engine Optimization Bookmarklets category. While some of them are of interest only to the search engine optimization community, many are useful for searchers and Web searching trainers. One numbers Google's search results. Another lists all words on a page and the frequency of each, which can be used to show how a search engine indexes words on a page. My list at searchengine showdown.com/bmlets includes the ones I find most useful.

The Pop-Up Presence

Advertising pays for many Web sites and is the primary support for Web search engines. Yet advertising has changed over the years. In the late 1990s, banner ads were the primary type, but then they lost popularity and were replaced by other types. In the early 2000s, pop-up and pop-under advertisements appeared all over the Web, along with the text ads favored by search engines. While pop-up and pop-under ads appear to be declining, they continue to rank high on the list of online annoyances. For any teacher using a live Web connection to show examples, pop-ups, pop-unders, and other media-rich ads can be very distracting for the teacher and the students.

Many strategies can remove most of these annoying, in-your-face ads. The most basic approach is to keep all the example searches and sites as academic as possible and stay away from sites that use lots of pop-ups. Modern browsers have built-in options that block pop-ups. Internet Explorer on Windows XP and Mozilla, Firefox, and Netscape can turn them off via a preference setting. For Internet Explorer users with older operating systems, many programs are available that eliminate pop-ups. For searchers, the easiest solution may be to download and install one of the search engine toolbars that includes pop-up suppression.

Toolbars from Google, Yahoo!, Dogpile, and others all have this capability.

Suppressing pop-ups and pop-unders prevents them from being a distraction during the session. It can certainly make life easier for the presenter, but a couple of precautions are in order. First, there is a risk that in suppressing pop-ups, information content may be lost. Some sites use JavaScript pop-ups to provide information content such as definitions. Tutorials often use pop-ups for informational purposes. However, these types of pop-up windows are typically "requested pop-ups," in which the user actually clicks on something to get the pop-up window. Most pop-up blockers do not block these types. Some commercial databases use pop-ups to provide information or links to other resources. All of these types of informational pop-ups may be blocked by toolbars or internal settings.

Second, by not blocking pop-ups, you are replicating what the students see and use rather than showing the expert-Internet-user view of the Web. Most users do see pop-ups and have to go through all the steps that a shortcut avoids.

Third, the toolbar approach requires that a search engine toolbar be visible to the students. While instructors may choose to promote one or more toolbars, using more than one search tool at a time tends to go against common instructional strategy. One option is for the instructor to have the toolbar loaded but to drag it toward the right side of the screen to make it less visible or to uncheck it from the View menu so it does not display. Instructors should also be sure to check the toolbar or other pop-up suppression settings. Some will ding every time one is suppressed, and if you thought the pop-ups were distracting, wait until the computer starts making those sounds. Fortunately, the noise can usually be turned off (or you can just turn down the speakers).

Despite all the concerns, some prefer to teach in a setting free of pop-ups. For users of Mozilla and Firefox, the Adblock plug-in (adblock.mozdev.org) can also block media-rich ads such as Flash animations or all graphics from a particular ad company. It can remove additional advertising from an instructional demonstration.

The Shortcut Advantage

From all of these tips, tricks, and shortcuts, each instructor may choose just a few. These keyboard shortcuts, bookmarks, bookmarklets, and pop-up suppressors offer a teacher many options for making a presentation smoother and less prone to distractions due to technology or advertising. In most of my teaching, I primarily use Firefox for its many keyboard shortcuts, the ability to increase the font size easily, the tabbed browsing, and the many pop-up and ad-blocking options. However, I also use Internet Explorer in most demonstrations to show its browser-specific search features.

Whichever browser and whatever shortcuts you choose to use, avoid wasting time waiting for a site to load or fixing some problem with the computer. Find the shortcuts that work best for you or that you are most likely to use. A toolkit of tips, tricks, and shortcuts makes for better presentations. Showing tricks your students may never have seen before also increases your reputation.

Chapter 13

Tales from the Trenches: Anecdotes, Examples, and Exercises

Including stories or examples in a training session is a great way to reinforce an instructional point. Jeff Humphrey has "held onto some … early Internet success stories and still uses some for practice exercises. It helps to show real examples of hunting down obscure information." Tales of successfully using a certain technique, search engine feature, strategy, or source help students understand why they should learn to do the same.

Most of us prefer not to get stuck using the same one or two stories over and over again. Even if our audience does not get tired of them, we will. Ran Hock tries to keep his spontaneous. "Most anecdotes are on the spur of the moment. Especially since I often have repeat attendees, I don't like telling the same story too often."

Analogies, Sayings, and Terminology Tales

Finding an apt analogy can help the attendees learn a point more quickly than just listening to an explanation. One of the more common analogies, especially among librarians, uses books to explain the difference between a search engine and a directory: The directory is more like a book's table of contents, giving a hierarchical, organized view of the content, while the search engine is more like the book's index, except it includes every word on every page. One trainer describes the Yahoo! Directory as a "tour guide," since it can be used to find key Web sites and starting points for further exploration. Another compares the Yahoo! Directory to a "man-made lake" and Google to the "deep end of the ocean." Gary Price says, "For older users, ... a card catalog has been a good analogy [for a directory]. I also mention that in many cases directories are built by hand. Mentioning that LookSmart and Yahoo! now charge commercial interests for inclusion is also worthwhile and might help illustrate the need and strengths of the LII and others."

To underline the importance of flexibility within searching, Gary advocates "the need to pivot." To stress choosing appropriate tools, he notes that "you don't start searching for a telephone number with an encyclopedia."

Paul Barron digs into the research literature to describe the content structure of the Web. He uses the "Bow Tie" theory to illustrate the way pages interconnect. Illustrated nicely at www.almaden. ibm.com/almaden/webmap_press.html, this theory comes from Andrei Broder's (2000) research on the structure of the Web.

To clarify the very fuzzy term *portal*, one teacher compares it to walking into a library, since you have so many information services to choose from once you come in. Similarly, a *portal* can be compared to walking into a shopping mall. Certainly shopping malls have information pathfinders and lots of product information (of varying quality, depending on the sales personnel), but its main goal is to provide a meeting place for shoppers and merchants. Many of the big portals on the Web serve the same function.

I often use "picture of the past" to explain the way search engine databases are built because I want to emphasize that the search engine searches a database of what the Web used to look like rather than searching Web pages of the present.

Joe Barker likes to advise students to "search with peripheral vision" to get them to learn from their searches and think more broadly about their information needs. He also compares metasearch engines to "expecting everything to be always at the same mall."

Ran Hock uses several phrases to highlight the importance of exploring all the options of a search tool. Many users never even look at advanced search forms, preferences, or help files. To encourage them to change that behavior, Ran tells students to look in all the "nooks and crannies" of a search engine and "click everywhere." See *The Extreme Searcher's Internet Handbook* (Hock 2004) for more detail.

Alice Fulbright uses the concept of "discriminating phrases" to help students find relevant search terms for their topic. "To teach students how to find the 'discriminating phrase' for something, I encourage them to do a search with *all* the words they can think of to describe what they are seeking. For example, for articles about parents who have their young children sleep with them, I do a Google search using all these words: mother father child sleep together in same bed. ... It will return articles about the 'family bed' and 'co-sleeping.' This demonstrates how to discover a phrase that describes a phenomenon."

Beware of confusing terminology. Jeff Humphrey advises to "avoid using popular names for Web sites when relaying the location of Web pages. I have been asked while working the reference desk if I was Edgar or Thomas because 'the librarian said Edgar [meaning the EDGAR database] has that information' or 'the other librarian said Thomas will have that.'"

To illustrate for librarians the difference between a directory and a search engine index, Jeff says, "a directory is like your reference collection, where you usually find a limited amount of information or a starting point, while an index is like the rest of your library collection, where you have plenty of items to choose from, but you'll need to open them up to see which one will work best."

Boolean Examples

When teaching traditional Boolean searching, Alice Fulbright offers the following example, which covers both Boolean searching and truncation:

> To teach nesting and truncation, I often use this example:
> (youth* OR adolescent* OR teen*) AND (media OR television) AND violen*
> I stress that the OR operator is most commonly used to name synonyms.

This Boolean syntax is commonly supported in traditional bibliographic databases, but among Web search engines, only Exalead will handle the search query properly. Using an example like this can help students understand the different approaches of Web searching and other database search systems.

But Alice also cautions that "because of the templates in the advanced search modes, I spend much less time teaching students how to write Boolean statements using nesting techniques."

Jeff Humphrey uses a different example when he illustrates Boolean searching: "two actors who ... worked in multiple movies together and separately. Usually it's Dean Martin and Jerry Lewis. Much better than the usual 'cats and dogs' example."

Exercises

For any training session with sufficient time, especially a hands-on session, exercises are an excellent way to reinforce instructional points through practice. Sheila Webber suggests the following strategies for helping students maximize the effectiveness of exercises:

- Working individually, in groups, and in pairs (as all have different benefits in terms of learning)

- Getting students to give feedback on how they planned and did the search, not just on what they found

- Encouraging students to listen to and critique other people's approaches to a search

- Giving quizzes

- Voting for your favorite search engine

- Evaluating and comparing sources and engines

One of Jeff Humphrey's favorite exercises is to have the students look up who said "Winning isn't everything" and to get the full quotation. This is an effective exercise since there are many conflicting answers on a variety of Web pages (most credit Vince Lombardi).

Rita Vine likes to customize examples and will "sometimes use the question of finding salaries for [her students'] professions as a way to explore search engine retrieval versus resource discovery in sources like LII." She also uses phone number and reverse phone number directory lookups, with the students' using their own phone numbers. As for teaching templates for searchable databases, Rita says, "Most people don't know that you don't have to fill out all the boxes in a search template in order to search successfully. For example, on the www.hockeydb. com Web site, there is a template to search for hockey team statistics [see Figure 13.1, from hockeydb.com/ihdb/stats/teams. html]. So we have them look for a local team, say the Toronto Maple Leafs, but we show them that they can fill in the *minimum* information and still find it. And every extra box filled in is a potential error" that could cause valuable information to be missed. In this example, entering simply *maple* into the team

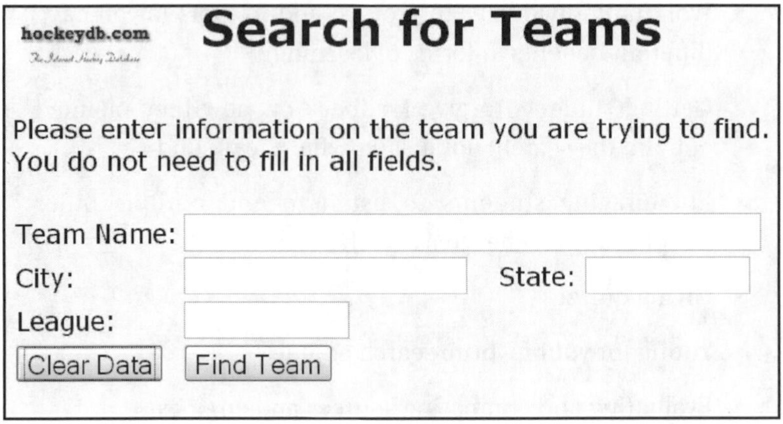

Figure 13.1 Hockey Database search screen

name box works very well, and entering *toronto* in the city box will work also.

Rita also has an effective exercise for identifying databases on the invisible Web. "We begin by introducing the textbook invisible Web database—PubMed (pubmed.gov). It's such a great example—everyone cares about health information, and PubMed has so much important research linked from it, but only through its searchable database." Rita then continues by having the class look at three other databases and "try to decide if search engines can theoretically grab all the content. The first one is completely browseable (so not at all invisible), the second is completely searchable (hence all invisible), and the third is a hybrid—some parts visible, some parts invisible. This exercise really helps people figure out the notion of the invisible Web from the inside out."

Sheila Webber gives two examples she uses to teach Web searching. First "students perform a search for the same topic on different search engines; for example, student 1 uses Google, student 2 uses AltaVista. The students then get together and compare their results and what they searched on, see how many hits the searches have in common, and decide which search engine [or] strategy was best." Her second example, from the health field, comes about 4 weeks into her Information Literacy class:

> [Students] get a lecture about the needs of health care professionals and of patients, which refers to a few key sources (like PubMed). They sign up for groups (of four or five students) and are given this briefing: A friend's child is of the age [when children are] expected to get the combined [Measles Mumps Rubella] vaccine; should [the friend] use this vaccine or not? Each group must produce a presentation which shows how [the group] carried out the search, identifies good sources, and summarizes the group's advice, and ... each group has to produce a handout that lists useful sources of information for [the] friend. The students are told that they must use at least one search engine and one specialist medical source. They work on the search in lab sessions (2-hour) in weeks 4 and 5, also getting a couple of short demonstrations and handouts about metasearch engines and PubMed ... from me. A teaching assistant and I circulate regularly to see how they are progressing, answer questions, [and] provide support. The students upload their presentations onto WebCT by the lab in week 6, when the groups give their presentations. Each group gets written feedback on [its] presentation. The following week, in the lecture, I draw out some general learning points.

While most of us never have the luxury of continuing an exercise over several weeks, some portions of this approach can be adapted for a daylong hands-on workshop. Sheila points out that while it is very helpful to have students report what they have done, provide feedback, and analyze what to do differently, it is also extremely time consuming and her exercise can provide valuable experience without them.

Joe Barker says, "As the last exercise of the day, I have everyone write down a question, and I randomly redistribute them and have everyone try to work on someone else's question. We then talk about what/how/why for each question answered successfully and brainstorm what to do for the ones that were stumpers. This synthesizes, makes real, and reviews the entire day's lessons. Then I collect all the questions [to add to] a huge treasure of questions to use in subsequent classes as I revise the materials."

Joe also offers advice on how to manage the hands-on portion of a seminar. "I provide lots of practice time with exercises in these classes, when the students work alone or in pairs while I walk around and see what they need to have reinforced from the materials just presented. We then go over all their experiences, and I give them 'answer sheets' with some searches I found effective for each question and for all the tools taught. The answers are the greatest part: People can use them to continue to learn after the class and to have models and detailed explanations of what works and what does not."

Paul Barron offers this example for combining the link field search with an evaluation exercise by doing a link search on the www.martinlutherking.org site:

> First have the attendees discuss what they would expect to find on the site. They usually say biography, speeches, historical writings, and images. Do a link check of the site. Usually the first return is the White Nationalist News Agency as well as K–12 schools and public libraries. This review leads into a discussion of what *is* www.martinlutherking.org. Open up the Web site, review the content, especially the text on the home page that says 'Download a flyer for your school.' Then have the attendees do a title search for 'martin luther

king' in AltaVista, AlltheWeb, and Google. Each search engine will return the site in the first 10 hits (research indicates and I can confirm that students usually look only at the first 10 returns). Review the site description and ask if students would likely select a site described by AlltheWeb and Google as portraying Dr. King as a 'corrupt communist.' Every teacher has always responded that students would look at that return. End the learning session with a WhoIs search for www. martinlutherking.org, which will indicate the site is maintained by Stormfront.org. Review the Stormfront Web site, noting the section 'Stormfront for Kids.'

This exercise dramatically illustrates the value of using an advanced syntax operator, in this case the field search, which looks for other pages that link to the given URL.

Need to come up with some new ideas for exercises? Phil Bradley says, "I try to change examples all the time to keep fresh. I'll ask delegates what they'd like to find, or have had difficulty finding, and will use those ... to explain search techniques." This unplanned approach can lead to some surprisingly good examples to use in later sessions. I have used the same approach, and the results can become excellent examples of some of the points made earlier in the session.

Humor can always help as well. Jeff Humphrey does his "best to have fun with sessions. This rubs a few attendees the wrong way, but most seem to appreciate a casual approach. You don't need to do 3 hours of stand-up to make the session fun. My practice exercises have a definite pop culture flavor to them, like who invented the plastic pink flamingo or what is the fax number for the British Lawnmower Museum? Some of the sites we visit have a sound effect, like the call of the bull moose, which gets a giggle from most attendees. I also try to make sessions as interactive as possible, not just trainer to student but attendee to attendee. ... Hearing how others in a similar situation approach using the Internet is often more helpful than me lecturing."

Unexpected Answers

Sometimes an exercise or other interaction with students may result in a completely unexpected response. Even a carefully planned exercise may suddenly end up going in a completely different direction when an unexpected answer comes up.

Many years ago I was teaching students about Usenet groups and the ability to search these discussion forums. I had been having good interactions with the class, and one student in particular had been very responsive to my questions, offering her own experiences to the rest of the group, until I got to the part about searching Usenet postings by name. I asked if anyone would like me to search their name to show a profile of their postings. This previously vocal attendee gave a very definite no and suddenly stopped participating. I used a random Usenet poster as the example instead of asking for a volunteer. One outcome of this unexpected turn of events was a lesson in the lack of privacy if you post to Internet discussion forums. A negative outcome was the sudden lack of participation from that certain attendee.

Paul Barron tells of a positive outcome from an unexpected answer:

> In one of my training sessions at the Virginia Military Institute, I asked the cadets to find the full text of Vannevar Bush's *Atlantic Monthly* article 'As We May Think.' The prize was a pizza and would be given to the cadet who had the least number of returns that contained the full text of the article. The goal was to have them construct a case-sensitive, sorted, title search,

which usually returns four results in AltaVista. Prior to building the search query, we brainstormed the process, and I asked one cadet how he would find the article. He replied, 'I wouldn't look for it!' When asked how he would find it, he said, 'I would ask a librarian.' He was awarded an honorary pizza for his incredible intelligence. I also reminded the cadets that the librarians in Preston Library 'are paid to help you! Use them.'

Then there are surprising or unexpected results to various searches. As Phil Bradley comments, you "can't believe what you see on the Net." He runs a search at Google on "cancer can now be cured," which places a site from Hulda Clark in the top position—a site that provides all kinds of dubious claims about healing cancer. Phil also mentions a "poor guy [who] did a search for 'legal 500' (without quotation marks) and got a porn site as his No. 1 hit." The *Legal 500* is an online guide to the U.K. legal profession, but the top hit was from a site with "one of the barely legal images you can find if you dial 0 500 etc."

In a hands-on session, I once had students guess the address for the United States Geological Survey's Web site. A retired professor and his wife were in the back of the room and suddenly started laughing. They said that instead of guessing www.usgs.gov they made the common mistake of guessing www.usgs.com, which brought up a single box on a page saying to "click here" to win a million dollars. Of course, the professor did not win a million dollars, and the link led to an adult Web site. Joe Barker reports a comparable event when "someone misheard me and typed in 'hotbox' instead of 'hotbot' and got the whole class blushing over the pornography on his screen."

Limitations of Search Engines

Rita Vine makes an important point about Web searching and the ways in which the search engine databases are constructed—

one she feels many searchers ignore: "the issue of Web page con-
struction design as an influencer of the keywords on the page.
Searchers never think that their keywords might be scattered on
different pages that together form a framed Web page, which is
rendered in a browser window. Search engine searches query
individual pages only, so many good but framed pages will go
unretrieved."

This is an important lesson for an instructor as well. The
"records" in a search engine's database are only for individual
pages, not for the whole of the information potentially available
from a specific Web site. Rita says another error "is trying to
include a geographic qualifier to their searches to limit their search
to materials in their country. (This is done all the time for
Canadian topics.) But many Web pages that might ... be relevant
contain no geographic keyword, and so are missed by the search
engine retrieval system. Again, it's a design question: The last thing
on the mind of most Web designers of non-commercial content is
how the page will be searched for in a search engine."

Rita has a great example that she uses to show this problem:

> One of my favorite examples to demonstrate the
> utter fallibility of search engines is the task of finding
> good summary information on Canadian legislation
> that restricts advertising of cigarettes. Learners try the
> question in a search engine and may use a variety of
> synonyms, truncation, and more—but they rarely find a
> good *summary*. Then they try the same search by
> browsing in an excellent Canadian directory called the
> Virtual Reference Library (www.virtualreference
> library.ca)—it's easy to browse to the smoking
> resources, where they discover only seven links. But the
> standout link is the one to the Canadian Council on
> Tobacco Control (www.cctc.ca), which has a fantastic

tobacco library *and* a full summary document of all the links to tobacco-control legislation in Canada [see Figure 13.2].

And when they find the page with the summary, they discover that it is in fact a framed Web page, and that the keywords they worked so hard to find in search engines don't all appear on any one page. *Plus* they [neglected] to think of the keywords that actually *do* appear on the page!

Canadian Law and Tobacco   home

CCTC-CCCT   ▸ Regions   ▸ Subjects   ▸ Analysis   ▸ Enforcement ▸ Français

Subjects
Promotion,
Packaging &   Blue link: Statute
Products ▸   Red link: Regulation

Restrictions on Promotion, Packaging, and Products

Promotion, Packaging
& Products
Manufacturers &
Distributors
Point of Sale
Smoking

Search This Site
 Search Law
 WebPages
Search
 Databases
▸ Tobacco Library
 Guildford
 Documents
CCTC WebSite
NCTH Website

		BC	AB	SK	MB	ON	QC	NB	NS
	Province								
	Ad restrict	TSABC S2.1		TCA S6.1	NSHPA S7.3.1.c-d		TAQ S24		
Promotion,	Lifestyle						TAQ S24.3		
Advertising,	Trade-marks						TAQ S27		TAA S9
and	Sponsor-ship	TSABC S2.1					TAQ S22		
Sponsorship	Mis-leading	TSABC S2.1					TAQ S24.2		
								TSANB	TAA

Figure 13.2   Canadian Law and Tobacco legislation page, within frames

Danny Sullivan, the most-quoted authority on search engines, gives examples of search engines' inability to answer all questions. "One woman wanted to see if there was a swimming pool in a town she was moving to. She did all types of queries and could see there was a swimming club, found the city hall, located a recreational center there, but couldn't tell from any of this whether there was a pool open to the public. This was all during a 'hands-on' part of a course I was doing. I talked with her and noted that for all of the places she did find, a phone number was listed. I had no doubt that if she called any of these places and asked if there was a swimming pool for the public, they'd know. However, as is all too common, she was fixated on finding that information via the Web because many people have become convinced that everything must be findable that way. Basic, common-sense information-seeking skills are being forgotten as a result."

Danny has a second example. "A woman I was teaching wanted to see if there was a particular type of conference being held in a subject area. We quickly found that a conference like the one she wanted had been held the year before, but we had no luck with various queries locating whether a new one was being offered. Ultimately, I said that while we could keep looking, there was a contact address for someone involved with the last conference. ... I was sure the person would probably respond in a day or so [to an e-mail] about ... similar upcoming conferences. It's another case where search engines take you part of the way, an important part of the way, but using some old-fashioned techniques ultimately get you the answer."

Failures

All of us occasionally run into problems during an instructional session. Equipment fails. The audience turns out to be completely different from what you expected. Students have a strong, adverse reaction to a carefully planned exercise that was designed to be clear. As Alice Fulbright notes about her audience, "The levels of ability and basic skills of the students in my classes are usually quite varied." That variation can lead to problems.

While most of us prefer not to dwell on such failures, they can become some of our own best learning experiences. Here are some stories of failures, even from some of the best-known Web searching trainers. It is only fair to begin with one of my own.

Back in 1998 I was giving a group of market researchers a workshop entitled "Power Web Searching: The Web and Beyond." During part of the workshop, I introduced Usenet newsgroups and the DejaNews search engine for searching newsgroups. Despite giving many caveats about its being a collection of personal and often very opinionated postings and describing it as a source for information on individuals, personal product experiences, competitive intelligence, and breaking news, one attendee got quite upset and gave a long diatribe about it being completely useless information and completely unreliable since it was not based on a statistical random sample.

Rita Vine shares a similar example: "I still have some stunning failures. For example, I was lecturing on effective Web search at an insurance firm [to a class] full of claims adjusters who often have to search for information on the Web related to a case or to track down missing persons. I had worked very hard to show the class invisible Web databases for public records, links to insurance ratings sites, insurance news, legislation for both Canada and the U.S., and at the end of it all, someone put up his hand and demanded to know why he wasn't being shown 'advanced' search techniques like Boolean searching and other typically 'advanced' options in search engines. I really thought that I had explained the limitations of search engines well, and in fact most of the class had understood the theory, but I felt so deflated by that comment." Both of these examples show that some students may have their own agendas and views, which may be in direct contrast with the instruction. The challenge is to find a way to still help such students learn something even if they disagree.

Sometimes the failures are hard to avoid. Trainers doing customized sessions often have to depend on the course requester to let them know what the audience needs. Sometimes the requester gets it wrong. Ran Hock describes such a failure when he based "a course design too much on a sponsor who was not familiar with the search needs of the audience."

Then there are the problems endemic to the Internet. Jeff Humphrey recalls "trying to do a demonstration on how to track a bill in the Indiana legislature on the opening day of a session. An overloaded server made a live demo impossible. Luckily, at the last minute, I had printed out screen dumps of the site and was able to show people what it would look like if we were live."

Sometimes the problem is the question itself. Diane Kovacs emphasizes the whole process of question analysis, recalling a patron who insisted an ancestor had served in the Civil War when all available information demonstrated otherwise. Another of Diane's examples is someone who wants to trace "Native American ancestors but cannot provide a name, birth date, death date, or identifiable tribal affiliation." As she notes, "The problem is not in the searching. It is in the formulation and expectation implicit in the research question."

Failures can be turned into an opportunity for teaching. Joe Barker notes that "frequently an answer or result that was there last week is morphed or gone. This becomes a basis for exploring how to find something in a reorganized site—or justifies finding another source and evaluating its merits."

Facilities Failures

From the workshops and sessions I have presented over the course of the past decade, I can certainly say that the overall reliability of computers and their Internet connections has improved. Yet failures still occur. Not long ago I was giving a talk at the Massachusetts Institute of Technology (MIT). As MIT is one of the most renowned engineering schools in the U.S. and possesses speedy Internet connections, I had absolutely no concerns about having a functioning connection during the whole session. So of course, right in the middle of the talk, the Internet connection died and did not come back up until several hours later.

Even with the best plans for backup, facilities can fail. At a 2002 Web Search University conference in Chicago, Reva Basch was delivering her keynote address, speaking into a microphone and using her laptop to run a PowerPoint presentation that was projected onto a large screen. Then the power went out. In the large room, she lost the sound system, the projection capabilities, and the Internet connection. The laptop was still running on its battery, but the audience was unable to see what the speaker was seeing. Undaunted by the power outage and since the audience had nowhere to go anyway, Reva continued with her talk, minus the demonstration ability. The power outage killed most of her possible backup options—transparencies, handouts, canned slides, and PowerPoint. So while you should plan for facility problems, be prepared for anything.

Rita Vine tells of a similar situation. "I have taught some classes where the Internet just stopped responding and, in one particularly memorable case, where a complete power failure brought the session to a grinding halt for over an hour." Gary Price mentions the necessity of "being ready to improvise if a live connection doesn't work. I once did a 90-minute session without a live connection. Not fun, but the session got rave reviews." With some facilities failures and other emergency situations, there is really nothing to do but postpone the session.

Beyond connection and power problems, other facilities failures can certainly get in the way. Sheila Webber remarks, "I find the constraints of teaching rooms a problem—either we have lecture rooms, practically none of them networked and too many of them with fixed seating, or labs, in which the less enthusiastic students may lurk behind the computer doing their e-mail during 'presenting' bits, as there isn't enough clear space to force them to haul out their chairs from behind the computers unless it's a very small class."

All the basics of a facility can make a difference, from chairs and desks to the heating, ventilation, and air conditioning equipment.

Jeff Humphrey once had "30 adults in a lab at a junior high school, in desks scaled for sixth graders, with a less-than-functional air conditioning unit, in July, for a full-day session." He had a second session scheduled in the same location but canceled it after the trials of the first one.

The Team Teaching Danger

Many times, a team-teaching environment is ideal. With more than one teacher to share the load, the planning can be much easier. Especially in a hands-on session, more than one instructor means that more students can get individualized assistance, quicker fixes for computing problems, and more question-and-answer interactions.

Successful team teaching nevertheless requires careful planning and the right combination of trainers. Here is Jeff Humphrey's story of "being volunteered by a higher-up to do a 'Train the Trainers' session ... with a consultant hired by a local department of education to help promote our statewide database services. She was constantly changing her mind as to what needed to be covered and which of us would cover it. I thought we finally had everything straightened out about 30 minutes before the session. She left for a lunch meeting during my part of the presentation, returned late for her part, then proceeded to cover the same material I had been teaching for the previous 2 hours. As a result, I'm now extremely picky about team teaching situations." So while team teaching opportunities can be successful, be cautious when the co-presenter is unknown.

Web Site Instruction and the Web Searching Paradox

Putting class tutorials, questions, answers, and exercises online makes sense when teaching Web searching. However, the paradox lies in the nature of the search engines. Once that information is posted on a Web page, that text is likely to get indexed by a search

engine. Joe Barker describes the problem of posting both questions and answers on a Web site. "My own answer sheets to the
exercise questions come up in Google first, as top results."

This can destroy the whole purpose of an exercise. To combat the
problem, Joe stopped making the answer sheets available online.
Another approach is to use the robots exclusion protocol via the
robots.txt file or the noindex robots metatag to keep the answer
sheets from being indexed by the search engines. Details on how to
do this are available at www.robotstxt.org/wc/exclusion.html.

Lost Interest

Keeping the interest of the audience is crucial to most instructional settings. You can lose the audience if you teach skills they
already know well. Diane Kovacs tells of the time she "was teaching
Advanced search skills to a group that already knew everything I
was teaching. I lost my flow and concentration because they were
all nodding at me." The opposite can happen as well. I have often
heard advice about getting the students involved by using topics of
interest to them. This advice probably holds in some subjects, but
I have found that it fails to work well for Web searching. First of all,
most people attending a session on Web searching are already convinced of the value of searching on the Web. If anything, they need
to be convinced to look in places besides their favorite search
engine. But the major danger in using topics of personal interest is
that they lead directly to full-text Web pages. Once, many years
ago, after asking attendees to search for some words that interest
them, I watched the class focus shift from the instructor to their
computer screens. Rather than focusing on the techniques and
strategies for Web searching that I was teaching, they were preoc-
cupied with the absorbing information they had found.

Now I never ask people to search for something of interest to
them. Instead, I use topics and examples of no particular interest
for both exercises and examples so that students can focus on the

instructional point rather than the information on the Web pages. The students can try the techniques on their own topics after the session is finished.

Formulas for Success

Different teachers find different formulas for success in instructional sessions. For Paul Barron, much is in the attitude. He says, "Associations and school divisions … ask me to present. That is due to the downright good time we have in the workshops. There are lots of prizes awarded, and the attendees learn something they can use immediately. Most importantly, I never embarrass anyone or make anyone feel foolish. I am surprised by the number of people who have told me that after a presentation."

Handouts help. Joe Barker likes "lots of handouts. I print out all the tables from my searching site on Search Engines, Directories, invisible Web, and more. I also print out the PowerPoint slides. The body of the class consists of hands-on keying following another handout explaining with graphics how each search engine works, what it looks like, model searches, and such. This makes it possible for people to walk away with the equivalent of a little book on searching, with cheat sheets and exercises to practice with." From his many classes, Joe has learned to "put less detail in the PowerPoint" and more details into the handouts that accompany the hands-on section.

Phil Bradley notes that "if you can show interest and enthusiasm as a trainer, clients will pick up on that and will get enthused themselves." Diane Kovacs connects with attendees by matching their needs to the instructional content: "I'm always a little surprised at how enthusiastic my students can be when we mesh their need for learning with what I'm teaching."

For Ran Hock, a successful session is "any course where attendees come back and comment that their time was well spent, that they learned something significant and useful, and comment to the effect that 'I didn't know I could do that!'" One final story from Ran makes a very clear example of successful teaching. "I sometimes use this in regard to simply knowing what a tool can do for you: The person who, only 2 days before, had spent over $6 on directory assistance for a German phone number and discovered in class that he could have gotten it for free in less than two minutes."

Afterword

We have come to the end of this journey through the topics and issues of teaching Web searching. Beyond the stories shared in these chapters, be sure to look at the sample handouts and other training materials included in Appendix B.

Web search training is a challenging topic. There is no single right way to teach Web searching, just as there is no single right way to search the Web. I hope that this exploration of the approaches of many trainers will help you come up with new ideas and innovative approaches of your own, and greater energy to continue teaching Web search skills.

Appendix A

The Trainers: Introduction to the Interviewees

In the interest of presenting a broad array of approaches and techniques in the book, I sent detailed e-mail surveys to 12 well-known and well-respected instructors. Their approaches, examples, quotations, lessons, and anecdotes are scattered throughout the book. Some samples of the handouts and Web sites they use in their instruction are available in Appendix B.

These instructors are listed in the Preface and following are their biographies as well as information about their training sessions, Web sites, and services.

Please contact them directly if you would like to learn more about the instructional materials included in Appendix B.

Joe Barker
Librarian
Program Coordinator Internet/Web Instruction
The Teaching Library
University of California
302 Moffitt Library
Berkeley, CA 94720
Phone: 510-643-1636
Fax: 510-898-1525
E-mail: jbarker@library.berkeley.edu

Joe Barker joined the Teaching Library in the summer of 1995 and has been with the University of California, Berkeley (UC Berkeley) library since 1983. Before his present incarnation in public service and instruction, Joe headed the acquisition department of the library. He began his library career in 1975 (MLIS from UC Berkeley) and worked for several years at Virginia Tech in circulation, acquisitions, serials control, budget management, and systems development. Joe chose librarianship as a career after completing a PhD in French literature (Emory University) and teaching for 5 years (State University of New York, Binghamton). His experience with academic research—and particularly his contact at Emory with several reference librarians whose knowledge amazed him—inspired him to pursue academic librarianship.

In the Teaching Library, Joe spends about 65 percent of his time at reference and in course-integrated bibliographic instruction. The Teaching Library specializes in tailored courses and other instruction to help students with research on any subject. Joe has enjoyed reconnecting with classroom instruction and teaching after many years in library management and technical services. He has become a fervent believer that every library manager and behind-the-scenes "techie" should have a thorough grounding in reference. The challenges and rewards of using library, Internet, and other resources to meet the research and information needs of the public are Joe's core reasons for working in a research library.

Joe also coordinates the Teaching Library's Internet/World Wide Web instruction—a series of courses offered year-round to students, staff, faculty of the university, and anyone in the community who wishes to learn about the Internet and how to find information on the World Wide Web. He maintains a complete series of Web pages containing all the current content of the classes offered. These pages may be found at Finding Information on the World Wide Web: A Tutorial (www.lib.berkeley.edu/TeachingLib/Guides/Internet/FindInfo.html).

Joe began teaching Web searching with the Infopeople project (infopeople.org) in 2000, conducting classes throughout California public libraries, getting to know colleagues who share his commitment to providing quality information and who rely heavily on the Web sometimes. In many ways, he feels that what he knows about Web searching is more directly valued in public libraries' reference and research than at the university, where students are ushered to "scholarly" sources and encouraged not to use the Web. Joe feels the Web contains valuable information that is often more up-to-date than published sources.

Paul Barron
Library Manager
James Monroe Center for Graduate and Professional Studies
Mary Washington College
121 University Blvd.
Fredericksburg, VA 22406
Phone: 540-286-8057
Fax: 540-286-8040
E-mail: pbarron@mwc.edu

Paul Barron is currently library manager at Mary Washington College's James Monroe Center for Graduate and Professional Studies in Fredericksburg, Virginia. After retiring from the Marine Corps, Paul earned a library science degree from the University of Texas at Austin in 1997. He was the head reference librarian at Rockbridge County Regional Library, the librarian and archivist at the George C. Marshall Foundation, and the technology director for the Rockbridge County Schools in Lexington, Virginia.

Paul is a National Teacher Training Institute (NTTI) Master Teacher, a former adjunct faculty member at the Virginia Military Institute and the Dabney S. Lancaster Community College in Lexington, Virginia, and Infography's (www.infography.com) subject matter specialist for Internet searching. He has led more than 40 workshops and presentations on Web searching in California, Maryland, Virginia, and Texas for college faculty; K–12 educators; library media specialists; and academic, public, and school librarians. His NTTI instructional technology lesson plans are available at www.wvpt4learning.org/lessons/pdf03/webwise.pdf and www.wvpt4learning.org/lessons/pdf02/nowaah.pdf. His recommended list resources for learning to search the Web are located at www.infography.com/content/813746743748.html.

Phil Bradley

Internet Consultant, Trainer, Web Designer, and Author
5 Walton Gardens
Feltham
Middlesex TW13 4QY
U.K.
Phone: 020-8844-1746
E-mail: philb@philb.com
Web site: www.philb.com

Phil Bradley is a qualified information professional, having obtained an honours degree in librarianship in the early 1980s. His early career was spent working with the British Council before becoming head of technical support (U.K. and Europe) for SilverPlatter. He then became global director of training and later Webmaster. In the mid-1990s, Phil became an independent Internet consultant. He spends much of his time teaching groups (librarians, doctors, lawyers, etc.) about various aspects of the Internet and has probably instructed more people in the U.K. than anyone else in how to use the Internet.

When he's not teaching, Paul writes about the Internet and has written several well-received titles about searching the Web, writing and designing Web pages, and promoting Web sites. He also writes a monthly column in the Chartered Institute of Library and Information Professionals (CILIP) magazine *Update* as well as columns and articles for professional journals. Phil is also a Web site designer and numbers among his clients various charities, an accountant, medical organizations, a chemist, and a stand-up comedian. Phil offers a Search Engine Optimization (SEO) service to provide help and assistance in improving the appearance and ranking of sites, and he is a well-known speaker (both in the U.K. and abroad) on Internet-related matters.

When he's not working, Phil indulges his hobbies of genealogy, the American Civil War, and reading science fiction. Contact Phil at philb@philb.com or via his Web site (www.philb.com).

John Ferguson
Retired Librarian
1914 Mission Drive
Garland, TX 75042
Phone: 972-272-0488
E-mail: jferguson3@verizon.net

John Ferguson was a reference librarian at Richland College in the Dallas County Community College District for 19 years before retiring in the summer of 2003. He was also a teaching librarian, and as a member of Richland College's adjunct faculty, he taught courses in English, the humanities, religion, and philosophy.

John was also the creator of the library's Web site in 1994. He managed the site for 10 years and the library's 44 public workstations for 7 years. As part of the Richland College Library Web site, John created the Conan the Librarian pages (www.rlc.dcccd.edu/lrc/conan.htm). Beyond his many activities at the Richland College Library, John has been a presenter at various national conferences, including Internet Librarian and Computers in Libraries.

In a more humorous vein, John, who joined the Richland College Library staff in 1984, has been around. During his 61 years on this planet, he has:

- worked as a soda jerk and short-order cook

- built and sold trampolines

- baptized and buried people—not necessarily the same ones—as a Christian minister

- managed a health club

- worked in a bookstore

- supervised people working on mainframe computers

- done artwork for a designer of integrated circuits

- worked in a video rental store

- worked in a college registrar's office

- sold Bibles door-to-door

- worked as an encyclopedia salesman

- owned and operated an information brokerage

- delivered Grit, the newspaper

Alice Fulbright
Reference Instruction Librarian
Richland College Library
12800 Abrams Road
Dallas, TX 75243-2199
Phone: 972-238-3725
E-mail: alicefulbright@dcccd.edu

Since 1992 Alice has been a reference librarian at Richland College. She is a graduate of Texas Tech University and received her MLIS from the University of North Texas in 1990. Before coming to Richland College, she taught elementary school in the Lubbock and Richardson school districts and completed ESL certification through East Texas State University.

Alice's duties at the Richland College Library (www.rlc.dcccd. edu/lrc/rlclib.htm) include working at the library reference desk with students on their various research projects, developing student handouts, and teaching formal classes that cover the use of the Internet and electronic databases as well as the use of print materials. In 1999 the library instruction program at Richland College Library won the national EBSCO Award, presented annually to one community college in the nation for excellence in library instruction.

With the help of colleagues and many materials previously developed for the *Richland College Library Handbook,* Alice developed the Dallas TeleCollege Library (ollie.dcccd.edu/library/tele college.htm) to assist distance learners in every aspect of the library research process. She is in the process of updating and maintaining this Web site to keep pace with the changing realm of electronic searching.

In the past, Alice taught a continuing education course titled Internet Searching, geared to the needs and interests of adults in the community who wanted to learn Internet searching techniques and become acquainted with many valuable Web sites.

Randolph (Ran) E. Hock, PhD
Online Strategies
9919 Corsica Street
Vienna, VA 22181
Phone: 800-871-4033 or 703-242-6078
E-mail: ran@onstrat.com
Web site: www.onstrat.com

Randolph (Ran) Hock has trained more than 10,000 online researchers over the past 20 years. He has held management and training positions with DIALOG and Knight-Ridder Information Services. He was also a reference librarian at the Massachusetts Institute of Technology (MIT) and was the first data services librarian at the University of Pennsylvania.

Ran has taught frequent continuing education and other courses for the University of Maryland College of Information

Studies and also teaches in Lesley University's Technology in Education program. He is active in the American Society for Information Science and Technology (ASIST), for which he has served on the board of directors and chaired committees and chapters.

Through his company, Online Strategies, Ran develops and presents customized on-site seminars in how to effectively and efficiently make use of Internet resources. These seminars have been presented for companies, government agencies, nongovernmental organizations, associations, conferences, universities, schools, and library systems. Courses have been given throughout the U.S. and in Austria, France, Hungary, Portugal, and the U.K. More information on these courses offered by Online Strategies can be found at www.onstrat.com.

Ran is the author of numerous books, including *The Extreme Searcher's Guide to Web Search Engines: A Handbook for the Serious Searcher* (CyberAge Books, 2001), *The Extreme Searcher's Internet Handbook* (CyberAge Books, Second Edition, 2007), *Yahoo! to the Max* (CyberAge Books, 2005), and *The Traveler's Web* (CyberAge Books, 2007). He is also a frequent contributor and columnist in professional publications, including *ONLINE* and *The CyberSkeptic's Guide to Internet Research*.

Jeff Humphrey

Interactive Media Specialist
Indiana Cooperative Library Services Authority (INCOLSA)
6202 Morenci Trail
Indianapolis, IN 46268
Phone: 317-298-6570 or 800-733-1899 (within Indiana)
E-mail: jeff@incolsa.net

Jeff Humphrey is a reformed reference librarian turned INCOLSA interactive media specialist and Internet trainer, offering courses in searching, Web design, and HTML. He has delivered workshops and presentations at local, state, and national conferences covering all aspects of the Internet and its use in libraries. He earned an MLS from Indiana University and, prior to joining INCOLSA, worked 8 years as a reference librarian and reference and technology trainer in public libraries.

INCOLSA is Indiana's statewide library network, serving 768 member institutions, including school corporations, public library systems, special libraries (corporations, hospitals, law firms, museums, correctional facilities, and more), and colleges and universities representing more than 2,200 libraries throughout Indiana. INCOLSA provides reference, interlibrary loan, videoconferencing and distance learning, training and continuing education, INSPIRE, technology support, and other services, such as OCLC member support, from its central office in Indianapolis and from seven field offices located throughout Indiana.

Diane Kovacs
President of Kovacs Consulting—Internet & Web Training
1117 Meadowbrook Blvd.
Brunswick, OH 44212
Phone: 330-273-5032
Fax: 330-225-0083
E-mail: diane@kovacs.com
Web site: www.kovacs.com

Diane Kovacs is president of Kovacs Consulting—Internet & Web Training. She has nearly 10 years' experience as a Web teacher and consultant. She teaches a variety of Web-based or Web-supported in-person classes in Web research skills. Diane received an MILS from the University of Illinois in 1989 and an MEd in instructional technology from Kent State University in 1993. She received her BA in anthropology from the University of Illinois in 1985.

Diane's first book, *The Internet Trainer's Guide*, was published in 1995 (Wiley) and was followed by *The Internet Trainer's Total*

Solution Guide (Wiley, 1997) and *Cybrarians Guide to Successful Internet Programs and Services* (Neal-Schuman, 1997), which she co-authored with her husband, Michael Kovacs. Her latest books include *The Kovacs Guide to Electronic Library Collection Development: Essential Core Subject Collections, Selection Criteria, and Guidelines* (Neal-Schuman, 2004), co-authored with Kara L. Robinson, and *The Virtual Reference Handbook: Interview and Information Delivery Techniques for the Chat and E-mail Environment* (Neal-Shuman, forthcoming). Diane's other books include *Genealogical Research on the Web* (Neal-Schuman, 2002), *How to Find Medical Information on the Internet: A Print and Online Tutorial for the Health Care Professional and Consumer* (Library Solutions Press, 2002), and *Building Electronic Library Collections: The Essential Guide to Selection Criteria and Core Collections* (Neal-Schuman, 2000). Since 1990 she has been editor-in-chief of the *Directory of Scholarly and Professional Electronic Conferences.*

Diane is the 2000 recipient of the Documents to the People award from the Government Documents Roundtable of the American Library Association. She was also the recipient of the Apple Corporation Library's Internet Citizen Award for 1992 and was the University of Illinois Graduate School of Library and Information Science Alumni Association's first recipient of the Young Leadership Award in 1996.

Gary Price
Gary Price Library Research and Internet Consulting
107 Kinsman View Circle
Silver Spring, MD 20901
Phone: 301-593-9311
E-mail: Gary@ResourceShelf.Com
Web site: www.resourceshelf.com

Gary Price, Director of Online Information Resources at Ask.com, is a librarian, information research consultant, and writer based in suburban Washington, DC. A native of the Chicago area, he earned his MLIS from Wayne State University in Detroit, Michigan. He also holds a BA from the University of Kansas in Lawrence, Kansas. From February 1995 through April 2001, Gary worked as a reference librarian at George Washington University.

Gary is the editor and compiler of the ResourceShelf (www.resourceshelf.com), one of the best sources of current information about all kinds of library- and information-related topics, including search engines. He is also the founder and a contributor to DocuTicker (www.docuticker.com), a daily listing of new reports from government agencies, think tanks, universities, and other groups. From August 2004 through January 2006, Gary was the News Editor of Search Engine Watch. These and other compilations have been mentioned in numerous publications, including the *Washington Post*, the *Guardian*, and the *Chronicle of Higher Education*.

Gary is a frequent speaker at professional and trade conferences, a contributor to *Searcher* magazine, and co-author with Chris Sherman of *The Invisible Web* (CyberAge Books, 2001). In the summer of 2002, he received the Innovations in Technology Award from the Special Libraries Association.

Danny Sullivan
Calafia Consulting and Search Engine Watch
Editor, SearchEngineWatch.com
Contact via sewatch.com/about/article.php/2155671
or feedback@calafia.com

Often described as a "search engine guru," Danny Sullivan helps Webmasters, marketers, and everyday Web users understand how search engines work. Danny's expertise about search engines is often sought by the media, and he has been quoted in publications such as the *Wall Street Journal, USA Today,* the *Los Angeles Times, Forbes,* the *New Yorker,* and *Newsweek.*

Danny began covering search engines in late 1995, when he undertook a study of how search engines indexed Web pages. The results were published online as A Webmaster's Guide to Search Engines, a pioneering effort to answer the many questions site designers and Internet publicists had about search engines. The positive reaction from both marketers and general search engine users caused Danny to expand the guide into SearchEngine Watch.com. The site is now widely recognized as an authoritative place to find the straight scoop on dealing with search engines.

Jupitermedia purchased SearchEngineWatch.com in 1997 and Danny continues to maintain the site for the company. An associated e-mail newsletter, the Search Engine Report, goes to more than 130,000 readers each month. SearchEngineWatch.com offers members an exclusive e-mail newsletter and access to premium content not available on the public site.

In addition to his work for SearchEngineWatch.com, Danny speaks widely on the topic of searching and organizes a popular conference series about search engine marketing called Search Engine Strategies. Danny gave training sessions on Web searching at the British Library for a number of years and continues giving training sessions for a large U.K. company.

Rita Vine
President
Workingfaster.com
1235 Bay Street, Suite 1000
Toronto M5R 3K4
Canada
Phone: 416-928-1405 or 800-343-9878
Fax: 416-928-2903
E-mail: rita@workingfaster.com

Web site: www.workingfaster.com

Rita Vine has been a professional librarian and instructor for more than 20 years. She is a co-founder and president of Workingfaster.com, which specializes in designing research tools and training programs for serious Web users.

Rita is the creator of Workingfaster.com's unique methodology of Internet searching, called Keep It Simple Searching, and a co-designer of the company's unique enterprise Web search tool, the Search Portfolio. She has designed and customized online and instructor-led courses for businesses, associations, and corporations throughout North America.

Workingfaster.com has been a leader in teaching Internet searching skills to information professionals for more than a decade. In addition to offering both instructor-led and online training courses in online searching and teaching, the company produces a unique Web-based licensed product called the Search Portfolio to help librarians and information professionals easily search the Web using the top 100 peer-selected starting points.

Designed for reference, Web collection development, and virtual reference, the Search Portfolio is the premiere starting point for users who want to maximize the value of their online research and avoid the commercial content of most search engines. Visit the Search Portfolio at www.searchportfolio.com to learn more about how this product delivers an enterprise solution for managing Internet research tools. To learn more about Workingfaster.com's courses and programs, visit www.workingfaster.com.

Sheila Webber
Lecturer
Department of Information Studies
University of Sheffield, Western Bank
Sheffield S10 2TN
U.K.

Phone: 0044-0114-222-2641
Fax: 0114-278-0300
E-mail: s.webber@sheffield.ac.uk

Sheila Webber is a lecturer in the Department of Information Studies, University of Sheffield, U.K. Her key areas of research and teaching are information literacy and business information. She is currently co-leader of a research project into U.K. faculty's conceptions of information literacy. Before coming to Sheffield, Sheila was head of the British Library's Business Information Service and head of BLAISE Online Services, responsible for marketing and training. She then taught in the Department of Information Science at the University of Strathclyde, Scotland. She says she is rather horrified to realize that she has been teaching for more than 20 years! Sheila is a Fellow of the Chartered Institute of Library and Information Professionals, a member of the committee of the IFLA Management and Marketing Section, a member of the American Society for Information Science and Technology (ASIST), and a member of the U.K.'s Institute for Learning and Teaching in Higher Education.

Sheila's Web sites include the Information Literacy Weblog (ciquest.shef.ac.uk/infolit) and the Information Literacy Place (dis.shef.ac.uk/literacy).

Sample Handouts and
Other Training Material

In many instructional sessions, handouts, Web sites, or other supplemental materials (such as PowerPoint presentations, workbooks, or Adobe Portable Document Format [PDFs]) can be a great help to students. Such materials can reinforce a concept or provide additional information about a search engine. Types of materials include exercises, outlines for lectures, or even lists of URLs with descriptions

The sharing of materials between trainers is a time-honored staple of bibliographic instruction; it saves us from having to reinvent a format or rewrite descriptions every time. Handouts and other training materials should be customized for a particular audience, however. Trainers must take into account the local access situation and possible peculiarities of the network setup, such as firewalls or other security measures that inhibit access to certain Internet resources. Also, the topics covered by training materials will always vary, as will the style and approach of the trainer.

Following the theme of learning from one another, this appendix includes a variety of handouts, Web pages, and instructional aids from many of the trainers who contributed to this book. The materials are arranged alphabetically by the trainer's last name. Think of it as an idea exchange. Look at the variety of supplementary training material here, and consider the varying designs, approaches, and content. Then consider adapting them to match your own teaching style and audience needs. (Since Web search engines can change so fast, do not depend on the specific search engine descriptions in these training materials to be accurate when you use them.)

My thanks to all those who have allowed their training materials to be reproduced here. Each item has been reproduced with permission; unfortunately, some formatting may have been lost in the translation to book form. The copyrights belong to the authors or their organizations. Please contact them (see the contact information in Appendix A) if you wish to reproduce any of these materials.

May these inspire you to create even better training materials and to one day share them with others.

Joe Barker, librarian and program coordinator of Internet/Web instruction, the Teaching Library at the University of California, Berkeley

- Begin the Pre-Searching Analysis (www.lib.berkeley.edu/ TeachingLib/Guides/Internet/form.pdf)
- Web Page Evaluation Checklist (www.lib.berkeley.edu/ Teaching Lib/Guides/Internet/EvalForm.pdf)
- Recommended Search Engines: Table of Features (www.lib. berkeley.edu/TeachingLib/Guides/Internet/SearchEngines.html)
- Recommended Search Strategy: Analyze Your Topic & Search with Peripheral Vision (www.lib.berkeley.edu/TeachingLib/ Guides/Internet/Strategies.html)

Here are four different documents from one of the best-known teachers and best-known sites for training materials on Web searching. The first two documents, Begin the Pre-Searching Analysis (Figure AppB.1) and Web Page Evaluation Checklist (Figure AppB.2), can be used to prepare for a Web search and to evaluate Web pages. These forms are available online in Adobe PDF format or can be provided to students as paper handouts.

Begin the Pre-Searching Analysis uses a spare design with ample room for the students to write their thoughts and answers to the topic analysis questions. The design works well with the intent of the handout, which is to get the students to think about their topic in different ways.

The Web Page Evaluation Checklist is much more detailed in design and asks very specific questions. Since the focus here is on evaluating the quality of the information on a Web page, this design, too, works well for the purpose of the handout. With check boxes and yes/no questions, it can be filled out quickly, even though finding answers on the Web page may be difficult.

The third document, Recommended Search Engines: Table of Features (Figure AppB.3), shows the beginning of one of Joe's Web pages. It is a long, information-packed table with a great deal of search engine details. Joe also provides a link to a PDF version of the Web page, which provides a better printout. The final document from Joe, Recommended Search Strategy: Analyze Your Topic and Search with Peripheral Vision (Figure AppB.4), shows the beginning of a linked page on search strategies. This five-step strategy is sequential, and the page goes on to note non-recommended strategies as well.

Figure AppB.1   Begin the Pre-Searching Analysis (©2002 Copyright Joe Barker, reproduced with permission)

TOPIC WORKSHEET

> **Jot down a topic or subject you'd like to explore on the Web:**

BEGIN THE PRE-SEARCHING ANALYSIS

1. **What UNIQUE WORDS, DISTINCTIVE NAMES, ABBREVIATIONS, or ACRONYMS are associated with your topic?**
   These may be the place to begin because their specificity will help zero in on relevant pages.

2. **Can you think of societies, organizations, or groups that might have information on your subject via their pages?**
   Search these as a "phrase in quotes," looking for a home page that might contain links to other pages, journals, discussion groups, or databases on your subject. You may require the "phrase in quotes" to be in the documents' titles by preceding it by **title:**[no space]

3. **What other words are likely to be in ANY Web documents on your topic?**
   You may want to require these by joining them with **AND** or preceding each by **+**[nospace]

4. **Do any of the words in your answers to Questions 1, 2, or 3 belong in phrases or strings—together in a certain order, like a cliché?**
   Search these as a "phrase in quotes" (e.g., "affirmative action" or "communicable diseases").

5. **For any of the terms in your answer to Question 4, can you think of synonyms, variant spellings, or equivalent terms you would also accept in relevant documents?**
   You may want to allow these terms by joining them by **OR** and including each set of equivalent terms in ( ). In Infoseek, allow any of them by **omitting +**[no space] **and** **-**[no space] before them.

6. **Can you think of any extraneous or irrelevant documents these words might pick up?**
   You may want to exclude terms or phrases with **-**[no space] **before each term,** or **AND NOT.**

7. **What BROADER terms could your topic be covered by?**
   When browsing subject categories or searching sites of Webliographies or databases on your topic, try broader categories.

Figure AppB.2   Web Page Evaluation Checklist (©2002 Copyright Joe Barker, The Teaching Library, University of California, Berkeley, reproduced with permission)

Web Page Evaluation Checklist

The column on the left lists questions to ask to investigate Web pages.
Evaluating Web pages requires two actions:
- Be suspicious
- Think critically about every page you find

	Title of page you are evaluating:	Title of page you are evaluating:
1. Look at the URL:		
Personal page or site?	□~ or %, or *users, members,* or *people*	□~ or %, or *users, members,* or *people*
What type of domain is it? Appropriate for the content?	□ com □ org/net □ edu □ gov/mil/us □non-US_____ □other:	□ com □ org/net □ edu □ gov/mil/us □non-US_____ □other:
Published by entity that makes sense? Does it correspond to the name of the site?	Publisher or Domain Name entity:	Publisher or Domain Name entity:
2. Scan the perimeter of page, looking for answers to these questions:		
Who wrote the page?	□E-mail □Name:	□E-mail □Name:
Dated?	Date _____ Current enough?	Date _____ Current enough?
Credentials on this subject? (Truncate back the URL if no useful links.)	Evidence?	Evidence?
3. Look for these indicators of quality:		
Sources well documented?		
Complete? If 2nd-hand information, is it **not altered or forged?**		
Links to more resources? Do they work?		
Other viewpoints? Bias?		
4. What do others say?		
Who links to it? Hint: In Google search: *link:all.or.part.of.url*	Many or few? Opinions of it?	Many or few? Opinions of it?
Is the page rated well in a directory? http://lii.org or http://infomine.ucr.edu or http://about.com		
Look up the author in Google		
Does it all add up?		
Why was the page put on the Web?	□Inform, facts, data □Explain □Persuade □Sell □Entice □Share/disclose Other:	□Inform, facts, data □Explain □Persuade □Sell/entice □Share/disclose Other:
Possibly ironic? Satire or parody?		

BOTTOM LINE: Is the Web page as good as (or better than) what you could find in journal articles or other published literature that is not on the free, general Web?

Figure AppB.3   Recommended Search Engines: Table of Features (©2006 Copyright Joe Barker, reproduced with permission)

Finding Information on the Internet: A Tutorial http://www.lib.berkeley.edu/TeachingLib/Guides/Internet/SearchEngines.html **The BEST Search Engines** *UC Berkeley - Teaching Library Internet Workshops*
About This Tutorial I Table of Contents I Handouts I Glossary

Recommended Search Engines: Tables of Features

Google appears still to have the largest database of Web pages, including many other types of Web documents (e.g., PDFs, Word, Excel, PowerPoint documents). Despite the presence of many advertisements and considerable clutter from blog sites and newsgroups, Google's popularity ranking often makes pages worth looking at rise near the top of search results. Our new "Googling to the Max" course (when offered?) reflects our recognition that Google currently is the winning web search engine and so people need to learn to use it really well.

Google alone is often not sufficient, however. Less than half the searchable Web is fully searchable in Google. Overlap studies show that about half of the pages in any search engine database exist only in that database. Getting a second opinion is therefore often worth your time. For a second opinion, we recommend Teoma or Yahoo! Search. We no longer recommend using any meta-search engines for web searching, although some of the features in Dogpile and Vivisimo's Clusty may prove useful for some searches.

Features in common among the search engines we recommend. Search engines have become a little bit standardized, allowing us to use some of the same search techniques in all of them:

Things You CAN Do in Google, Yahoo!, and Teoma	Things NOT Supported in Google, Yahoo!, or Teoma
• **Phrase Searching** by enclosing terms in double quotes • **OR** searching with capitalized OR • **- excludes, + requires** exact form of word • **Limit** results by language in Advanced Search	• **Truncation** - use OR searches for variants (airline OR airlines) • **Case sensitivity** capitalization does not matter

Some Ways the Recommended Search Engines Differ:

Search Engine	Google www.google.com	Yahoo! Search search.yahoo.com	Ask.com www.ask.com
Links to help	Google help pages	Yahoo! help pages	Ask help pages
Size, type Size varies frequently and widely. See tests and more charts.	HUGE. Size not disclosed in any way that allows comparison. Probably the biggest. Biggest in tests.	HUGE. Claims over 20 billion total "web objects."	LARGE. Claims to have 2 billion fully indexed, searchable pages. Strives to become #1 in size.
Noteworthy features and limitations	Popularity ranking using PageRank™. Indexes the first 101KB of a Web page, and 120KB of PDFs.	Shortcuts give quick access to dictionary, synonyms, patents, traffic, stocks, encyclopedia, and	Subject-Specific Popularity™ ranking. Suggests broader and narrower terms.

Figure AppB.3 (cont.)

	~ before a word finds synonyms sometimes (~help > FAQ, tutorial, etc.)	<u>more</u>.	
Phrase searching <u>(term definition)</u>	Yes. Use " ". Searches common "<u>stop words</u>" if in phrases in quotes.	Yes. Use " ".	Yes. Use " ". Searches common "<u>stop words</u>" if in phrases in quotes.
Boolean logic <u>(term definition)</u>	Partial. AND assumed between words. Capitalize OR. - excludes. No ( ) or <u>nesting</u>. In <u>Advanced Search</u>, partial Boolean available in boxes.	Accepts AND, OR, NOT or AND NOT, and ( ). *Must be capitalized.* You **must** enclose terms joined by OR in parentheses (classic <u>Boolean</u>).	Partial. AND assumed between words. Capitalize OR. - excludes. No ( ) or <u>nesting</u>.
+Requires/ - Excludes <u>(term definition)</u>	- excludes. + will allow you to retrieve "<u>stop words</u>" (e.g., +in).	- excludes. + will allow you to search common words: "+in truth".	- excludes. + will allow you to retrieve "<u>stop words</u>" (e.g., +in).
Sub- Searching <u>(term definition)</u>	Sort of. At bottom of results page, click "Search within results" and enter more terms. Adds terms.	Add terms.	Sort of. Add terms.
Results Ranking <u>(term definition)</u>	Based on page popularity measured in links to it from other pages: high rank if a lot of other pages link to it. <u>Fuzzy AND</u> also invoked. Matching and ranking based on "cached" version of pages that may not be the most recent version.	Automatic <u>Fuzzy AND</u>.	Based on Subject-Specific Popularity™, links to a page by related pages. More <u>info</u>.

Figure AppB.4   Recommended Search Strategy: Analyze Your Topic and Search with Peripheral Vision (©2006 Copyright Joe Barker, reproduced with permission)

Finding Information on the Internet: A Tutorial
http://www.lib.berkeley.edu/TeachingLib/Guides/Internet/Strategies.html

Recommended Search Strategy: Analyze your topic & Search with peripheral vision

UC Berkeley - Teaching Library Internet Workshops

About This Tutorial I Table of Contents I Handouts I Glossary

---

The Five-Step Search Strategy We Recommend

Step #1. Analyze your topic to decide where to begin.
Click here for a printable FORM you may use to Analyze Your Topic (PDF file). **PDF files** are supported in Netscape 4.x and some other browsers. To view, search, or print the PDF files, you will need to use Adobe® Acrobat® Reader software, which is available free from Adobe if you need it.

Does your topic...	have distinctive words or phrases?
	    methernitha, unique meaning
	    "affirmative action," specific, accepted meaning in word cluster
	have NO distinctive words or phrases you can think of? You have only common or general terms that get the "wrong" pages.
	    "order out of chaos," used in too many contexts to be useful
	    sundiata, retrieves a myth, a rock group, a person, etc.
	seek an overview of a broad topic?
	    victorian literature, alternative energy sources
	specify a narrow aspect of a broad or common topic?
	    automobile recyclability, want current research, future designs, not how to recycle or oil recycling or other community efforts
	have synonymous, equivalent terms or variant spellings or endings that need to be included?
	    echinoderm OR echinoidea OR "sea urchin," any may be in useful pages
	    "cold fusion energy" OR "hydrogen energy," some use one term, some the other; you want both, although not precisely equivalent
	    millennium OR millennial OR millenium OR millenial OR "year 2000," etc., pages you want may contain any or all.
	Make you feel confused? Don't really know much about the topic yet? Need guidance?

Step #2. Pick the right starting place using this table:

YOUR TOPIC'S FEATURES:	Search Engines	Subject Directories	Specialized Databases "Invisible Web"	Find an Expert	LUCK
Distinctive word or phrase?	Enclose phrases in " ". **Test run** your word or phrase in Google.	Search the broader concept, what your term is "about."	Want data? Facts? Statistics? All of something? One of many like things?	Look for a specialized subject directory on your topic. E-mail the author of a good page you find.	Always on your side. Keep your mind open.
NO distinctive words or phrases?	Use more than one term or phrase in " " to get fewer results.	Try to find distinctive terms in Subject Directories.	Schedules? Maps? Look for a specialized database on the Invisible Web.	Ask a discussion group or expert.	Learn as you search.
Seek an overview?	NOT RECOMMENDED	Look for a specialized Subject Directory focused on your topic.	Hard to predict what you might find.	Never hurts to seek help.	

Figure AppB.4 (cont.)

Narrow aspect of broad or common topic?	Boolean searching as in Yahoo! Search.	Look for a Directory focused on the broad subject.			
Synonyms, equivalent terms, variants?	Choose search engines with Boolean OR, Truncation, or Field limiting.	NOT RECOM- MENDED			
Confused? Need more information?	NOT RECOM- MENDED	Look for a Gateway Page (Subject Guide). Try an **encyclopedia** in a Virtual Library. Ask at a **library** reference desk.			

Step #3. Learn as you go & VARY your approach with what you learn.

Don't assume you know what you want to find. Look at search results and see what you might use in addition to what you've thought of.

Step #4. Don't bog down in any strategy that doesn't work.

Switch from search engines to directories and back. Find specialized directories on your topic. Think about possible databases and look for them.

Step #5. Return to previous strategies better informed.

Search Strategies We Do NOT Recommend

Because of their inefficiency and often haphazard and frustrating results, we do not recommend either of the following two approaches to finding Web documents:

- **Browsing searchable directories.** If you can find a search box, search a directory. BROWSING is sometimes fun, rarely as efficient. The term "directories" refers here to any collection of Web resources organized into subject categories or some other breakdown appropriate to the content (Subject Directories or directories of specialized databases or of gateway pages). Browsing locates documents by your trying to match your topic in first the top, broadest layer of a subject hierarchy, then by choosing narrower sub-subject-categories in the hierarchy that you hope will lead to your target. Browsing encounters the difficulty of guessing under which subject category your topic is classified. The taxonomy in every directory differs, making browsing inconsistent from one search tool to another. The category "health" may contain documents on medicine, homeopathy, psychiatry, and fitness in one directory. In another "medicine" may

Figure AppB.4 (cont.)

include health, mental health, and alternative medicine, but not the term psychiatry and may classify fitness only under "lifestyle." *Searching (typing keywords in a search box) retrieves occurrences of your words no matter where they may be classified by subject. Use broad terms in searching any directory.*

- **Following links to sites recommended by heavy use or commercial interest.** Often in search engine results, you will see links to sites that are selected based on how often they are visited by others, or based on fees paid to the browser. Or you may see recommended "cool" sites. Use these with caution! Others may visit sites for reasons having no relation to your information interests, and the best sites for you may still be largely undiscovered by the vast public searching the Web. Taste varies and should vary. Make your own <u>evaluations</u>.

Table Matching Your Search Needs with the Features Search Engines Offer

The purpose of thinking about your topic before you start searching is to **determine what terms to search for** and **what features you need** to search successfully. The table below lists on the left features of many search inquiries. Use it to determine which features your searches need. On the left, the table describes search tool features designed to support each of the search needs listed on the left.
The links take you to the <u>table of search engines</u>—so you can pick a search engine with the features you need.

Features of your search inquiry	Matching Search Tools Features worth learning and using

Are you looking for a **proper name** or a **distinct phrase**?
 	
 • The name of an organization or society or movement
 • A proper name or an individual
 • A distinctive string of words generally associated with your topic
 	
 Can you think of an organization, proper name, or phrase to search for? It might help zoom in on the pages you want.
	PHRASE SEARCHING is a feature you want in every search tools you choose.
	     Requires your terms all to appear in exactly the order you enter them.
	     Enclose the phrase in double quotations " "
	 Examples:
	     "affirmative action"
	     "world health organization"
	     "a person's name"

Are some of your terms **common words** with **many meanings and contexts**?
 	
 • *Children* in conjunction with *television* and also *violence*
 • *Censorship* as an aspect of *ethics* in *journalism*
	BOOLEAN AND will help:
	   children AND television AND violence
	   journalism AND ethics AND censorship
	 Google and **AlltheWeb** and most other search engines put AND in between words automatically (by default):
	   children television violence journalism ethics censorship

Do you anticipate lots of search **results with terms you do not want**?
 	
 • Your search for *biomedical engineering* and *cancer* brings you lots of academic programs, and you want research reports. So you try to exclude documents containing *Department of* or *School of*.
	BOOLEAN AND NOT will help:
	   "biomedical engineering" AND cancer AND NOT
	   "Department of" AND NOT "School of"
	 or its **-EXCLUDES** near equivalent:
	   "biomedical engineering"
	   cancer -"Department of" - "School of"

Paul Barron, librarian and former Technology Director, Rockbridge (VA) County Schools

- Locating Web-Based Educational Resources (two PowerPoint slides)
- Web Wise by Who Is-ing (www.wvpt4learning.org/lessons/pdf03/webwise.pdf)

Using PowerPoint presentations, especially ones with many screen shots, can be a session saver when no Internet connection is available or the connection crashes. Paul has often used very large PowerPoint presentations successfully in such situations. Figures AppB.5 and AppB.6 are examples of slides from one of Paul's presentations, Locating Web-Based Educational Resources. (In the actual presentation, the slides are in color and also contain many animations.) In the first slide, Paul combines the humor of the animation with a portion of a screen shot and several key informational points, getting his point across in a very effective way. The second slide demonstrates excellent use of a reminder placed in a highlighted box.

Another training document Paul uses is a lesson plan he wrote for the National Teacher Training Institute titled Web Wise by Who Is-ing (Figure AppB.7). It shows how search engine training can be incorporated into a Web evaluation session using link searching and domain name ownership searching. This lesson plan is available online in PDF format.

Figure AppB.5   Locating Web-Based Educational Resources, PowerPoint Slide
                 Example No. 1 (©2003 Copyright Paul Barron, reproduced with
                 permission)

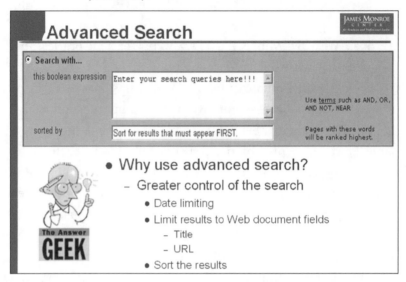

Figure AppB.6   Locating Web-Based Educational Resources, PowerPoint Slide
                 Example No. 2 (©2003 Copyright Paul Barron, reproduced with
                 permission)

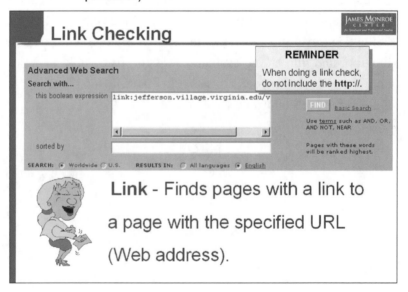

Figure AppB.7 Web Wise by Who Is-ing (©2003 Copyright National Teacher Training Institute and Paul Barron, reproduced with permission)

Grades 11 - 12

Web Wise by Who Is-ing!

Paul Barron, WVPT

NTTI

Overview

Topic: Technology, Staff Development. Among the influences that shape students' thinking skills, the Internet and the World Wide Web are some of the most influential. The majority of students rely on the Web to research topics for school projects; however, they may be weak at determining the quality of a website's content. They may value information-gathering over deliberation, breadth over depth, and other people's arguments over their own. Students should be skeptical about information on a website; they must determine who is the author, the author's credentials, and the author's agenda. This Web resource evaluation session provides information literacy training for instructional personnel and students who will identify what content they expect to find on the Martin LutherKing.org website, conduct a review of the website's content and a check to determine the registrant of the MartinLutherKing.org site.

Time Allotment

One 1-hour session

Media Components

Computers with Internet access; one to three
  instructional personnel or students per computer
Netscape Navigator or Microsoft Internet Explorer
  browser
Projection Device (optional)
Display Device (optional)
Websites for: Evaluation, Performing Registrant
  Checks, and Title Field Searching & Link Checking
**Anti-Dr. Martin Luther King Propaganda
Websites**
www.martinlutherking.org. A biased site, maintained by the racist organization Stormfront.org,
  that alleges that Dr. King was an agent of com-
  munism, a disruptive force in American history,
  and accuses him of numerous acts of plagiarism.
www.stormfront.org. An extremist site promoting a
  message of "White Pride World Wide." The
  www.martinlutherking.org. site is registered and
  maintained by Stormfront.org.

> **Caution for Instructional Personnel**
> There is profanity on the homepage of the
> www.martinlutherking.org Web site.
> When conducting the session,
> www.martinlutherking.org/flyer.html
> will be used as the homepage for the site.

Pro Dr. Martin Luther King Website
www.mlkonline.com. The official website of the
  estate of Martin Luther King, Jr. The site that
  provides copyrighted writings, documents, and
  recordings of Martin Luther King, Jr.
How to Recognize an Advocacy Page
www2.widener.edu/Wolfgram-Memorial-
  Library/webevaluation/advoc.htm. The Widener
  Library site provides a checklist to evaluate an
  advocacy page. An advocacy page is usually
  a .org site maintained by an organization attempt-
  ing to influence public opinion.
Website Registration Check Sites
www.easywhois.com and www.netsol.com/
  cgi-bin/whois/whois. These Web search tools can
  check a website's registration, administrative and
  technical contacts, and when the site was updated.

1

Figure AppB.7 (cont.)

Web Wise by Who Is-ing!

AlltheWeb, AltaVista, and Google Search Engines
www.alltheweb, www.altavista.com, and www.google.com. The search engines support title field searching and link checking.

Learning Objectives

The student will be able to:
• evaluate website content for reliability, validity, accuracy, authority, and point of view and bias. Specifically they will evaluate a website resource for its:
  1. Content – Recognize that the www.martin lutherking.org site is biased and attempts to deceive and to manipulate the reader with the site's biased content.
  2. Source – Determine by performing a "Who Is" check that the instructional personnel or students will determine that the developers of the extremist website Stormfront.org are the source of the content on the www.martin lutherking.org site.
  3. Quality — Demonstrate an understanding that the content of the www.martinlutherking.org site presents a one-sided view and expresses opinions rather than facts.

Instructional personnel and students will be able to:
• use the World Wide Web search engines as tools to aid in research. Specifically, instructional personnel and students will be able to conduct: Title searches and Link searches
(This lesson addresses Va. SOL Computer/Technology 12.2, 12.3, 12.4; and English Research 9.8, 10.10, 11.9, 12.8)

Materials

Handouts:
• One copy of the "Bring the Dream to Life" flyer available at: www.martinlutherking.org/flyer.html
• One copy of the "Widener University Wolfgram Memorial Library Advocacy Web Page" evaluation criteria available at: www2.widener.edu/ Wolfgram-Memorial-Library/webevaluation/ advoc.htm

Teacher Preparations

• Ensure all computers are connected to the Internet and that either the Netscape Navigator or Microsoft Internet Explorer browser is open
• Preview, bookmark, and print copies of the:
  a. Widener University Wolfgram Memorial Library Advocacy Web Page evaluation criteria published at www2.widener.edu/Wolf-gram-Memorial-Library/webevaluation/advoc.htm
  b. The Martin Luther King Jr. flyer published at www.martinlutherking.org/flyer.html
• Preview the content categories on www. martinlutherking.org/flyer.html; develop a detailed familiarity with the content of the following link *Truth About King: What He Fought and Fought For*
• Practice the following searches:
  a. Title searches using the advanced search options in AlltheWeb, AltaVista, and Google's basic search option. (see attached)
  b. Link check using AltaVista's advanced search option. (see attached)
  c. Practice a "Who Is" Check of www.martin lutherking.org using either www.easywhois.com or www.netsol.com/cgi-bin/whois/whois noting who registered the site and that is kept updated. (see attached)

Introductory Activity

1. Handout the "Bring the Dream to Life" flyer to the instructional personnel or students.

2. Ask the instructional personnel or students:
a. Since the website has Martin Luther King in the address and the site is an organization (.org) website: Do you think that www.martinlutherking.org is the official website of the Martin Luther King organization?
b. Would they expect that the site seeks to promote the ideals of Dr. Martin Luther King, Jr.?

3. Assign three- or four-person teams of instructional personnel or students to collaboratively brainstorm and develop a list of subject areas they would expect to find on the website.

2

Figure AppB.7 (cont.)

Web Wise by Who Is-ing!

4. Direct the teams to discuss the content lists that they developed.

Focus For Media Interaction

Focus the instructional personnel's and students' attention to the necessity of evaluating website content. Explain that, unlike the traditional "gatekeeper" filtering of editors and peer reviewing, there is no "gatekeeper" on the Web—anyone can publish a Web page! Explain to the instructional personnel or students that they will compare their content lists with the subject categories on the www.martin lutherking.org website and that they will evaluate the website's content by using the evaluation criteria of: authority, accuracy, objectivity, currency and coverage.

Learning Activities

1. Direct the instructional personnel or students to connect to the Web page www.martinlutherking.org/flyer.html

2. Compare the list of subject areas developed by the instructional personnel or students with the subject areas on www.martinlutherking.org/flyer.html.

3. Ask the instructional personnel or students:
a. Are the subject areas on the Web page what you expected to find on a website dealing with Dr. Martin Luther King?
b. Is there any reason to expect that, after reviewing the section titles, the content would not be favorable toward Dr. Martin Luther King and his ideals?

4. Direct the instructional personnel or students to connect to the link titled: Truth About King: What He Fought and Fought For.

5. Ask the instructional personnel or students:
a. What is the title of the article?
b. Are you surprised with the article's title?

6. Direct the instructional personnel or students to read the first paragraph beginning with, "WHEN

THE COMMUNISTS TOOK OVER a country…" and the first paragraph of the section titled, "Communists Beliefs and Connections."

7. Ask the instructional personnel or students:
a. Is the information biased?
b. How would they characterize the website?

8. Ask the instructional personnel or students:
a. How many results do they normally review when searching the Web?
b. Do they think that the website would be located in the first ten results by a search engine?

9. Illustrate and guide the instructional personnel or students as they perform the title field searches in AlltheWeb, AltaVista and Google and note which number of the result the www.martinlutherking.org website is in each search engine; for example, result 6 of 100.

10. Have the instructional personnel review the description of returns from the three search engines.
a. Ask the students: Would you look at the returns from AlltheWeb and Google if those search engines described the site as, "Attacking Dr. King as a corrupt communist, under the control of a Marxist Jewish conspiracy?"
b. Focus the instructional personnel's or student's attention on the value of the Who Is in determining

11. Illustrate and guide the instructional personnel or students as they perform a "Who Is" check of the www.martinlutherking.org using either www.easy whois.com or www.netsol.com/cgi-bin/whois/whois.

12. Ask them: What organization is responsible for the www.martinlutherking.org website by finding, "Name Server: ISERVER.STORMFRONT.ORG" in the search results.

13. Direct the instructional personnel or students to connect to and to review the content of and to determine the orientation of www.stormfront.org.

14. Direct the instructional personnel or students to connect to the "Kids Page" link. Ask them:
a. Can you find the hyperlink to www.martin lutherking.org on the "Kids Page" link?

3

Figure AppB.7 (cont.)

Web Wise by Who Is-ing!

15. Ask the instructional personnel or students to summarize the process of Web resource evaluation and "Who Is" checking and how the two websites, www.martinlutherking.org and www.stormfront.org are related.

Culminating Activities

Have instructional personnel or students demonstrate their information literacy proficiency by:
1. Evaluating the content on the official website of the estate of Martin Luther King, Jr., www.mlkon line.com, that provides copyrighted writings, documents, and recordings of Martin Luther King, Jr.

2. Comparing and contrasting the quality of the information on the www.martinlutherking.org and the www.mlkonline.com sites.

3. Selecting the site that provides an unbiased or unprejuiced appraisal of the contributions of Dr. Martin Luther King.

Assessment

Inform the instructional personnel or students that they are researching photographic evidence of the Holocaust. Evaluate their ability to critically evaluate the content of the website, www.air-photo.com, using the criteria and answering the questions below.
Authority:
- What organization created the page?
- Does the quality of the photos influence your evaluation of the site?

Accuracy:
- Does the title of the page match their expectation of the site's content?
- Is the purpose of the page indicated on the home page?
- Does the information contradict something you found somewhere else?

Objectivity:
- Is the information true?
- Does the information appear biased?
- Is the information useful for your research project?

Currency:
- Are there dates on the page to indicate when the page was last revised?
- Does that matter?

Coverage:
- Does the website clearly address the topics that you expected?
- Is the point of view of the organization clearly presented with supporting arguments?

Community Connections

Have instructional personnel or students perform a link check to www.martinlutherking.org using the AltaVista advanced search option. Determine if there are K-12 websites that are linked to the site. Determine whether the school is using the site for Web resource evaluation or failed to review the content on the site. If the K-12 sites are not using the site for Web resource evaluation, have the students e-mail the site's Webmaster, recommend that the content www.martinlutherking.org be evaluated and the link removed from the school's website.

Cross-Curricular Extensions

Technology: Have students evaluate the quality and accuracy of the information on the following websites using the evaluation criteria described in the "Checklist for an Advocacy Web Page."
www2.widener.edu/Wolfgram-Memorial-Library/webevaluation/advoc.htm
a. GENOCHOICE - Create Your Own Genetically Healthy Child Online! www.genochoice.com/
b. DreamTech International. www.d-b.net/dti/
c. Welcome to the Raelian Revolution. www.rael.org/

Research: Have instructional personnel or students conduct research on Kevin Alfred Strom and David Duke, the author of two sections of the www.mar tinlutherking.org website, to determine their beliefs on civil rights.

Figure AppB.7 (cont.)

About the Author

Paul Barron
Paul Barron is the Technology Director for the
Rockbridge County Schools in Lexington, Virginia.
After retiring from the Marine Corps he earned a
Masters Degree in Library and Information Science
from the University of Texas at Austin. He has provided staff development training on the use of the
Web for research at workshops for school systems
in the Shenandoah Valley and the New River Valley
and at conferences sponsored by the Shenandoah
Valley Technology Consortium, the Virginia Department of Education, the Virginia Electronic Media
Association, the Virginia Library Association, and
the Virginia Society for Technology Educators. He
is also an adjunct faculty member at the Virginia
Military Institute and Dabney S. Lancaster Community College.

March 2003

A publication of the 2002-03 NTTI—Virginia

5

Figure AppB.7 (cont.)

Web Wise by Who Is-ing!

PRACTICE TITLE FIELD SEARCHES
AlltheWeb Title Search (Use the Advanced Search Option)

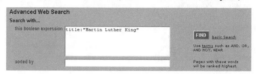

AltaVista Title Search (Use the Advanced Search Option)

Advanced Web Search
Search with...
this boolean expression   title:"Martin Luther King"

FIND   Basic Search
Use terms such as AND, OR, AND NOT, NEAR

sorted by   Pages with these words will be ranked highest.

Google Title Search (Use the Basic Search Option)

| Web | Images | Groups | Directory | News-New! |

intitle:"Martin Luther King"

Google Search   I'm Feeling Lucky

· Advanced Search
· Preferences
· Language Tools

PRACTICE LINK CHECKS
AltaVista Link Check for K-12 Web Sites (Use the Advanced Search Option)

Advanced Web Search
Search with...
this boolean expression   link:www.martinlutherking.org AND url:k12

FIND   Basic Search
Use terms such as AND, OR, AND NOT, NEAR

sorted by   Pages with these words will be ranked highest.

Practice a "Who Is" Check of www.martinlutherking.org using either www.easywhois.com or www.netsol.com/cgi-bin/whois/whois noting who registered the site and that it is kept updated.

Easily look up the whois record for any domain ... .COM, .NET, and .ORG domains, and most country-level Top Level Domains.

look up a domain

Domain name: www.martinlutherking.org

next ▶

Phil Bradley, U.K.-based Internet consultant, trainer, Web designer, and author

• Internet Tools for the Advanced Searcher (www.philb. com/adint.htm)

Phil's Web page is primarily text based, and it is full of information about search engines. The extracts shown here from a few years ago (Figure AppB.8) describe search engines and give a brief Google review; the section discussing intelligent agents is also shown.

Contrast Phil's basic design of an instructional Web page, which looks more like a presentation in a book, with that of Gary Price, shown later. Both use long Web pages with a variety of links. But Phil's is designed more for reading, while Gary takes the outline approach with long lists of links. In part, the design is based on the use of the Web page. Phil's can be used as a self-contained instructional tool, while Gary's is specifically designed to accompany his talks.

Figure AppB.8   Internet Tools for the Advanced Searcher (©2003 Copyright Phil Bradley, reproduced with permission)

Internet Tools for the Advanced Searcher

Contents:
Search engines
Virtual libraries
Intelligent Agents
More effective ways of searching
A list of useful search engines

Search Engines

What types of search engines are there?

The number of different types of search engines breaks down into several major types:

- Free text search engines
  - o   AltaVista
  - o   Google
  - o   Teoma
  - o   AlltheWeb
- Directory or Index based search engines
  - o   Yahoo!
- Multi or Meta search engines
  - o   Ixquick
  - o   eZ2www
  - o   Kartoo
- Natural Language search engines
  - o   Ask Jeeves
- Site or subject specific search engines
  - o   Electronic Telegraph archive
  - o   BT enquiries
  - o   Genealogical databases

How do search engines actually work?

Depends on the type of search engine. Some will employ robot or spider programs that wander around the Web, and when they find a new page or site will copy the data back to their home base and will include the information when they next update their index. Other search engines, such as the Directory-based services, rely on Web page authors visiting the engines and registering directly.

Those search engines that employ a ranking service will then also take into account a variety of things about the Web page that they have returned to the user at the completion of a search. Some of the things that will be considered are:

- Location of the word in the title element
- Location of the word in the major headings on a page
- Number of times the words are found
- Number of words found against the number of words asked for

Figure AppB.8 (cont.)

- Proximity of the terms to each other
- Terms in the URL
- Keyword density

Searching using Google

Basic search functionality - type in a number of keywords - generally up to about 4 or 5 to focus your search
Use '-' to exclude terms from your search by placing it immediately before the word you wish to exclude, such as Everton -Liverpool
Phrase search by using "..." to search for an exact phrase - up to 10 words in length, such as "Everton Football Club"
Exclude phrases by using the minus sign immediately before the phrase, such as - "Liverpool Football Club"

Advanced search functionality - options to run AND OR NOT and phrase searches.
Language options, which are reasonably full
File formats - varied, and better than other engines. These include Adobe, PowerPoint, Word, Spreadsheet
Date - limited and not impressive in comparison to AlltheWeb
Occurrences - specific places on the page. Most of these are automatically taken into consideration by relevance ranking, so are of limited use.
Domain - specific site, domain, country or combination of the last two
Similar pages - can be helpful to broaden out a search
Links - also broadens out a search

Multimedia - fine with images, but very limited with other multimedia. Better is AltaVista or AlltheWeb

Groups - the best (only!) resource for searching for newsgroup information

Directory - Yahoo! lookalike approach

- **News** - over 4,000 resources constantly checked and updated

Intelligent Agents

What are these things?

Intelligent agents can be defined as pieces of software that must conform to a certain number of points:

- They should be able to operate without direct intervention of human beings
- They should be able to exert some control over their actions
- They need to be able to interact with human beings via some sort of interface
- Agents will be able to exchange messages between each other and other interfaces
- They need to be aware of their environment and have to be able to respond to changes as they occur

Figure AppB.8 (cont.)

- They should be able to act without direct commands by taking the initiative

Early implementations of intelligent agents

The very first intelligent agents were, as you might guess, very basic indeed, and hardly deserved the term "intelligent." The one that most people recognise as the forerunner of what we have today is a program called Eliza at http://www-ai.ijs.si/eliza/eliza.html. "She" was designed to be a psychotherapist, and did little except echo back comments that you made to her. Although you can ask Eliza questions, she generally throws the question back to you, so the conversation is rather one-sided! However, since she was written in only just over 200 lines of code she is still quite impressive, and it's possible to sit and chat to her for several minutes before you fall asleep from boredom!
Another version is ALICE - An Artificial Linguistic Computer Entity at http://www.alicebot.org/, which I personally didn't find very effective, but which is still worth taking a look at.
Alternatively, have a chat with Brain!
All three of these are known as *Chatterbots* for obvious reasons.
If you don't like any of these, you can visit the Botspot Chatterbot page at http://www.botspot.com/search/s-chat.htm to find some others.

Intelligent agents which learn from your preferences

There are a variety of agents that will learn from your likes and dislikes and will then attempt to make suggestions based upon your preferences. There are several nice examples of these on the Internet at the moment, and in particular I liked:
Alexandria Digital Literature Library at http://www.alexlit.com/. This agent asks you to rate a number of books that you have read, and once you have input data rating a minimum of 40 titles it will be able to suggest other titles that it thinks you would probably enjoy reading. I tried the system out, and it seemed very top heavy with science fiction titles, but there is an option of choosing your own favourite authors and rating those as well. I was quite impressed with the results that were returned to me.
If you don't like this version, you may wish to explore the The Readers Robot, which can be found at http://www.tnrdlib.bc.ca/rr.html.
The Amazon bookshop at http://www.amazon.com/ has a facility which will update you every time books are added to its catalogue that match your own particular interests. It is pushing a point rather a lot to call it an "intelligent agent," since it is very basic, but having said that, it is a useful feature of their Web site.

John Ferguson, reference librarian, retired, Richland College Library, Dallas

- Searching the Invisible Web (www.rlc.dcccd.edu/lrc/ppt/ invisible.ppt)

Figure AppB.9 is an outline version of a PowerPoint presentation that John used when teaching a subject-specific, 90-minute workshop at Richland College Library. Unfortunately, the outline version doesn't show the colorful background, the animated text entry, and the colored words that John incorporated.

This presentation is a fairly standard use of PowerPoint. But in terms of the instructional design, note the beginning quotation from one of the founding fathers of the Internet. It grabs the attention of the audience and makes a strong point about the importance of the content to be covered. A horizontal line indicates where each slide ends.

Figure AppB.9 Searching the Invisible Web (©2002 Copyright John Ferguson, reproduced with permission)

"If people believe that they have searched the entire Internet when they run a search on a search engine, they are sadly mistaken—they are only seeing a subset of what is available."

Vint Cerf, *Financial Times*, 12/5/01

Searching the Invisible Web
Richland College Library

April 2, 2002

Your Presenter:
John Ferguson

What is the Invisible Web?

· "Stuff" that search engine crawlers (spiders) cannot—or **will not**— add to their databases

· Two to 50 times larger than the visible Web

· Invisible Web resources often much higher quality than the visible Web

Why the Invisible Web?

· Non-HTML file formats (AVI, MOV, MPEG, PDF, Flash, Office files, streaming media)

· Most real-time data (stock quotes, weather, airline flight info, etc.)

· Depth-of-crawl and page-size restrictions

· Dynamically generated pages
(cgi, Javascript, asp, or most pages with "?" in the URL)

· Web accessible databases that have their own "local" search engines

· Site requires registration before use or is fee-based

Figure AppB.9 (cont.)

- Information contained in Javascript pop-up windows or in frames

- Lag time in crawling and refreshing search engine databases

- Different search engines crawl and index pages differently—no two are alike

---

So How Can I Find What's on the Invisible Web?

- SearchAbility (metasite)
- Direct Search
- Virtual Acquisition Shelf and News Desk
- Invisible Web.com
- Invisible-web.net
- Librarians' Index to the Internet
- InfoMine

Surface Web, Deep Web, Invisible Web, Opaque Web, Dark Web: What Are the Differences?

- The Surface Web refers to Internet resources indexed by general search engines.
- The Deep Web refers to everything else.
- The Invisible Web refers to Internet resources accessible only by specialized search tools.

- The Opaque Web refers to Internet resources that are unlinked.
- The Dark Web refers to Internet resources that are off limits (except to the privileged few).

Alice Fulbright, reference librarian, Richland College Library, Dallas

- How to Download Text from the Web (www.rlc.dcccd.edu/lrc/ pdfs/download.pdf)

Figure AppB.10 shows one of the handouts that Alice and her colleagues at the Richland College Library have made available online in PDF format. It is an excellent example of a very function-specific instructional aid. While not part of searching, download-ing information from the Web is certainly an activity many searchers will want to do at some point.

This kind of handout can be a very useful adjunct to a Web searching session. The instructor can focus the session on the pri-mary instructional points, then provide additional how-to resources, like this one.

By making a handout like this one available on the Web, the trainer could even cover the concept briefly in a classroom setting, then refer the students to the handout for more details.

While this handout does not have the look and feel of a profes-sionally designed graphic masterpiece, it presents important information clearly and includes screen shots at appropriate points. In addition to how-to information, it includes good advice, such as "Get the URL (Web address)—the URL will not automati-cally be saved on the disk." Such added advice makes handouts even more valuable to the users.

Figure AppB.10 How to Download Text from the Web (©2003 Copyright Richland College Library, reproduced with permission)

How to Download Text From the Web
(Note: The procedure for downloading text from DCCCD **subscription databases** may differ from these instructions.)

Follow These Instructions Carefully
Use a 3.5 inch DOS *formatted* disk.   Make sure your disk is not locked or write protected.

Your disk should look like this one:
closed write protect hole ⇒      ⇐ open write protect hole

Insert formatted disk into the **A** drive of the computer.

To Download a Text Document:

1. When the document you wish to download is visible on your monitor, click once with the left mouse button on the FILE menu in the upper left corner of your screen and highlight *"Save As."* The *"Save Web Page"* box will appear.

2. In the *"Save in"* box:
    *   This should show that the file will be saved to the A Drive. Do not worry, if it says something else, because the next step will take care of this problem.

If you cannot change this box to the A Drive,   ⇒

typing **"a:"** here will force the file to go to the A Drive. ⇒

3. In the *"File name"* box:
    *   Click in the left end of the box and type **"a:"** so that the file will be saved to the disk in the A drive.
    *   Next, type a name for your file. (If a file name already appears, you may choose to use it.)
    *   *Now, add the file name extension **.txt** at the end of the file name (e.g., **a:File Name1.txt**).

4. *In the *"Save as type"* box:
    *   Click on the down pointer at the end of the box and **change the file type** from "**Web Page, complete (*.htm, *.html)**" to "**Text File (*.txt).**"

5. Click on the *"Save"* button.

6. **Get the URL** (web address) - **the URL will not automatically be saved on the disk.**
    *   If you are downloading from the web, copy the URL so you can write a proper MLA citation for your works cited page.
    *   If you are downloading from a subscription database, ask a librarian for a handout that will show you how to cite your source with the correct URL.

NOTE: If you save a file as a **.html** file type, you must be sure that whatever other computer you will be using has a browser (*Internet Explorer* or *Netscape*) that can open and read .html files. **The computer lab in Del Rio (D257) at Richland College will print only .txt files for students. They will not print .html files.**

Figure AppB.10 (cont.)

How to Download Pictures or Graphics From the Web

(Note: The procedure for downloading pictures or graphics from DCCCD **subscription databases**
may differ from these instructions.)

To Download a Picture or Graphic:

1. Place your mouse pointer in the center of the picture or graphic that you wish to download, and
    click once with the **RIGHT** mouse button.
2. Highlight *"Save Picture As"* and click.
    The *"Save Picture"* box will appear:
3. In the *"Save in"* box:
    *   This should show that the file will be saved to the A Drive. Do not worry, if it says some-
        thing else, because the next step will take care of this problem.

If you cannot change this
box to the A Drive,   ⇒

typing "**a:**" here will force
the file to go to the A Drive. ⇒

4. In the *"File name"* box:
    *   Click in the left end of the box and type "**a:**" so that the file will be saved to the disk in the A
        drive.
    *   Next, type a name for your file. (If a file name already appears, you may choose to use it.)
    *   Now, add the file name extension **.gif**, **.bmp**, or **.jpg** at the end of the file name. Use the
        same file type that appears in the lower box. (e.g., **a:Graphic1.gif**)
5. In the *"Save as type"* boxes:
    *   Use whatever file type appears. It will not need to be changed.
6. Now click on the *"Save"* button.
7. **Get the URL** (web address) - the **URL will <u>not</u> automatically be saved on the disk.**
    *   If you are downloading <u>from the web</u>, copy the URL so you can write a proper MLA citation
        for your works cited page.
    *   If you are downloading <u>from a subscription database</u>, ask a librarian for a handout that will
        show you how to cite your source with the correct URL.

**Note: The computer lab in Del Rio (D257) at Richland College will print only .txt files for
students. They will not print graphics or pictures.**

⇒ Pictures and graphics can be found on the web at *Google Images* at <u>http://www.google.com/imghp</u>.
⇒ Pictures and graphics can also be found in the following DCCCD Online Subscription Databases:
   Academic Search Premier, Master File Premier, and *Student Resource Center.*

Ran Hock, Online Strategies
- Using the Web Effectively for Research
- The Internet for the Pharmaceutical Researcher

Ran is known for his extensive handouts. Workbooks might be a more appropriate label since they often are 50 or more pages long. Figures AppB.11 and AppB.12 show the table of contents for two of his "workbooks," giving a sense of the incredible extent and scope of Ran's handouts.

The first handout excerpt, Using the Web Effectively for Research (Figure AppB.13), is from a presentation Ran gave to a government agency in 2001. The second, The Internet for the Pharmaceutical Researcher presentation (Figure AppB.14), was made later in 2002. Note the difference in what search engines were covered and also how the content differed depending on the audience.

The metasites section from Using the Web Effectively for Research (Figure AppB.13) includes title, URL, a description, and a screen shot of each of the sites covered. The screen shots provide a visual reminder of the demonstration that attendees saw during the session.

In the extract from The Internet for the Pharmaceutical Researcher (Figure AppB.14), note how Ran uses arrows to point to almost every link on the Google search page. Each arrow is tied to a number with an explanation of the capabilities of that link or function. Few people know anything about the many options Google and other search engines provide. Ran's approach helps users see how much is available.

Figure AppB.11   Using the Web Effectively for Research—Table of Contents
(©2003 Copyright Ran Hock, reproduced with permission)

Using the Web Effectively for Research

Table of Contents

Figure AppB.12 The Internet for the Pharmaceutical Researcher—Table of Contents (©2003 Copyright Ran Hock, reproduced with permission)

The Internet for the Pharmaceutical Researcher

Table of Contents

Figure AppB.13　Using the Web Effectively for Research—Excerpt (©2003 Copyright Ran Hock, reproduced with permission)

The Web Reference Shelf

Metasites for General Reference

Internet Public Library Reference Ready Reference – *www.ipl.org/ref/RR/*

From the School of Information, University of Michigan

A great collection of ready reference links, including almanacs, biographies, census data, dictionaries, encyclopedias, etc.

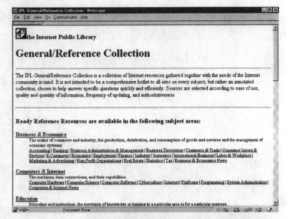

Research-It!
www.itools.com/research-it/research-it.html

Contains biographical dictionary, birthdays of famous people, Bible (several translations), Bartlett's, links to maps, CIA Factbook, etc.

Arranged by the following collections of tools:
LANGUAGE - Dictionaries, (pronouncing dictionary, rhyming dictionary, French, Spanish, Japanese, German and Italian dictionaries, etc.), thesaurus, translator, etc.
LIBRARY - Biographical dictionary, Bible, quotations
GEOGRAPHICAL - Maps telephone numbers, etc.
FINANCIAL - Currency converter, stock quotes, ticker symbol lookup
SHIPPING – ZIP Codes, FedEx and UPS package tacking
INTERNET – Link to Liszt newsgroup/listserv directory

Figure AppB.13 (cont.)

Using the Web Effectively for Research   37

Virtual Reference Desk
thorplus.lib.purdue.edu/reference

Not fancy, but a straightforward,
useful collection of ready
reference tools

From Purdue University Libraries

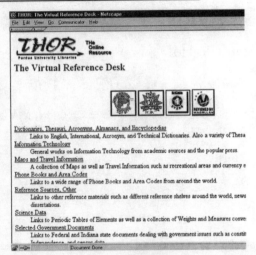

Yahoo! Reference
www.yahoo.com/Reference

A very extensive collection,
though not particularly
selective. 38 categories,
including some fairly unique,
such as flags, weights and
measurements, and calendars.

Remember that Yahoo! is
searchable within a category,
i.e., you can search within the
Reference category for specific
topics such as "flags."

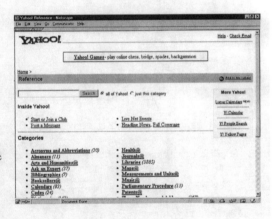

**Figure AppB.14   The Internet for the Pharmaceutical Researcher—Excerpt
(©2003 Copyright Ran Hock, reproduced with permission)**

The Internet for the Pharmaceutical Researcher   10

Search Engines

Remember the following about Web search engines:

If you want to be exhaustive (and/or very precise), **search more than one**. Each will often find things the others miss.

The **largest**:

AltaVista	altavista.com
Google	google.com
AlltheWeb	alltheweb.com
WiseNut	wisenut.com

Most major search engines provide an **Advanced Search page** that provides considerable additional search power, including field searching (title, etc.) and other capabilities.

All of the major search engines provide substantial **Boolean** capabilities allowing for a very precise, yet exhaustive search.

Use the following to **refine** your search:

Additional terms (all major search engines automatically "AND" all terms)

Narrow to pages with your words in the title

Search for phrases where appropriate, by using quotation marks

Use Boolean

See **Appendix I** for details.

We will look at Google in some detail.

For detail on the Web's second most powerful search engine, AlltheWeb, please see Appendix II.

Figure AppB.14 (cont.)

The Internet for the Pharmaceutical Researcher	11

Google
www.google.com

Overview

Google is the largest of the Web search engines and ranks records based on their popularity, i.e., the degree to which other pages refer to a page. A measure of "importance" is assigned to a page dependent upon that measure of "popularity." The "importance" of a page is independent of your query. Retrieval options have been greatly enhanced in the last year or so. Google retrieves records based on an ANDing of all terms and ranks the output by popularity and the proximity of your search terms within the record. Google's output is unique in that it allows you to go to the page as it is currently on the Web, or to go to a "cached" copy that Google stored when it retrieved the page. Google is at present also the best source for **newsgroup** searching (with USENET file back 20 years.), for **images**, and for **PDF files**. Google contains about 2 billion Web pages.

Strengths 👍	Weaknesses 👎
Its "popularity" approach results in very good ranking. "Cached" option for finding slightly earlier versions of a page, etc. **Largest** database Strong **language** searching capability **Covers newsgroups** **Results include PDF files** **Best image search available** Lots of gems on results pages (**translations**, etc.)	No truncation No NEAR operator

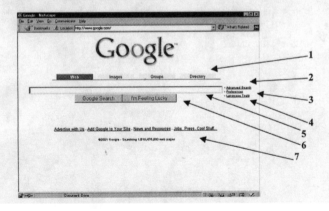

Figure AppB.14 (cont.)

On Google's home page you'll find:

1. **Links to special searches:**
   Web - the default
   Images - Lead to the largest image search database available on the Web
   Groups - Search of 650 million Usenet postings back to 1995!
   Directory - Link to Google's implementation of Open Directory

2. Link to **Advanced Search**

3. **Language and Display Preferences -**
   - Language search and interface preference
   - # of results per page
   - Option to have results opened in new window
   - Safe Search option (adult content filter)

4. **Language Tools** provides:
   - A search box to limit retrieval to a specific language or country-of-origin
   - A box for translating a specific Web page between English and five languages (French, German, Italian, Spanish, Portuguese, or Russian) or between French and German
   - Choice of having the Google interface in any one of over 60 languages
   - Links to the Google country-specific versions for 23 countries

5. **Query box** - Enter one or more words. Minus and OR can be used. Google will ignore small, very common words unless you insert a plus sign in front of them. Google will ignore quotation marks.

6. **"I'm feeling lucky"** - Will automatically take you to the page that Google would have listed first in your results. If you're really lucky, it works. Mostly a gimmick.

7. Various **special options**

Figure AppB.14 (cont.)

The Internet for the Pharmaceutical Researcher   13

Advanced Search

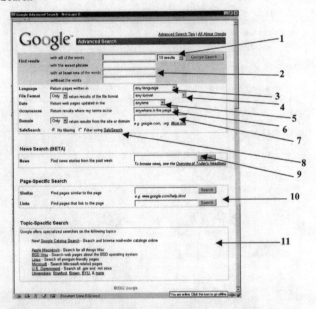

1. Choice of 10, 20, 30, 50 or 100 results per page
2. Boxes to perform simple Boolean combinations
3. Choice of search in 35 languages
4. File Format (PDF, xls, doc, ps. ppt. rf)
5. Date restriction (anytime, last 3 months, Last 6 months, last year)
6. Window to limit retrieval to title or URL fields
7. Box for limiting to (or excluding) a particular domain or URL
8. Adult content filter option
9. News search
10. Page-specific search
    for pages that are *similar* to a particular page, Enter URL
    for pages that link *to* a particular page, Enter URL
11. Topic-specific search
    Catalog Search, Apple Macintosh, BSD Unix, Linux, U.S. Government,
    Universities (selected)

Figure AppB.14 (cont.)

The Internet for the Pharmaceutical Researcher   18

Language Tools Page

Provides another place where you can search by language and also here, by country. Provides translations (Systran) between various combinations of: English, German, French, Italian, Portuguese, Spanish.

Catalog Search

This is accessible from either the bottom of the Advanced Search page or at catalogs.google.com. The main page contains a subject directory and also a search capability. There is also an Advanced Catalog Search.

Google Toolbar

Go to the "All About Google" link on the home page to find out about this.

This is a free downloadable feature that allows you to have the Google search box and additional features as a toolbar on Internet Explorer.

It provides:
Google **Search**: The search box can always appear on your browser screen.
Search Site: To search only the pages of the site currently displayed
PageRank: See Google's ranking of the current page.
Page Info: Get more information about a page, similar pages, and pages that link to a page. You also get a cached snapshot.
Highlight: Will highlight your search terms (each word in a different color.)
Word Find: To find search terms wherever they appear on the page.

It can be customized to include most of the features on the regular Google home page (and in several languages.)

Most Important Things to Know About Google

It has the **largest** Web database.
It's **ranking** is excellent.
Use it when you want to search **newsgroups**. (Click "Google Groups" on its home page.)
It has the largest **image** database on the Web. (Use the Advanced Search page.)
It automatically includes **PDF files** as well as Web pages in results.
To search **titles**, use the "Occurrences" window on the Advanced page.
Terms are automatically ANDed. To OR terms, put an OR between the terms.

Jeff Humphrey, Internet training specialist, INCOLSA, Indiana's statewide library network

- Web Resources: Ready Reference Sites (www.incolsa.net/hand outs/int004.htm)

Jeff's Web page is designed to function as an online companion to one of the workshops he offered. The design of the site is basic, a common trait of Web pages designed to accompany training sessions. By avoiding superfluous graphics and extra elements, Jeff communicates the information directly and easily.

After the INCOLSA graphic to brand the page, the design provides one long list of a wide variety of ready reference sources (Figure AppB.15). This kind of instructional material is a great addition to Web searching sessions. It can be used to emphasize specific information-rich resources that provide answers to specific questions more quickly than a search engine can.

Since this is designed as a Web page, the URLs do not need to be displayed. Jeff could have simply linked the title to the URL, shortening the page. But there are advantages to both listing the URLs and creating links, as Jeff has done. First of all, the file can double as a print handout. In addition, with the URLs displayed clearly, it is easier to talk about the preliminary evaluation steps you should take before visiting a resource. A careful look at a URL may tell much about the organization that is providing the information. For example, the United States Gazetteer obviously comes from the Census Bureau since its URL begins www.census.gov, but SoYouWanna comes from an unknown .com site.

Figure AppB.15   Web Resources: Ready Reference Sites (©2000–2003
Copyright INCOLSA, reproduced with permission)

Web Resources: Ready Reference Sites INT 004

This is an online companion for one of our Internet searching workshops. Sites covered in the workshop will change from time to time depending on their availability.

General Sites

Information Please Almanac
http://www.infoplease.com/

Infoplease.com is the online version of the all-purpose print Information Please Almanac. This site is both browseable and searchable. Items are grouped into categories, and separate encyclopedia, dictionary, and biography search mechanisms are available. The front page includes a daily almanac and some breaking news stories.

SoYouWanna
http://www.soyouwanna.com/

SoYouWanna.com "teaches you how to do all the things nobody taught you in school."

OneLook Dictionaries
http://www.onelook.com/

Need to look up the meaning of a word, but not sure where to start? Try Onelook. Onelook has access to over 900 dictionaries, both general and subject specific. If your search returns no results, Onelook gives links to other suggested sites.

Perpetual Calendar
http://www.wiskit.com/calendar.html

Java based version of a traditional perpetual calendar. Type in a month and year, and the Sunday to Saturday style calendar appears.

Date and Time Conversion
http://www.bsdi.com/date

Choose a country and the current date and time for that area appears at the top of the page. Countries are grouped by region.

Standard Industrial Classification Code
http://www.osha-slc.gov/oshstats/sicser.html

Figure AppB.15 (cont.)

Most versatile SIC lookup site I have been able to locate. You can search by keyword to identify a four digit SIC code, or enter a code for detailed description of the items that fall into a specific category.

Acronym Finder
http://www.acronymfinder.com/

Acronym Finder is a searchable database of over 295,000 acronyms. The search box is squeezed into the top right corner of the screen. Type in your acronym and results are returned ASAP.

Nom De Guerre
http://go.to/realnames

Fancy way to say pseudonym finder. Nom de Guerre does not include a keyword search, so you are limited to browsing a list by clicking the first letter of the person's last name (or only name for those ultra-celebrities.)

Baby Names
http://babynamer.com/

Babynamer.com has a database of over 20,000 names and meanings. First choose boy or girl, then type in a name or browse through one of four categories: Reviewers, Popularity, Notables, or Meaning.

United States Gazetteer
http://www.census.gov/cgi-bin/gazetteer

The Census Bureau has created a site where you can type in the possible name of a county, city, or town and locate any area with that name. The gazetteer automatically stems all entries (for example Jeff brings up Jefferson, Jeffersonville, etc.)

Household Helpers

Better Homes and Gardens Home Improvement Encyclopedia
http://www.bhg.com/bhg/category.jhtml?catref=cat10002

Does somebody need help with a project, but all of your Time-Life books are checked out? Better Homes and Gardens has excerpts from their Step-by-Step guides available online. Projects are broken into 5 categories, and all entries include pictures.

Repair Clinic
http://www.repairclinic.com/

This is intended as an electronic parts store, but Repair Clinic has a troubleshooting section covering 15 household appliances. Also includes how it works and preventive maintenance tips.

Fabric Stain Removal Guide
http://www.chemistry.co.nz/stain_frame.htm

Figure AppB.15 (cont.)

Ordinary cleaning not quite getting the job done? Consult the Fabric Stain Removal Guide for the proper remedy. Treatments are listed by stain source, and usually require everyday household items.

Carpet Stain Removal Guide
http://www.rainbowintl.com/corporate/spot.asp

Rainbow International has put together this nice site for step-by-step carpet spot and stain removal. Remedies are listed by source of the stain, and read the general instructions at the top of the page before using the rest of the guide.

Money Matters

Full Universal Currency Converter
http://www.xe.net/ucc/full.shtml

A very easy to use currency converter, type in the total units, then pick your variables from the two lists.

Amortization Calculator
http://list.realestate.yahoo.com/realestate/calculators/amortization.html

Easier to use than a print version. Type in your lending amount, the length and term of the loan, the rate, and start date, and get a nice table showing the payment amount and a principle and interest breakdown.

Big Charts Historical Stock Quotes
http://www.bigcharts.com/historical/

I am often asked, "Do you know a place on the Internet that gives historical stock quotes?" Finally, I can say yes. Other places give the quotes, but Big Charts has a much easier to use interface. Type in the symbol, type in the day, and click look up.

Sperling's Best Places
http://www.bestplaces.net

"In 1985, Bert Sperling developed a software program named "Places U.S.A." which allowed people to enter their personal preferences to find their own best place. BestPlaces.net is a natural extension of our work over the last fifteen years regarding demographics, preferences, and the selection of "Best Places" to live, work, or retire."

Entertainment

Internet Movie Database
http://www.imdb.com/

The Internet Movie Database is a fun resource. Type in the name of a film, television show, actor, actress, etc. and find out all kinds of information. Includes production notes and trivia, too.

Figure AppB.15 (cont.)

All Music Guide
http://www.allmusic.com/

The All Music Guide is a very extensive guide to all music genres. You can search for artists, songs, albums, and labels.

Medical

American Medical Association Online Doctor Finder
http://www.ama-assn.org/aps/amahg.htm

The AMA created this online database listing "virtually every licensed physician in the United States and its possessions. Searchable by physician name or specialty, the only drawback is that you must enter a state to execute a search.

Mayo Clinic First Aid & Self Care Guide
http://www.mayoclinic.com/findinformation/firstaidandselfcare

"MayoClinic.com's guide to First-Aid and Self-Care offers practical and easy-to-use information on everything from how to treat a sunburn or recognize the signs of a heart attack to ways to avoid back injuries or deal with a range of aches and pains."

Politics and Government

Political Parties, Interest Groups, and Other Special Movements
http://www.psr.keele.ac.uk/parties.htm

Collection of links to web sites for political parties and interest groups around the world.

United States Historical Documents
http://www.law.ou.edu/hist/

Eclectic mix of official documents and transcripts of famous speeches assembled by the University of Oklahoma Law Center. Includes treaties and Presidential inaugural addresses.

Stateline.org
http://www.stateline.org/

Stateline.org is intended as a source for state level news, but it includes background information and data for all 50 states.

Science and Math

Periodic Table of Elements
http://www.webelements.com/

Figure AppB.15 (cont.)

Click the element's square on the main page, and get its basic chemical properties and a brief description.

Unit Conversions
http://www.onlineconversion.com/

Comprehensive site that helps to convert various units of measure.

Weather Underground Historical Weather Information
http://www.wunderground.com/

Weather Underground gives you current weather conditions, but it also has historical weather information. You need to find the city first, then look for the Historical Conditions box in the middle of the page.

Diane Kovacs, Kovacs Consulting

- Beyond Boolean: Effective Web Reference Strategies
- Analyze the Reference Question, Conduct a Good Reference Interview, and Develop a Search Strategy

Diane offers a variety of Web-based instruction and Web-supported classes. These examples of her instructional material come from her Beyond Boolean self-paced workshop. More information about her currently offered workshops is available at kovacs.com/training.html.

Diane's self-paced workshops include lectures, discussions, reviews, and Web-based readings and activities. She estimates 8 hours for completing the Beyond Boolean workshop. The first screen shot (Figure AppB.16) is from an online "overhead," which is the second of 16 for her course. Note the buttons at the bottom of the screen. The Next and Back navigation buttons move through the overheads, and Agenda goes back to the main page. This particular slide also has a Lecture link that brings up a lengthier description of the topic and may also include discussion questions. The Review button provides additional information.

After students go through the Lectures and Discussions pages, this workshop has four Web-based activities. The first one, "Analyze the Reference Question, Conduct a Good Reference Interview, and Develop a Search Strategy," is reproduced in Figure AppB.17. Note that Diane's online course provides a form so that a student's answers on the worksheet can be e-mailed to Diane for instructor feedback.

Figure AppB.16   Beyond Boolean: Effective Web Reference Strategies (©2002–2003 Copyright Diane K. Kovacs, reproduced with permission)

Use the Right Reference Tool?

Web Search Engines are the equivalent (roughly) of Online Catalogs. Generally it is best to use them to locate resources that contain needed information.

A given Web Search Engine may or may not search Subject Reference Sources that have Web-based interfaces. Most search only published Web pages and not the database content that may be stored 'behind' a Web-based interface. This database content has been referred to variously as:

- The "Deep" Web or "Deep Content"
- The "Invisible" Web
- Web-based Subject Reference Sources (free and fee)

©2002-2003 Diane K. Kovacs
Revised Sept. 1, 2003

Back   Lecture   Review   Agenda   Next

Overhead 2 of 16

**Figure AppB.17   Analyze the Reference Question, Conduct a Good Reference
Interview, and Develop a Search Strategy (©2002–2003
Copyright Diane K. Kovacs, reproduced with permission)**

**Activity 1.   Analyze the Reference Question, Conduct a Good Reference
Interview, and Develop A Search Strategy**

Overview of this Activity

Choose at least one of the reference questions from the list provided on the page
<u>Reference Questions to Use in Comparing and Evaluating Web Subject
Reference Sources, Directories/Electronic Libraries, and Web Search Engines</u>
or
Write down a question or questions of your own, and begin analyzing the
reference question, conduct a good reference interview* and develop a search
strategy.

Please type your name and e-mail address if you would like instructor feedback.

STEP 1.	Analyze the Reference Question: What question(s) are you working with?
	Answer the following questions for each reference question you choose from the list or use from your own experiences. 1. Given the questions you choose - what more do you need to know from the patron? 2. What type of information does the patron need? Known Item or General Information? 3. What type of question was asked? Direction, Ready Reference, Specific-Search, or Research? 4. What questions do you need to/will you ask of the patron in order to clarify the reference question and the exact information needed? 5. Would you recommend a print or other electronic format source to answer this question (rather than a Web source)? Why? Why not?
STEP 2.	Conduct a Good Reference Interview - Optional Role-Play Activity - Below

Figure AppB.17 (cont.)

STEP 3.	Develop a Search Strategy: What subject area does this question generally fall into? Do you/Did you know of a Web Subject Database that will answer the question? What Web Subject Database will you use first? Why?
STEP 4.	Write down the keywords and Boolean operators you would use if searching these questions in a general Web search engine (CD-ROM or fee-based database or library catalog). In a subsequent activity you will compare your results using Web Subject Reference Sources, and Web Directories or Electronic Libraries with your results using a Web search engine. You will need the keyword and Boolean search strategies for these questions in Activity 4.

OPTIONAL ROLE-PLAY ACTIVITY	Role-Play and Observe: You are the reference person. You will be observing your own responses and actions. You may work with a real-role play partner to play the patron or imagine the interview based on your prior experience.
	
	Use the following format to record your observations.
	
	What type of information did the patron need? Known Item or General Information? What type of question was asked?
	
	  o **Direction**
	  o **Ready Reference**
	  o **Specific-Search**
	  o **Research**
	
	What do you say or do in response to the question

Figure AppB.17 (cont.)

(you chose above? Do you "Conduct a Reference Interview"? That is, do you try to determine the real information need of the patron? Will you show the behaviors outlined by the ALA Code of Ethics "Behavioral Guidelines" for reference staff?

- o **Be Approachable**
- o **Show Interest**
- o **Conduct a Reference Interview**
- o **Conduct a Search (Activities 2-4)**

What will the patron do or say in response to the reference person? How is the reference interview concluded? How does the reference person interpret the patron's questions? Use your imagination and experience.

Other things to consider for real-life practice that you do not need to respond to for this optional role-play activity:

1. Does the patron seem satisfied with the response to their question? How do you know?
2. Describe the patron's appearance. (e.g., male/female, color, age, clothing quality, etc.)
3. Describe the patron's attitude. (e.g., friendly, forthcoming, belligerent, short, etc NO NAMES)
4. Describe the reference person's appearance. (e.g., male/female, color, age, clothing quality, etc.)
5. Describe the reference person's attitude. (e.g., friendly, forthcoming, belligerent, short, etc. NO NAMES)
6. What are your impressions or feelings? Did the appearance or attitude of the patron or the reference person affect the reference interview process? Describe what you noticed.

SEND Your Responses to the Instruc | Clear Your Answers and Start Ov

Greg R. Notess, reference librarian, Montana State University

- Searching the Internet and the World Wide Web: A Crash Course
- Basic Internet Searching

After commenting on others' handouts and teaching aids, it is only fair to include a few of my own. These two handouts are from very different times and are aimed at very different audiences.

The first handout, Searching the Internet and the World Wide Web: A Crash Course (Figure AppB.18), is from a course I taught in 1996 at the Online World conference. The audience was made up primarily of librarians and information professionals, and the Internet was still new to some of them, so I took time to explain how to read URLs and how to understand host names, and I even covered gopher, ftp, and telnet protocols.

I still use some of the handout design principles I used then. I like to use tables to present information about search engine features because they provide a quick visual comparison of search engine capabilities. Tables also allow me to squeeze more information onto each page. I have always liked information-dense resources myself, but I have realized that most others prefer much more white space, so I no longer use this condensed format for handouts.

The second handout, Basic Internet Searching (Figure AppB.19), from 2001, is one I used at Montana State University for a seminar for students, staff, faculty, and even the general public. It was a hands-on session that used the framed approach discussed in Chapter 11. Much of the content in the handout was exactly the same as the information on the framed Web page used during the session, but the handout provided attendees with something to take notes on and take with them after it was over.

Figure AppB.18 **Searching the Internet and the World Wide Web: A Crash Course (©1996 Copyright Greg R. Notess, reproduced with permission)**

Searching the Internet and the World Wide Web: A Crash Course

Oct. 1996 c Online World
by Greg R. Notess

Welcome to the eclectic information resources of the Internet. Successful searching of the Internet requires a basic understanding of addresses, Uniform Resource Locators, and WWW browser functions. E-mail and other communication tools are also useful in exploring the depth, or lack of depth, in Internet information resources.

Internet Address Basics

Each computer on the Internet has a unique machine address such as **universe.digex.net**.

univers = Computer name
digex = Company (Digital Express)
net = type (network)

An e-mail address adds a user name. My account name is gnotess. Thus gnotess@universe.digex.net is one of my e-mail addresses while root@universe.digex.net would be a different person at the same site.

Uniform Resource Locator (URL)

URLs add a bit more to uniquely identify specific Internet resources. The basic syntax is

[protocol] :// [host] / [path] / [filename]

For example, the http://www.cas.org/index.html uses the Web's hypertext transport protocol to connect to STN's machine and retrieves the index.html file.

Pay close attention to URLs, as they can change. Understanding the structure can help in trying to locate a new location for an old URL.

Major Protocols

http is the World Wide Web protocol and the most common beginning for URLs.

telnet (remote login) is the protocol to log in to a remote computer. With this command, an Internet user can connect to systems such as library catalogs, specialized databases, and search services. Telnet is one of the few functions that Web clients do not handle by themselves. Some kind of telnet software is necessary.

FTP (File Transfer Protocol) is used to transfer files between two computers.

Gopher offers a menu format. Gophers were popular before the widespread use of graphical Web browsers, but they can still include substantial information resources.

Communication

E-mail and Usenet news are two primary means of Internet communication. For **e-mail**, there are many different mailer programs include Netscape Navigator.

Lists: E-mail-based discussion groups can be one of the best ways to get familiar with resources available on the Internet. Each list will have two e-mail addresses: one for all of the people on the list and one for the e-mail management program. To subscribe to a LISTSERV list, send a message to

listserv@address

and include the subscription request in the body of the message

sub group my name

Usenet news: Rather than sending individual messages to each subscriber, Usenet newsgroups can be browsed at any point before the articles expire. Beginners should try reading groups such as **news.answers** first. Be sure to read any Frequently Asked Questions (FAQ) files available.

Search Tools

There are now many search engines and finding aids available that link to all sorts of Internet information resources. There are two main categories:

Subject Directories: These select and classify resources into subject categories and subcategories. Some include reviews and/or ratings. Access to resources is by keyword search of the database or by browsing the classifications. Examples include Yahoo! and the Excite Reviews.

Search Engines: These attempt to find and index as many sites as possible. Search

Figure AppB.18 (cont.)

features vary greatly, as does the actual scope, currency, and accuracy of the databases.
See **http://imt.net/~notess/compeng.html** for more details on search engines.
See **http://imt.net/~notess/compeng.html** for the online, up-to-date versions of these
tables with additional information and explanations of terms used.

Subject Directories

These are some of the best known subject directories. There are two numbers in the #
of categories column. The first designates the number of main categories and the second
is the number of main categories and subcategories on the top-level page.

	Selection Criteria	Database Size	Review Length	Ratings Range	# of Categories	Review Style
Yahoo www.yahoo.com	User Submitted	400,000	0-2 lines	Cool	14/72	Descriptive
Excite Reviews www.excite.com	Selected	60,000	4 lines	1-4	16	Popular
Magellan www.mckinley.com	Selected	unknown	10 lines	1-4	26	Popular
Sites by Subject www.lycos.com	Link Rates	50,000	5 lines	None	16/66	Descriptive
Top 5% Sites www.lycos.com	unknown	10,500	10 lines	0-50, 3 sections	16/66	Popular -descriptive
WebCrawler Select www.webcrawler.com	Selected	4,000	4 lines	None	18	Popular -descriptive

Search Engines

Based on my own search comparisons, the following four search engines appear to have
the largest databases as of October 1996. They also have some of the most advanced search
features. Of the four, HotBot is the largest.

	Boolean	Proximity	Truncation	Fields	Limits	Sorting
AltaVista altavista.digital.com	Full	Phrase, near	Yes *	Yes, title, URL, link, image, etc.	Date	Relevance
Excite www.excite.com	Full	No	No	None	No	Relevance, site
HotBot www.hotbot.com	+ - system	Phrase	No	URL only	Date, more	Relevance
Infoseek Ultra ultra.infoseek.com	+ - system	Phrase	No	Yes, title, URL, link, site	No	Relevance, date

Other Search Tools

Usenet: Try Dejanews for searching Usenet archives - www.dejanews.com
E-mail Lists: For e-mail lists and discussion groups, try Liszt - www.liszt.com
Telnet: Use Hytelnet to find telnet resources - galaxy.einet.net/hytelnet/START.TXT.html
Gopher: Veronica is the classic gopher search engine -
gopher://liberty.uc.wlu.edu:70/11/gophers/veronica

Figure AppB.19   Basic Internet Searching (©2001 Copyright Greg R. Notess, reproduced with permission)

Basic Internet Searching
An MSU-Bozeman Library and ITC Computing Seminar
Greg Notess, Reference Librarian
align@montana.edu

Welcome to the eclectic information resources of the Internet. This workshop covers how to use the portals to their best advantage, techniques for combining search words, and how to guess organization's Web address.
Web site:
http://www.lib.montana.edu/~notess/li/basicsearch.html

Lesson 1: URL Guessing
For many sites, you do not need a directory or search engines. Guess at the central URL for a relevant organization.
1. Leave off **http://**
2. Use the common **www** to start the machine address
3. Add the name, acronym, or brief name of the organization (nra, honda, uwyo)
4. Add appropriate top level domain:
   com for commercial
   edu for U.S. higher education
   org for other organizations
   gov for U.S. federal government and **mil** for U.S. military
   net for Internet companies & Internet service providers

> **Basic Principle #1**
> Think of the organization most likely to provide an answer to your question. Then try to go directly to their Web site.

Lesson 2: Combining Words When Searching
See the Web page for more details. Can use Boolean operators (AND, OR, NOT) or the plus and minus symbols. Try using a plus (+) directly in front of required words and a minus (-) directly in front of words or phrases to exclude from search results.
Whenever possible, try a phrase search first.

> **Basic Principle #2**
> Use phrase searching whenever possible. Almost all search engines can do phrase searching B searching for the words entered adjacent to each other and exactly in the order submitted. Use double quotes to identify a phrase: "this is a phrase"

Examples:
Using a phrase search: Aapples pie recipe@
Using the + and - :   +apples +strawberries -kiwi
Using Boolean operators: (apples AND strawberries) NOT kiwi

Figure AppB.19 (cont.)

> **For More Information**
> See Search Engine Showdown
> http://searchengineshowdown.com/

Lesson 3: The Portals

Use a portal, directory, or search engine to finding the Web site of organizations when you can't guess the URL. The portals offer subject directories, which select and classify resources into hierarchical categories. The Portals also offer Internet services, specialized pages for frequently requested topics, search engines, and more.

Beyond just finding the Web sites of organizations, use the portals for finding

- Popular interest topics (music, film, shopping)
- Web pages on broad, general subjects
- Commercial products (and shopping searches)
- News and Current Events (but also see Academic Universe on the library page)

Selected Portals, Directories, & Search Engines

	Use for	Comments
Google www.google.com	Top pages based on link popularity.	Large database, cache, but no portal features
Yahoo! www.yahoo.com	Browsing, general subjects, finding organizations, news, free e-mail, shopping, etc.	Best known but getting old and out of control?
SearchEdu www.searchedu.com	Finding academic pages from .edu sites	Search is limited to only .edu sites and also has cached copies of pages
Britannica www.britannica.com	Finding academic topics and views and not commercial sites and products	Combination of *Encyclopædia Britannica*, 75 magazines, and a small Web directory
Excite www.excite.com	Browsing, news, personalization, commonly asked questions, more	Also try their searchable news database and NewsTracker
Lycos www.lycos.com	Searching Open Directory and Fast databases	Large search engine database and many services
AltaVista www.av.com	Specialized search centers, multimedia, directory, and search engine	Large search engine with advanced search features
Northern Light northernlight.com	Research on the Web and beyond, and organizes results into folders	Has large search engine and special collections

Gary Price, Gary Price Library Research and Internet Consulting

*   Web Search Update
*   Current Issues in Internet News Research

Gary keeps very busy between keeping up his ResourceShelf Web site and traveling around speaking and teaching about the Web and searching the Internet. His presentation style always packs information about many resources into whatever amount of time he has available.

Gary uses a Web page rather than PowerPoint for his presentations. At the top of each presentation, in a nice large font, is the URL for the whole presentation. As long as attendees get that one URL written down, they will have access to all of the other links, so Gary can provide a long list of links, and the students don't have to write them all down. Gary often uses a shortened version of the URL, using a tool like TinyURL, so that the one address that attendees need to write down is as short as possible.

These Web pages are published on Gary's own server. Even when doing a conference presentation, for which the pages could be published on the conference Web site, Gary puts his pages on his own server. The advantage is that when a page is hosted on his own server, it is immediately available even before the session. If it were on the conference Web server, it might not be available right away.

In contrast to Jeff Humphrey's use of a Web page both for online links and as a printable handout, Gary links from titles directly to the resources. This works perfectly with his style of instruction. Sometimes Gary offers a printout of his Web page to help students follow his lecture. In addition, some of the links are rather lengthy and would be very unwieldy to type in directly.

Many of the URLs not only link to the search engine but include the search statement and options set. So the link from the phrase "Reverse Linking Strengths" actually points to the 114-character

URL of www.alltheweb.com/search?cat=web&cs=utf-8&q=link%3
Awww.nlm.nih.gov+site%3Aorg+title%3Aresearch&_sb_lang=any

The two Web pages reproduced here are from presentations
Gary gave in August 2003. The first (Figure AppB.20) is from his
Web Search Update class, and the second (Figure AppB.21) is from
Current Issues in Internet News Research, which focuses on
searching the Web for news.

Figure AppB.20 **Web Search Update (©2003 Copyright Gary Price, reproduced with permission)**

Web Search Update--APRA 2003

Gary Price, MLIS
gary@resourceshelf.com
Dallas, Texas
August, 2003

This Page is Available at:
http://tinyurl.com/jklw

An Invitation to Visit My Daily Update
The ResourceShelf
Updated With Tools, New Resources, and News

Comments Before Content

- Marketing Means More Than Telling People We're Available
  - Demonstrate How Can We Save them Time?
  - Demonstrate is Not All in Google, That Good Info Still Costs $$$
- Authority, Scope, of Content Still Matter
- Where To Start? (Open Web, Fee-Based)

Web Search Comments

- More **Invisible** Material is Becoming Visible But is It Any Easier to Find?
- **"If It's Not in the First Ten Results, It's Invisible To Most People"**
  --Comment from a Person at One of My Sessions
- What Are Web Engines, Even Google Finding? Google and Limitations? I'm Not Kidding!

Figure AppB.20 (cont.)

Walt Mossberg of the *Wall Street Journal* on Google's (and Web Search) Limitations!

"But as brilliant as Google is, this process has several limitations. First of all, in most cases Google doesn't actually provide you an answer, just a list of links to Web pages where information might be found. So getting the exact information you want requires more steps: You have to browse through the links Google offers, pick out one that looks good, then go to it and look for the relevant material."

"Second, you're doing all this in a general, undifferentiated piece of software called a Web browser that isn't designed to help you drill down into information."

"Third, neither the browser nor Google gives you a good sense of the credibility of the sources that turn up, just their popularity."

(*Wall Street Journal* 3/6/2003)

Some of These Limitations are Things That an Information Professional Can Deliver On!

- Saving Time and Getting to Quality Answers Quickly
- Prior Knowledge (Collection Development, Learning Resources) With Direct Links to Specific Databases, This Can Save Time!
- These Sources Can Also Add More Usability to the Data
- Understanding and Judging Credibility Most Important

Part of the Mindset that Makes a Good Information Professional in 2003

- **Understand No Single Search Tool is Perfect, Even Google**
  Variety is the Spice of Life and the Good Info Professional
- Develop Collections and Learn "Specialized Search Tools".
- When It Comes to Web Engines Like Google, Be Able to **Exploit the Technology**
  (Knowledge of Each Tools Strengths, Weaknesses, Advanced Searching Options)
  Exploit **Quality** Free Material, Great Free "Stuff" is Available
- Knowledge of a Wide Variety of Resources (Free and Fee), Keep Current With Changes
  4 Tools That Can Help
  The ResourceShelf ||| Search Day ||| Search Engine Showdown ||| TVC Alert

Figure AppB.20 (cont.)

- How I View the Open Web, What I Try To Remember
  - o Info Still Costs Money
  - o It's Not All "on the Web" (Crucial To Demonstrate to Your Boss)
  - o The "Open Web" as a directory to potential answers
  - o *Understanding the Differences Between "On the Web" and "Via the Web"*

Web Search Engines

- A Time of Consolidation, Let's Look at What Remains as of Today
- Each of these Tools Use a Database That's Unique to the Engine
- From *Forbes*, May 2003:
  "Even Google's engineers admit Fast and Teoma deliver results comparable to theirs."
- A Great Year for **AlltheWeb!!!**
  - o URL Investigator
    Access by entering any URL
  - o Full-Text of Documents
    Remember, Google Stops Indexing after 101kb (HTML), 120kb (pdf)
  - o Reverse Linking Strengths (Google Example)
  - o Query Rewrites
  - o Calculator, Conversions
- **Teoma**
  The Resources Feature is VERY Useful
  Ask Jeeves is Much Improved
- **AltaVista Still Around, Still Powerful**
  - o Special Attention to the AV Image Database
  - o AltaVista News
    Btw, You Can Use All of AV's Syntax (including Truncation and NEAR)
- FirstGov Also Improves With More State Content
  - o Also Clustering FirstGov with Vivisimo
- **Hotbot Returns With a New Look, Functionality**
  - o Very Useful
- **How Could I Forget Google?**
  - o No Truncation
  - o Not All Pages Crawled in the Entirety
  - o Reverse Linking Issues
  - o Google Powers Yahoo

Becoming An Advanced Searcher With General Web Engines

- One Constant for All Web Engine, Limiting By Date is Not A Good Idea
- Clustered Results, Be Careful
- Using Limits is Very Important
  - o Site:
  - o Filetype:
  - o Link:
  - o Phrases in Quotation Marks
  - o Changing the Number of Results on a Results Page

Figure AppB.20 (cont.)

A Review of Specialized Tools, Databases, and More

- **WebSite-Watcher**
  Essential Resource!
- **What's a Wayback Machine?**
- **Secondary E-Mail Accounts**
  Are Essential These Days
- **How I Keep Spam to a Minimum**
- **"Key" Corporate Developments via MSN Money**
- **Non-Commercial Directories**
  InfoMine
  RDN
  LII
  Global Edge (International Business)
- **TinyURL (A Crowd Pleaser)**
- **What's a DocMorph?**
  Convert to PDF, Free!
- **EDGAR IQ & SECInfo.Com**
  IQ Offers Full-Text Searching
  SECInfo Offers Free Alert Service
  New: InsiderScoop (Fee-Based Service)
- **SurfSaver and Scopeware**
  Save it and then find it FAST!
- **Price's List of Lists is Back Thanks to SpecialIssues.Com**
- **SearchSystems.Net**
  Most public record databases sill sit on the Invisible Web
- **Peter Jacso's "PolySearch Bio"**
- **National Public Radio Archives**
- **Lookups from MelissaData**
  Zips, Addresses, Other Stuff
- **Another Example of OCR Searching**
  (Make sure term must be contained in the picture as text is checked)
  See Also: Google Catalogs
- **Delight Your Users Explain the "Canned Search"**
  Nothing More Than Bookmarking/Publishing a Search URL, A Good Use For
  Blogs
- **SmartBrief**
  Daily newsletters (free) with info about various industries
- **Basic NLP Demos**
  Lycos Finance
- **T-O-C Services**
  Free Alerts Direct from Publishers
- **Retail: Amazon Light**
  Simple, Get to The Point Interface
- **Spybot**

Additional Links
++ Federated Search Report (Search Mulitple Databases Simultaneously)
+++ MuseGlobal as an Example, Mentioned in Report
++ Speechbot (Demo, Voice Recognition Searching)

Figure AppB.21   Current Issues in Internet News Research (©2003 Copyright
Gary Price, reproduced with permission)

Current Issues in Internet News Research
APRA 2003

Gary Price, MLIS
gary@resourceshelf.com
Dallas, Texas
August, 2003

This Page is Available at:
http://tinyurl.com/jkse

An Invitation to Visit My Daily Update
The ResourceShelf
Updated With Tools, New Resources, and News

Understand the Limitations

- It's Not All Free
- Limited Searchability
- Limited Archives (2-4 Week Limit, In Most Cases)
- How Much Time Are You Wasting Looking For A News Article That Doesn't
  Exist "On the Web"?
- Information Still Costs Money
- Bottom Line: You Still Need Traditional Databases and Print Sources

News Search Engines

- AltaVista News
  Utilize AV Advanced Syntax
- Rocket News
- Google News
  Advanced Syntax Available
- MarketWatch.Com
- Yahoo News
  Advanced Syntax Available
- NewsNow
- Daypop

Don't Forget You're Able to "Can" Your Searches

News Software (Fee-Based)

- RocketInfo Desktop

Figure AppB.21 (cont.)

News Search and Publish Solution (Fee-Based)

- Nexcerpt

E-Mail News Alerts

- Yahoo News Alerts
- Marketwatch.Com Alerts
- Google Alerts (New)
- BizJournals News Alerts
- Secondary E-Mail Accounts
  Are Essential These Days

Other Important Tools

- WebSite-Watcher
  Essential Resource! (TrackEngine.Com or WatchthatPage.Com as Alternatives)
- SECInfo.Com
- National Public Radio Archives
- Trade Magazines III #2 III #3 III #4 Can Be Useful
- The SmartBrief
- What's A Weblog? Why Might this Technology Be of Value to You?

Rita Vine, president, Workingfaster.com

- Good Web Search Practices: The Basics for Effective Searching
- Search Planning Worksheet

Like Ran Hock, Rita Vine uses an extensive workbook as a handout. Rita's is more than 20 pages long. The extract reproduced in Figure AppB.22 is just a small portion of the workbook. The Search Planning Worksheet (Figure AppB.23) is also a part of the workbook.

Note the design of the pages and the variety of ways Rita emphasizes points. The workbook includes student exercises for reinforcement through practice. Screen shots help students remember featured Web sites. Special points are highlighted in boxes titled "Remember . . ." and "Using Search Boxes on Web Pages." She created a clear graphic flowchart to show the search engines' spidering process.

Rita not only makes great use of design elements and white space, but she carefully does not pack too much information into any one section, and she uses bulleted lists of points rather than large blocks of text.

Figure AppB.22 Good Web Search Practices: The Basics for Effective Searching
(Copyright © 1998–2003 Workingfaster.com Inc. All rights
reserved. These excerpts are reproduced with permission. No
portion of this document may be copied without express written permission of Workingfaster.com. Keep-It-Simple-
Searching™ and Search Portfolio™ are trademarks of
Workingfaster.com Inc.)

How do we search the Web right now?

Exercise

This exercise is designed to help you understand the types of tools that you use today to search the Web, and to learn from others in the class about different tools that exist.

Write down the topic that your instructor will give you in the space below.

Topic: _____

Write down the names of up to three (3) Web tools that you would use to find information on this topic.

1) _____

2) _____

3) _____

Class Discussion: Use this space to write down some additional Web resources to consider.

_____

_____

_____

Remember...

There are many different kinds of resources on the Web.

Most of us know only the best-branded, best funded resources.

Many excellent resources are not well known.

Figure AppB.22 (cont.)

Why use directories?

Use directories to find good quality, pre-selected links to topical resources, including many "invisible Web" databases that might not be indexed by search engines.

Directories enable you to browse a selective list of resources rather than search a giant database of undifferentiated Web pages.

Example: Librarians Index to the Internet (http://www.lii.org)

Key Directory Features

*   A browseable list of choices – you point and click

*   Covers many different topics

*   Number of resources is much smaller than search engines, but more selective

Tips for Using Directories Effectively

1) Try to browse rather than search with keywords.

2) If you use keywords, keep them very general.

3) Collect information from several directories for best results.

Figure AppB.22 (cont.)

Exercise

Using one of the directories discussed in class, try finding good
starting points for any of the following topics:

Topic: Car buying guides for new cars
Topic: Information on the major political parties in Canada
Topic: Databases for searching journal articles in medicine
            and health
Topic: A good starting point for finding appliance repair
            manuals
Topic: Looking for any Canadian patents owned by Nortel
            Networks

Tip: Use the keyword search box
only if you are unable to browse your
way to the right subject area.

* * *

Tip: If you search directories by
keyword, try to use one single, very
general keyword that describes your
topic category.

Example:

Use **salaries** not **accountants
salaries**
Use **cars** or **automobiles** not **ford
taurus**

Using Search Boxes on Web Pages!

Many Web sites offer an 'internal search' -- a search box that lets
you search the internal contents of that site alone.

Internal search boxes are not search engines! They usually offer
very basic search options. Recent research has shown that most
internal search options *do not work as stated.*

The solution? Try to browse instead of search. Do not rely on
internal searches alone to find what you are looking for.

Figure AppB.22 (cont.)

When to use Web Directories

- When you need an expert's help to discover the best quality sites in a particular subject

- When you are looking for a database to conduct a special literature search in a particular subject

How do Search Engines Work?

- Robot-generated! No humans at work!

- Special proprietary software program ("spider") starts at a page and "crawls", following links to other pages, crawls those, etc. etc...

- Partial content of Web page is captured into a very large database

- Other software "indexes" the pages in the database – removes common words, leaves the rest

- Users run *keyword searches* against the database to find pages with the words in their search

- Search engine fetches pages that match keyword search, rank orders them by "relevance" and delivers results instantly

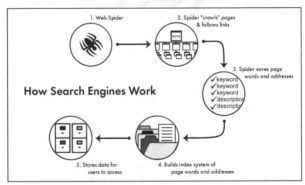

Figure AppB.22 (cont.)

How to Search using Search Engines – Basic Tips

- Search using KEYWORDS.

- Keywords are automatically treated as if you want ALL the words to appear in the same Web page.

- Your keywords must match EXACTLY against the pages in the database in order to be retrieved. (e.g. searching the keywords **canadian patents** will *not* find pages that have the word **canada** instead of **canadian)**

- If you don't succeed at first, try using word variations (**canada** instead of **canadian**) or synonyms (**carpal tunnel** as an alternative to **repetitive strain** or **repetitive stress)**

- Avoid unnecessary words if they are already implied by the essential words. (e.g. use **repetitive strain** not **repetitive strain injury**)

Exercise

Find Information Using Search Engines

Write down the topics that your instructor will give you in the space below.

Topic1:

_____

Topic 2:

_____

Using the recommended search engines listed under **Error! Reference source not found.** on page **Error! Bookmark not defined.**, find resources on this topic.

Compare results between topics and between search engines.

Record any notes here.

_____

_____

_____

When to Use Search Engines

1) To find very specific information -- names, companies, associations, and institutions (e.g. *rockefeller institute of government*)

Figure AppB.22 (cont.)

2) To find very specific "needle-in-a-haystack" topics (e.g. *mediastinoscopy, louisiana tax forms*)

3) To find detailed subject information that has little commercial value for consumers.

Search Engine Advanced Tips

1) If you don't find what you're looking for in the first ten search results, move on to another search engine or another type of tool.

2) **Use lower case** when typing in search terms. By typing words in lower case you will retrieve mixed case, upper case, and lower case versions of your words.

3) If you put a phrase inside of **quotation marks** (e.g. "rockefeller institute of government") most search engines will limit retrieval to those pages which contain the exact phrase.

Exercise: What type of search tool should I use?

Question	Search Engine?	Directory?	Neither?
Address of the New York State Bar Association			
Information on the process of botox injections			
A site to help a Grade 5 student learn more about the mating behavior of cats			
Finding lists of museums in London to help plan a trip			
Finding as many newspapers as possible that are published in New York City			

Why Don't Search Engines Always Find What I Want?

Reasons	What to Do About It?
Robots cannot download data from searchable databases	Use directories to find the database and search it directly

Figure AppB.22 (cont.)

Size of Net makes it hard to crawl fast enough to keep up with changes	Search current news sources directly for hot-topic data
Some sites purchase keywords and make deals with search engines	Avoid most search engines except for recommended ones
Human error--spelling and typos	Consider spelling variations (British vs. American spellings)
Your keywords aren't the ones used in the document	Consider synonyms, variant tenses, singular/plural and other possibilities

Figure AppB.23   Search Planning Worksheet (Copyright © 1998–2003
                  Workingfaster.com Inc. All rights reserved. This document is
                  reproduced with permission. No portion of this document may
                  be copied without express written permission of
                  Workingfaster.com. Search Portfolio™ is a trademark of
                  Workingfaster.com Inc.)

Search Planning Worksheet

Question: What am I trying to find out?

Classify the type of question

❑ Quick fact	❑ Topical search	❑ Known web site	❑ Distinctive name or needle-in-a-haystack
↓	↓	↓	↓
Quick Fact Lookup	Subject Starters	Search Engines	Search Engines

Develop a keyword search strategy

Concept 1		Concept 2		Concept 3
	and/or		and/or	

Keep It Simple Searching™ Tip: Try multiple keywords or phrases in search engines; use single keywords in subject starters

Assess the results

URL List
www.notess.com/teaching

Chapter 2

Google Toolbar
toolbar.google.com

SpyBot
www.safer-networking.org

QHOSTS trojan fix
software.brown.edu/dist/w-cleanqhosts.html

Finding Information on the Internet: A Tutorial
www.lib.berkeley.edu/TeachingLib/Guides/Internet/
FindInfo.html

Chapter 3

Classroom Control Systems
www.ala.org/ala/acrlbucket/is/iscommittees/webpages/
teachingmethods/classroomcontrol.htm
or
snipurl.com/6ktr

Snip URL
snurl.com

TinyURL
tinyurl.com

Chapter 4

Web Search Guide Tutorial: Research—Web Searching
www.websearchguide.ca/tutorials/tocres.htm

Finding Information on the Internet
www.lib.berkeley.edu/TeachingLib/Guides/Internet/
FindInfo.html

Internet Tutorials from Laura Cohen, University Libraries, University at Albany
library.albany.edu/internet

LearnAndGo—Searching the Web
www.ozline.net/tutor/tutorial.html

Quick Tutorial on Searching the Internet
bigdog.lib.purdue.edu/phys/inst/searchinginternet.html

net.TUTOR: Using Web Search Tools
gateway.lib.ohio-state.edu/tutor/les5/

Internet Search Tips and Mouse Exercise
www.hclib.org/pub/training/
www.hclib.org/pub/training/SearchTips/
www.hclib.org/pub/training/MouseExercise/

Tutorial: Site Clustering and Filtering
www.searchengineshowdown.com/tutorials/cluster.html

Information Cycle
www.libraries.psu.edu/instruction/infocyle.htm

TILT: The Texas Information Literacy Tutorial
tilt.lib.utsystem.edu

eManual: Online Information Literacy Learning (University of Winnipeg)
cybrary.uwinnipeg.ca/learn/emanual/

The Internet Navigator (University of Utah)
www-navigator.utah.edu

Tales from the MSU Stacks (Michigan State University)
tales.lib.msu.edu
tales.lib.msu.edu/Content/m07/t2/m7t2.html

QuickStudy: A Library Tutorial (University of Minnesota)
tutorial.lib.umn.edu

InfoTrekk (Curtin University, Australia)
library.curtin.edu.au/infotrekk/

MindMapping (James Cook University, Australia)
www.jcu.edu.au/studying/services/studyskills/mindmap/

Library Instruction Tutorials, Library Instruction Round Table
www3.baylor.edu/LIRT/lirtproj.html

Librarians' Internet Index
www.lii.org/pub/subtopic/5118

The RDN Virtual Training Suite
www.vts.rdn.ac.uk

Innovative Internet Applications in Libraries
www.wiltonlibrary.org/innovate.html#tutorials

Searching the WWW: Tutorials, Techniques, Tips
www.keithstanger.com/search.htm

Peer-Reviewed Instructional Materials Online Database
cooley.colgate.edu/dbs/acrlprimo/showrec.html

Learn the Net—Find Information Fast Online from ULiveandLearn
www.uliveandlearn.com/courses/cdetail.cfm?courseid=47

Chapter 6

Ask.com Site Features
sp.ask.com/en/docs/about/site_features.shtml

Yahoo!'s Shortcuts
help.yahoo.com/help/us/ysearch/tips/tips-01.html

Google's Special Features
www.google.com/help/features.html

The Argus Clearinghouse
www.clearinghouse.net

Chapter 7

Web Search University Conference
www.websearchu.com

Search Engine Strategies Conference
www.searchenginestrategies.com

Search Engine Showdown Reviews
www.searchengineshowdown.com/reviews

Search Engine Showdown Features Chart
www.searchengineshowdown.com/features/

Chapter 8

Librarian's Internet Index (LII)
www.lii.org

Resource Discovery Network (RDN)
www.rdn.ac.uk

Bibliography on Evaluating Web Information
www.lib.vt.edu/help/instruct/evaluate/evalbiblio.html

Mind Mapping
www.mind-mapping.co.uk

Overture
www.overture.com

Google Keyword Tool
adwords.google.com/select/KeywordToolExternal

Census Bureau
www.census.gov

Chapter 9

CRAYON (Create Your Own Newspaper)
www.crayon.net

Google News
news.google.com

Yahoo! News
news.yahoo.com

NewsNow
newsnow.co.uk

Rocketinfo
www.rocketnews.com

Daypop
www.daypop.com

Feedster
www.feedster.com

Google Groups
groups.google.com

Yahoo! Groups
groups.yahoo.com

Epinions
www.epinions.com

Ditto
ditto.com

Picsearch
www.picsearch.com

Singingfish
singingfish.com

Wayp
wayp.com

AnyWho
anywho.com

Switchboard
switchboard.com

192
192.com

TheUltimates
theultimates.com

Google Scholar
scholar.google.com

Windows Live Academic
academic.live.com

Scirus
scirus.com

Chapter 10

Proteus
www.thrall.org/proteus.html

Ask
www.ask.com

Exalead
www.exalead.com

Gigablast
www.gigablast.com

Google
www.google.com

Google Inconsistencies
searchengineshowdown.com/features/google/inconsistent.shtml

MSN Search
search.msn.com

Windows Live
www.live.com

Yahoo!
search.yahoo.com

Yahoo! Directory
dir.yahoo.com

Open Directory Project
dmoz.org

Librarians' Internet Index (LII)
lii.org

Resource Discovery Network (RDN)
www.rdn.ac.uk

Chapter 11

Basic Internet Searching Tutorial
www.searchengineshowdown.com/strat/basicsearch.html

Advanced Internet Searching
www.searchengineshowdown.com/strat/advancedsearch.shtml.

Chapter 12

Jesse Ruderman's Bookmarklets
www.squarefree.com/bookmarklets

Google Browser Button Bookmarklets
www.google.com/options/buttons.html

Bookmarklets.com Search Bookmarklet
bookmarklets.com/tools/search/srchbook.phtml

Bookmarklets.com Make Search Bookmarklet Tool
bookmarklets.com/mk.phtml

Search Engine Showdown Bookmarklets
searchengineshowdown.com/bmlets

Adblock Plug-in for Mozilla and Firefox
adblock.mozdev.org

Chapter 13

Researchers Map the Web
www.almaden.ibm.com/almaden/webmap_press.html

The Internet Hockey Database Team Search Form
hockeydb.com/ihdb/stats/teams.html

PubMed
pubmed.gov

Virtual Reference Library
www.virtualreferencelibrary.ca

Canadian Council on Tobacco Control
www.cctc.ca

Robots Exclusion
www.robotstxt.org/wc/exclusion.html

Appendix A

Finding Information on the World Wide Web: A TUTORIAL
www.lib.berkeley.edu/TeachingLib/Guides/Internet/FindInfo.html

Infopeople Project
infopeople.org

Infography Search
www.infography.com

National Teacher Training Institute Web Wise by Who Is-ing Lesson Plan
www.wvpt4learning.org/lessons/pdf03/webwise.pdf

National Teacher Training Institute No Waah! Lesson Plan
www.wvpt4learning.org/lessons/pdf02/nowaah.pdf

The Infography about Internet Searching
www.infography.com/content/813746743748.html

Phil Bradley
www.philb.com

Conan the Librarian pages
www.rlc.dcccd.edu/lrc/conan.htm

Richland College Library
www.rlc.dcccd.edu/lrc/rlclib.htm

Dallas TeleCollege Library
ollie.dcccd.edu/library/telecollege.htm

Online Strategies
www.onstrat.com

Kovacs Consulting—Internet & Web Training
www.kovacs.com

The ResourceShelf
www.resourceshelf.com

Price's List of Lists
www.specialissues.com/lol

Search Engine Watch
SearchEngineWatch.com

Search Engine Watch Feedback Form
sewatch.com/about/article.php/2155671

Workingfaster.com
www.workingfaster.com

Search Portfolio
www.searchportfolio.com

Information Literacy Weblog
ciquest.shef.ac.uk/infolit/

The Information Literacy Place
dis.shef.ac.uk/literacy/

Appendix B

Begin the Pre-Searching Analysis
www.lib.berkeley.edu/TeachingLib/Guides/Internet/form.pdf

Web Page Evaluation Checklist
www.lib.berkeley.edu/TeachingLib/Guides/Internet/EvalForm.pdf

Recommended Search Engines: Table of Features
www.lib.berkeley.edu/TeachingLib/Guides/Internet/
SearchEngines.html

Recommended Search Strategy: Analyze your Topic & Search with Peripheral Vision
www.lib.berkeley.edu/TeachingLib/Guides/Internet/Strategies.html

National Teacher Training Institute Web Wise by Who Is-ing Lesson Plan
www.wvpt4learning.org/lessons/pdf03/webwise.pdf

Internet Tools for the Advanced Searcher
www.philb.com/adint1.htm

Searching the Invisible Web
www.rlc.dcccd.edu/lrc/ppt/invisible.ppt

How to Download Text from the Web
www.rlc.dcccd.edu/lrc/pdfs/download.pdf

Web Resources: Ready Reference Sites
www.incolsa.net/handouts/int004.htm

Kovacs Consulting: International and Web Training Workshops List
kovacs.com/training.html

Bibliography

Auer, N. J. (2004, Aug. 13). Bibliography on Evaluating Web Information. Retrieved May 14, 2006, www.lib.vt.edu/help/instruct/evaluate/evalbiblio.html

Berkman, R. (2004). *The Skeptical Business Searcher:* The Information Advisor*'s Guide to Evaluating Web Data, Sites, and Sources.* Medford, NJ: CyberAge Books.

Brandt, D. S. (1997, May). Tutorial, or Not Tutorial, That Is the Question .... *Computers in Libraries,* 17(5), 44–46.

Broder, A., Kumar, R., Maghoul, F., Raghavan, P., Rajagopalan, S., Stata, R., Tomkins, A., and Wiener, J. (2000, June). Graph Structure in the Web. *Computer Networks,* 33(1), 309–320.

Dale, A., Johnston, B., Webber, S., and O'Flynn, S. (2003, April). Information: It's All in the Mind. *Library + Information Update,* 2(4), 30–34. Retrieved January 4, 2004, www.cilip.org.uk/update/issues/april03/article3april.html

Hansen, C. (Summer 2001). The Internet Navigator: An Online Internet Course for Distance Learners. *Library Trends,* 50(1), 58–72.

Hock, R. (2004). *The Extreme Searcher's Internet Handbook: A Guide for the Serious Searcher.* Medford, NJ: CyberAge Books.

Notess, G. R. (1995, July–August). Searching the World Wide Web: Lycos, WebCrawler and More. *ONLINE,* 19(4), 48–53. Also available online at www.onlinemag.net/OL1995/JulOL95/notess. html

Notess, G. R. (1998, May). Keyboard and Navigation Shortcuts. *ONLINE,* 22(3), 48–50. Also available online at www.onlinemag. net/OL1998/net5.html

Notess, G. R. (1999, October). A Multiplicity of Databases on Search Engines. *EContent*, 22(5), 60–62. Also available online at www.notess.com/write/archive/9910econtent.html

Notess, G. R. (2000, May). The Never-Ending Quest: Search Engine Relevance. *ONLINE*, 24(3), 35–40. Also available online at www.notess.com/write/archive/200005quest.html

Notess, G. R. (2003a, July). Bookmarklets, Favelets, and Keymarks: Shortcuts Galore. *ONLINE*, 27(4), 38–40. Also available online at www.infotoday.com/online/jul03/OnTheNet.shtml

Notess, G. R. (2003b, September). The Google Dance: Their Database Update Saga. *ONLINE*, 27(5), 42–44. Also available online at www.infotoday.com/online/sep03/OnTheNet.shtml

Notess, G. R. (2004, January). Toolbars: Trash or Treasures? *ONLINE*, 28(1), 41–44. Also available online at www.infotoday. com/online/jan04/OnTheNet.shtml

Olson, J., Christensen, R., Jeffries, S., et al. (2005, May 2). Classroom Control Systems. Retrieved May 14, 2006 from ACRL Instruction Section Teaching Methods Committee Web site, www.ala.org/Content/ContentGroups/ACRL1/IS/ISCommittees/ Web_pages/Teaching_Methods/Classroom_Control_System.htm

Oxford English Dictionary. 3rd ed. OED Online. Oxford: Oxford University Press. Retrieved May 14, 2006, dictionary.oed.com

Sherman, C., and Price, G. (2001). *The Invisible Web: Uncovering Information Sources Search Engines Can't See*. Medford, NJ: CyberAge Books.

Udell, J. (2005, May 16). Secrets of Screencasting: With a little diligence, short online videos can become powerful educational tools for IT. *InfoWorld*, 27(20), 21. Also available online at www.infoworld.com/article/05/05/11/200Pstrategic_1.html

About the Author

Greg R. Notess, a reference librarian at Montana State University, has been teaching Web searching and other Internet topics since 1991. A three-time Information Authorship award winner, he is the "On the Net" and "Internet Search Engine Update" columnist for *ONLINE*. A graduate of the University of Washington's librarianship program, Greg also holds two degrees in music. Greg is a popular conference speaker who has presented at conferences from Alaska to Florida and San Diego to Boston. International invitations have taken him to five continents for meetings in London, Montreal, Sydney, Tel-Aviv, Pretoria, Copenhagen, Oslo, Stockholm, Paris, Zagreb, and India. On the Web, Greg maintains SearchEngineShowdown.com, which reviews, compares, analyzes, and comments on the rapidly changing Web search environment.

Index

A

About.com, 108–109, 170
abstracting services, 7
academic settings, 45, 51
accuracy, 9, 142–143
Acxiom, 162
ad bidding engines, 105–106,
    151
adaptability, change and, 26–27
Adblock plug-ins, 205–206
address confusion, 23–24
addresses, 113–114, 153–154
Advanced Internet Searching
    tutorial, 181
advertisements, 150–153,
    204–206
adwords, 151
age/aging, user needs and, 14
Agricola, 112
Albany, University of, 59
alert services, 158
Allmusic.com, 165
AlltheWeb, *43*, 54
Alt key, 195
Alt-V, 198
AltaVista, 127, 161–162, 191
Amazon.com, 110–111
America Online (AOL), 3, 9, 23,
    24, 25

*American Heritage Dictionary
    of the English Language,*
    97
analogies, 207
answer engines, 106–107
AnyWho.com, 163
Argus Clearinghouse, 108
ARPANET, 4
arrows, navigation with, 198
Ask.com
    description, 171–172
    function, 98, 106–107
    news databases, 157
    picture search engines, 161
assignments, 50
Association of College and
    Research Libraries
    (ACRL), 33, 71
asterisks, 126
audiences
    assessment of, 17–19
    attitude of, 226
    characteristics, 13–16
    failures and, 220–226
    loss of interest, 225–226
    needs of, 11–12
    for online tutorials, 50
    session length variation and,
        81–83
audio files, 49, 162

V

Venn diagrams, 120
vertical portals, 103
ViewletBuilder, 50
ViewletCam, 50
Vine, Rita
  approach to know-it-alls, 15
  on audience assessment, 18
  on audience burnout, 86
  on Boolean searching,
    122–123
  on content, 37–38, 145,
    147–149
  on exercises, 211–212
  facility failures, 223
  on failures, 221
  on goal setting, 86, 90, 91, 94
  on image searching, 161
  on instruction environment,
    45
  on mechanical problems, 40
  on phone number
    searching, 163
  on phrase searching, 120
  on the research process,
    136–137
  on search engine math, 125
  on search engines, 217–218
  on search tool selection, 139
  on session length, 84–85
  terminology, 100, 101
  workbook approach, 42
Virtual Reference Library,
  218–219
Virtual Training Suite, 71
visual searching, 170
Vivisimo, 104, 170
vocabulary, technical, 80
vortals, 103

W

Wayp.com, 163
Web addresses, 153–154
Web pages, 51, 181–192,
  187–188
Web portals, 102–103
Web presentations, 44
Web Search Guide, 56–57, *57*
Web Search University
  conferences, 117
Webber, Sheila
  on content, 150
  on exercises, 210–211,
    212–213
  on facilities failures, 223
  on relevance ranking, 132
  on the research process, 136
  on search engines, 170
  on search features, 118
  on session length, 81
  on session organization,
    79–80
  on terminology, 114
  on Web search education, 46
WebCrawler, 55
Wilton Library, 71
Windows Live, 176–177
Windows Live Academic, 164
Windows Media players, 162
Windows shortcuts, 195
Wink, 50
Winnipeg, University of, 69
workbooks, 42
Workingfaster.com, 18
workshops, 16–17, 181–192
World Wide Web history, 2–4

More Great Books from Information Today, Inc.

The Extreme Searcher's Internet Handbook, 2nd Edition

A Guide for the Serious Searcher

By Randolph Hock

This revised edition is essential for anyone who uses the Internet for research. Randolph (Ran) Hock covers strategies and tools for all major areas of Internet content. Readers with little to moderate searching experience will appreciate Hock's helpful, easy-to-follow advice, while experienced searchers will discover a wealth of new ideas, techniques, and resources.

320 pp/softbound/ISBN 0-910965-76-5 $24.95

Teach Beyond Your Reach

An Instructor's Guide to Developing and Running Successful Distance Learning Classes, Workshops, Training Sessions and More

By Robin Neidorf

Distance learning is enabling individuals to earn college and graduate degrees, professional certificates, and a wide range of skills and credentials. In *Teach Beyond Your Reach*, teacher and author Robin Neidorf takes a practical, curriculum-focused approach designed to help new and experienced distance educators develop and deliver quality courses and training sessions. She shares best practices and examples, surveys the tools of the trade, and covers key issues.

248 pp/softbound/ISBN 0-910965-73-0 $29.95

The Skeptical Business Searcher

The Information Advisor's Guide to Evaluating
Web Data, Sites, and Sources

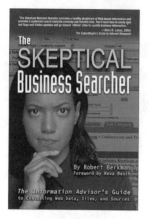

*By Robert Berkman • Foreword by
Reva Basch*

This is the experts' guide to finding
high-quality company and industry data
on the free Web. Information guru Robert
Berkman offers business Internet users
effective strategies for identifying and
evaluating no-cost online information
sources, emphasizing easy-to-use
techniques for recognizing bias and
misinformation. You'll learn where to go
for company backgrounders, sales and
earnings data, SEC filings and stockholder reports, public records,
market research, competitive intelligence, and more. The author's
unique table of "Internet Information Credibility Indicators"
allows readers to systematically evaluate Web site reliability.

312 pp/softbound/ISBN 0-910965-66-8 $29.95

Best Technology Practices
in Higher Education

Edited by Les Lloyd

A handful of progressive teachers and
administrators are integrating technology in
new and creative ways at their colleges and
universities, raising the bar for all schools.
Editor Les Lloyd (*Teaching with
Technology*) has sought out the most
innovative and practical examples in a range
of key application areas, bringing together
more than 30 technology leaders to share
their success stories. The book's 18 chapters
include firsthand accounts of school technology projects that have
transformed classrooms, services, and administrative operations.

264 pp/hardbound/ISBN 1-57387-208-3 $39.50

Yahoo! to the Max

An Extreme Searcher Guide

By Randolph Hock

With its many and diverse features, it's not easy for any individual to keep up with all that Yahoo! has to offer. Fortunately, Ran Hock—"The Extreme Searcher"—has created a reader-friendly guide to his favorite Yahoo! tools for online research, communication, investment, e-commerce, and a range of other useful activities. In *Yahoo! to the Max*, Ran helps Web users take advantage of many of Yahoo!'s most valuable offerings—from its portal features, to Yahoo! Groups, to unique tools some users have yet to discover. As with all Extreme Searcher guides, the author's regularly updated Web page helps readers stay current.

256 pp/softbound/ISBN 0-910965-69-2 $24.95

Super Searchers Go to School

Sharing Online Strategies with K–12 Students, Teachers, and Librarians

By Joyce Kasman Valenza • Edited by Reva Basch

Twelve prominent K–12 educators and educator-librarians share their techniques and tips for helping students become effective, life-long information users. Through a series of skillful interviews, Joyce Kasman Valenza—techlife@school columnist for the *Philadelphia Inquirer* and herself a tech-savvy high school librarian—gets the experts to reveal their field-tested strategies for working with student learners and educator peers. You'll discover techniques for teaching search tool selection, evaluating result lists and Web sites, deciding when to use a professional database or the Invisible Web, and much more.

272 pp/softbound/ISBN 0-910965-70-6 $24.95

Information Representation and Retrieval in the Digital Age

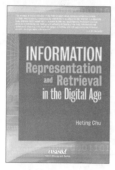

By Heting Chu

This is the first book to offer a clear, comprehensive view of Information Representation and Retrieval (IRR). With an emphasis on principles and fundamentals, the author first reviews key concepts and major developmental stages of the field, then systematically examines information representation methods, IRR languages, retrieval techniques and models, and Internet retrieval systems.

264 pp/hardbound/ISBN 1-57387-172-9 $44.50

Theories of Information Behavior

Edited by Karen E. Fisher, Sanda Erdelez, and Lynne (E. F.) McKechnie

This unique book presents authoritative overviews of more than 70 conceptual frameworks for understanding how people seek, manage, share, and use information in different contexts. Covering both established and newly proposed theories of information behavior, the book includes contributions from 85 scholars from 10 countries. Theory descriptions cover origins, propositions, methodological implications, usage, and links to related theories.

456 pp/hardbound/ISBN 1-57387-230-X $49.50